Lecture Notes in Artificial Intel

Subseries of Lecture Notes in Computer Sc

Edited by J. G. Carbonell and J. Siekmann

Lecture Notes in Computer Science

Edited by G. Goos, J. Hartmanis and J. van Leeuwen

Springer
Berlin
Heidelberg
New York
Barcelona
Hong Kong
London
Milan
Paris
Singapore
Tokyo

Frank Dignum   Carles Sierra (Eds.)

Agent Mediated Electronic Commerce

The European AgentLink Perspective

Springer

Series Editors

Jaime G. Carbonell, Carnegie Mellon University, Pittsburgh, PA, USA
Jörg Siekmann, University of Saarland, Saabrücken, Germany

Volume Editors

Frank Dignum
Utrecht University, Institute of Information and Computing Sciences
P.O. Box 80.089, 3508 TB Utrecht, The Netherlands
E-mail: dignum@cs.uu.nl

Carles Sierra
IIIA, CSIC
Campus UAB, 08193 Bellaterra, Catalonia, Spain
E-mail: sierra@iiia.csic.es

Cataloging-in-Publication Data applied for

Die Deutsche Bibliothek - CIP-Einheitsaufnahme

Agent mediated electronic commerce : the European agentlink
perspective / Frank Dignum ; Carles Sierra (ed.). - Berlin ;
Heidelberg ; New York ; Barcelona ; Hong Kong ; London ; Milan ;
Paris ; Singapore ; Tokyo : Springer, 2001
   (Lecture notes in computer science ; Vol. 1991 : Lecture notes in
   artificial intelligence) ISBN 3-540-41671-4

CR Subject Classification (1998): I.2.11, C.2, K.4.4, H.3.4-5, H.4.3, H.5.3, I.2, J.2

ISBN 3-540-41671-4 Springer-Verlag Berlin Heidelberg New York

This work is subject to copyright. All rights are reserved, whether the whole or part of the material is
concerned, specifically the rights of translation, reprinting, re-use of illustrations, recitation, broadcasting,
reproduction on microfilms or in any other way, and storage in data banks. Duplication of this publication
or parts thereof is permitted only under the provisions of the German Copyright Law of September 9, 1965,
in its current version, and permission for use must always be obtained from Springer-Verlag. Violations are
liable for prosecution under the German Copyright Law.

Springer-Verlag Berlin Heidelberg New York
a member of BertelsmannSpringer Science+Business Media GmbH
© Springer-Verlag Berlin Heidelberg 2001
Printed in Germany

Typesetting: Camera-ready by author, data conversion by PTP-Berlin, Stefan Sossna
Printed on acid-free paper   SPIN: 10782060   06/3142   5 4 3 2 1 0

Preface

It is now no longer necessary to argue the importance of agent technology. Besides numerous conferences and workshops on specific aspects of agent technology there are also many companies that are exploring its exploitation possibilities. In the light of these developments and in order to foster the transfer of agent technology from research labs to business, the EU has funded a "network of excellence" devoted to agent technology. This network of excellence, called AgentLink (http://www.agentlink.org/), aims at bringing together research groups from different countries and industrial developers. The ultimate goal is to create synergy among the different projects and groups to improve the competence of European industry and the excellence of academia. In order to achieve this goal, Agent-Link organises educational activities (summer schools), builds agent-related literature repositories, and facilitates collaboration between member nodes. One of the main activities related to the last point are the regular meetings of "Special Interest Groups" (SIGs). At this moment six SIGs are functioning, focusing on topics ranging from agent based social simulation to intelligent agents for telecommunications applications and telematics.

The current book combines two results from the activities of the SIG on "Agent Mediated Electronic Commerce". This SIG gathers the main research groups and industrial partners interested in the use of agent technology in electronic commerce.

First and foremost the book contains a roadmap of research and current technological developments in the area of agent-mediated electronic commerce. This roadmap is a direct result of the discussions between the participants of the meetings conducted by this SIG. Probably the most interesting part of this roadmap is the (joint) perspective on future developments in this area for research in Europe. This perspective is built on the foundation of current research and development in Europe.

The book also contains a number of papers that fill in parts of this roadmap in a European context. Some of these papers describe significant current developments in this area while other papers indicate some clear directions for future research. Together they compose an interesting overview of the area as it stands in Europe at this time. We have structured the book around four themes: Negotiation, Markets, User Preferences, and Security.

The book contains four papers around negotiation. The paper by A. Lomuscio, M. Wooldridge, and N. Jennings gives a classification scheme for negotiation and thus can function as a framework in which different research topics on negotiation can be placed. The paper by J.-L. Koning discusses one such issue, namely the designing and testing of negotiation protocols. Also the paper by S. Paurobally and J. Cunningham focuses on the specification of negotiation protocols (using an alternative specification mechanism). In the paper by E. Oliveira and A. Rocha the features of the agents partaking in a negotiation are discussed.

The section on markets also contains four papers. The paper by F. Dignum discusses the general advantages of using agents in electronic markets and draws some conclusions about the desirable properties of agents operating on these markets. The papers of M. Viamonte et al. and M. Esteva et al. both give formal descriptions of electronic market places. The last paper in this section, by M. Vetter and S. Pitsch, describes an actual market place, CASBA, that supports flexible trading using agents.

The section on user preferences contains one paper on user preference modeling (by M. Dastani et al.). Besides this paper there is also a paper describing how agents can be used to build adaptive web stores, by L. Ardissono et al. This section concludes with a paper from M. Torrens et al., which uses techniques from constraint satisfaction in order to build scalable catalogs.

The last section of this book contains only one paper on the topic of security. In this paper V. Roth and V. Conan describe how encrypted Java archives can be used to ensure security for mobile agents.

Hopefully this book will be an inspiration for researchers and will encourage them to take up the challenges indicated in the papers and for practitioners to start using some of the technology described in their new systems.

October 2000   Frank Dignum (Utrecht, The Netherlands)
                                      Carles Sierra (Barcelona, Spain)

Table of Contents

AMEC: Scientific and Technological Roadmap

Section I: Negotiation

Section II: Markets

Section III: Preferences

Section IV: Security

Agent-Mediated Electronic Commerce: Scientific and Technological Roadmap

Carles Sierra[1] and Frank Dignum[2]

[1] IIIA–CSIC (Barcelona),
sierra@iiia.csic.es,
http://www.iiia.csic.es/~sierra
[2] Institute of Information and Computing Sciences
Utrecht University (Utrecht),
dignum@cs.uu.nl

1 Introduction

Internet continues to spawn new markets and electronic commerce is changing many market conventions. Old commercial practices are being adapted to the new conditions of immediacy brought forth by the global networks, and new products, services, as well as new practices are beginning to appear. Agent-based technologies could play a critical role in this regard with the potential of eventually delivering unprecedented levels of autonomy, customization and general sophistication in the way electronic commerce is conducted. At the same time a number of theoretical, technological, economic, sociological and legal issues will need to be addressed before such opportunities become a reality.

Internet growth is surpassing the most optimistic forecasts. From 17 million users in 1992 to 195 million users world-wide in 1999, 47 millions of whom are in Europe. The activity is quite unbalanced from countries with high activity, like Sweden with a 40.9% of the population using Internet, to countries with a moderate activity, like Italy with 8% of usage. Reasons for these disparities can be found on different sociological attitudes towards technology or even on climatic factors. What is most relevant for this report is that a big part of Internet users have already sampled buying over the web (e.g. 40% in the UK), and a significant part qualify themselves as regular shoppers (e.g. 10% in the UK). Again, important differences between countries may be detected with respect to the expenses produced. For instance, Finland spent 20 times more than Spain on a per capita basis. The forecasts for European buying goods and services for the year 2002 suggest that the current 5.2 million shoppers will increase to 28.8 millions, and the European revenues from the current EUR3,032 million to EUR57,210 million. Finally, a significant increase in the number of European executives that believe in the future of electronic commerce has been observed (33% in 1999 up from 23% in 1998).

What the previous figures clearly state is that electronic commerce through Internet is reaching critical mass in Europe. The European Community is aware of all these changes and has been funding research in information and communication technologies, including electronic commerce, since the mid eighties.

F. Dignum and C. Sierra (Eds.): Agent Mediated Elec. Commerce, LNAI 1991, pp. 1–18, 2001.
© Springer-Verlag Berlin Heidelberg 2001

Different programs have served this purpose: ACTS/RACE, TELEMATICS, ESPRIT. Several projects have been funded in the past where agent technology was central. For instance, the well-known project ARCHON, and about 50 projects are currently being funded where agent technology is their *raison d'être*. The efforts and aims of all these different research programs have been recently fused into the "Information Society Technologies" (IST) program. This Program has a total budget of EUR3,6 billion during a period of four years and aims at supporting the use of agent technologies, specially in the area of Electronic Commerce. In the United States, the NSF last year launched a specific program for multi-agent systems with a budget of $65 million.

Other evidences of the interest for the use of agents in Electronic Commerce can be found in the series of workshops on Agent mediated Electronic Commerce of recent years (Seoul, April 1998; Minneapolis, May 1998; Stockholm, August 1999; Barcelona, June 2000).

In what follows a description of the current main research activities in Agent-mediated Electronic Commerce in Europe is presented and a scientific and technological roadmap, in terms of the research and development lines foreseen for the next years, is outlined. The references that exemplify each of the lines of research are by no means exhaustive, as there are many research groups, publications and running projects fitting in each of them. Most of the material has been gathered via three meetings of the AMEC Special Interest Group funded by the EU through the AgentLink Network of Excellence (Brussels, October 1998; London, April 1999; Barcelona, September 1999). Many of the attendants to these meetings have contributed ideas and, more importantly, pieces of their texts that have been integrated in this document. The references to the different European projects can be found through the CORDIS database [12].

2   Mediation by Agents in Electronic Commerce

Up to now a number of techniques have been used to structure the relation between customers and suppliers over the Internet. Users have been allowed to specify the attributes of goods to be acquired (sold), users have been modelled through profiles in order to better target offers, banners or to determine which negotiation strategy to use. However most developments made up to now are centered on a passive web query type of interaction. Richer and more flexible ways of interaction is what we will witness soon with the help of agents mediating in many of the steps of commercial transactions. Mediation is the corner stone of commerce. Mediators guarantee the infrastructure of trade: regularity, payment and financial conditions, back-up, delivery, etc. Software agents can similarly be of extreme utility for electronic commerce due to several reasons:

- **Autonomy** Agents may work proactively, reactively and independently of human intervention. They can wait for good deals without diverting our attention.
- **Personalization** Agents can be equipped with a personal profile to reflect its user preferences.

– **Social ability** The communication ability of agents permits them to negotiate over prices, services and transactions.
– **Intelligence** Agents can learn and hence perform better over time. In EC
  scenarios this may equate to making more money. Many AI techniques can
  be applied.

In [15] a more thorough analysis is given as to how these characteristics of agents
might be beneficial in mediating EC. Of course, the effectiveness of the agents
is for a large part determined by the marketplace on which they operate. In [57]
a model for an electronic marketplace for agents is described.

One of the first agents that was used in electronic commerce was Persona-
Logic [44]. It assisted customers to select automobile features by giving a set
of hard constraints that the car must satisfy and a series of graded soft constraints representing the preferences of the customer. The agent used constraint
satisfaction techniques to maximize the satisfaction of soft constraints. This line
of research is continued in the work presented in [52], which also makes use of
constraint satisfaction to satisfy as many preferences of clients as possible.

3 Current Developments in AMEC

In this section we outline some of the activities in Europe along those lines
identified by the SIG meetings participants as the right dimensions for AMEC.

3.1 Interaction

Commerce is all about interaction between buyers and sellers at all stages: finding, purchasing, delivery. In order to support interaction, autonomous agents
are being increasingly used in a wide range of industrial and commercial domains
[13]. In [56] a marketplace is described that makes use of agents to trade products. These agents have a high degree of self determination —they decide for
themselves what, when and under what conditions their actions should be performed. In most cases, such agents need to interact with other autonomous agents
to achieve their objectives (either because they do not have sufficient capabilities or resources to complete their problem solving alone or because there are
interdependencies between the agents). The objectives of these interactions are
to make other agents undertake a particular course of action (e.g. perform a particular service), modify a planned course of action (e.g. delay or bring forward a
particular action so that there is no longer a conflict), or come to an agreement
on a common course of action. The two basic mechanisms currently used are
Auctions and Negotiation which are the subject of the next two subsections.
Each interaction is governed by the protocol that is used by the participants
in the interaction. E.g. in an auction this can be a Dutch (or English) bidding
protocol. In the last subsection we indicate some developments in the area of
protocol modeling and verification for EC applications.

Auctions. The design of electronic auctions is receiving attention from several groups. Focus is both on platforms (e.g. IIIA in Barcelona [29]) and on formal modelling (e.g. University of Bath [21,41]). As the notion of trust plays a central role in trade, methods for enforcing the actions taken by agents are necessary. The design of the electronically equivalent institution similar to traditional ones seems to be a reasonable research direction [38]. It is thus not strange that time-honoured institutions such as Auction Houses have become one of the first electronic market places inter-mediated by agents (FM [23]). Different groups are looking for the development of electronic market places in Europe ([29,6, 49]). The European Union has funded several projects with this objective in mind: MEMO, ACTIVE, AIMEDIA, and GAVEL.

Negotiation. Perhaps the most fundamental and powerful mechanism for managing inter-agent dependencies at run time is negotiation. This is so because negotiation can be used to co-ordinate or share limited resources between two or more autonomous self-interested entities. In other words, an acquaintance needs to be convinced to act in a particular way (e.g. accept a deal). Since the agents have no direct control over one another, they must persuade their acquaintances to act in particular ways (they cannot simply instruct them). That is, agents have to engage in negotiation - a process by which a joint decision is made by two or more parties. The parties first verbalize contradictory demands and then move towards agreement by a process of concession making or search for new alternatives [45].

Different European groups are looking at this mechanism from different perspectives: models for negotiation [43,39,33,50], argumentation [42] or simulation [27].

Negotiation problems can be categorized in many ways (see also [34]). One way to classify these problems is according to the underlying incentive and information structures:

1. The actual size of the limited resource to be shared is unknown (e.g. two agents must agree to split a "cake" the size of which is unknown at the time of signing of contracts)
2. The set of agents who are, or may be, interested in the limited resource is unknown.
3. The set of agents is known, but their characteristics are unknown (e.g. agents bargaining with deadlines which are private information, or several agents competing for buying an object the worth of which is private information).
4. Everything is known but the strategy: For example, two agents with known time preferences bargain over how to split a dollar.

Depending on the category in which our problem fits, a different negotiation model may be applied. When building an autonomous agent which is capable of flexible and sophisticated negotiation, three broad areas are considered in defining such a negotiation model [37]: what negotiation protocol will be used, what are the issues over which negotiation takes place, and what reasoning model will the agents employ. Papers describing research in this area focus on one or more of the above aspects. For instance, [22] concentrates predominantly on the final point and presents a formal account of a negotiating agent's reasoning component. In particular, it concentrates on the processes of evaluating incoming proposals and generating counter proposals. The model specifies the key structures and processes involved in this endeavor and defines their inter-relationships. The model was shaped by practical considerations and insights emanating from the development of a system of negotiating agents for business process management (see [32] for details). In addition, some convergence and experimental results of certain types of negotiation using this model have been reported [50, 22]. Also, in [39] a reinforcement learning algorithm has been designed to enable agents to adapt themselves according to the changing environment, including the competitor agents.

This research area is receiving an increasing interest in the recent years, the NSF initiative for 'Negotiation technologies', or the specialised workshops during the last two years are clear evidences.

Protocols. One of the key determinants of interactions is the interaction protocol. That is, the ways interacting participants are allowed to progress towards deals. Agents may interact in order to reach agreements in many different ways: they may privately communicate their preferences to a third party that finds an acceptable deal for both sides, they can offer and counteroffer proposals in an iterative way, they can reach agreements on an issue by issue basis or on all issues at the same time, etc. The design of protocols, or mechanisms —in game theoretical terminology, is extremely important from the point of view of efficiency. The company Enersearch [18] is a good European referent with respect to the design of efficient market-protocols, mainly for power management. A very interesting approach using Petri nets can be found in [33].

3.2 Applications

There is a rich variety of interests in application domains. Applications range from market places, electricity management (Enersearch AB [18]), business (ADEPT project), banking, telecommunications, finance, marketing, insurance (DIALS project), and shopping assistants. In spite of such diversity, probably the most common application domain is retailing. An important aspect of retailing is to optimise targeted advertising. Companies are interested in producing the most appropriate advertising to increase the efficiency of their commerce. Techniques like data mining (to cluster shoppers) or profiling (to permit personalised communication) belong to the technological repertoire that the European projects MIMIC, NECTAR and AIMEDIA and the University of Torino [51] are using. In this book both [14] and [2] report on how agents can be used to personalize business transactions over the Internet. Case-based reasoning is being used in the project WEBSELL to design shopping assistants. The NECTAR project also uses agent technology to design virtual shops.

3.3   Engineering

Different groups are following a deliberative approach to agent design, like modeling agents that use BDI, goals, plans, persuasion. Different approaches to agent architectures are used, for instance using case-based reasoning or fuzzy rules [35].

Currently, there are several platform developments in Europe. We have already mentioned different European projects like AIMEDIA, whose objective is to end up with a product to be commercialised in the short term. In their case a kind of electronic "one-stop shop" that will provide users with profile managers, shopping agents and shopping assistants. The ZEUS agent toolkit, developed at BT Labs, permits programmers to develop agents to participate in market places [9]. At the Swedish Institute of Computer Science an agent-based market infrastructure has been developed that includes facilities for signing contracts, advertising, searching, brokering, matchmaking and negotiating [19]. At the Artificial Intelligence Research Institute (IIIA, [29]) of the Spanish Scientific Research Council a platform for designing electronic auction houses has been developed. It permits the use of different auction strategies and provides programmers with templates to define agents [47].

Different European research groups have applied formal techniques to the analysis of interaction protocols, mainly π-calculus [4], and dynamic logic [43, 31].

3.4   Products

Most of the engineering work is still confined to the laboratories of the research organisations and Universities and the R&D departments of (large) companies. However, there are already several software products oriented to the definition of agent applications in general. Some in Europe, like Grasshopper [30], a mobile agent platform specialised in tele-command internet applications; Mole 3.0 [36] that was the first mobile agent platform developed in Java at the University of Stuttgart; or FM 1.0 [23] a free platform for the creation of auction houses. No product specifically oriented at electronic commerce exists as yet, although several research products are aiming at generating such products and commercialising them (e.g. AIMEDIA [1], CASBA [7,56]).

3.5   Standards

There is a commonly shared belief within Europe on the importance of producing standards and specification environments as outcomes of current research. To this end, FIPA (the foundation for Intelligent Physical Agents - see http://www.fipa.org/) with its agenda for developing open interoperability standards for agents, is currently the main focus of attention.

3.6   Security

While companies, banks, and administration organizations presumably take care of their security features themselves, customers use commercial tools to participate in electronic commerce. If these tools do not provide effective security features, electronic commerce will not receive a global acceptance from individual customers.

The reason is clear: all known security threats apply to electronic commerce systems and especially to agent mediated electronic commerce systems: disclosure, alteration, copy and replay, denial of service, repudiation, spoofing and masquerading. However, the good news is that the security techniques for defending such attacks are known: authentication, access control, encryption, signatures, auditing and traceability, public key infrastructure and certification.

On the other hand, the need for mobile agents is acknowledged by many groups [24]. Many researchers and developers see agents as programs roaming a network to collect business-related data in order to help users to buy goods. The research efforts concentrate on how to guarantee termination, security or exactly-once protocols. To protect agents against malicious hosts agents should contain time-limit validity, and electronic money with expiration date, apart from the need for third parties to provide security for transactions. Proposals have been made to provide anonymity in transactions and off-line trusted third parties for secure contract signing [17]. Projects like MULTIPLECX look for secure transactions that can be scalable over the Internet. Among the results obtained so far we could mention the Mole software developed at the University of Stuttgart [36]. In this book the issue of security in the light of mobile agents is explicitly addressed in [48].

From the point of view of trust, certification services can nowadays guarantee the identity of the sellers. It appears that the eBay method is not good enough. A number of services like TRUSTe [55], ConsumerInfo.com [10] or a Better Business Bureau like BBBOnLine [5] or WAB [60] guarantees the honesty of the other party, or escrow [20] services like iescrow.com [28], Trade-direct.com [53] act as third parties for the delivery of goods and money. Trade-direct charges 5-6% of the contract price as escrow fee.

3.7 Legal Issues and Privacy

There are different companies delivering software for personalisation, like Broadvision, Net Perceptions or Vignette. Others, bundle online shopping and personalisation, like Interworld, or inTouch.

The modelling of user preferences is essential if an agent is to be instructed to perform an automated mediation task. The agent will be faced with different choices and it must be able to establish preferences among them. Different techniques to model profiles, like for instance rough sets (VUA, [58]), are being used. As already said before, data mining is another candidate for profile generation being explored in projects like MIMIC and AIMEDIA. A similar approach is being taken within the project TREVI to determine the relevance of information.

There are several European Directives that regulate the protection of individuals with regard to the processing of personal data, on the free movement of data and on misleading advertising. These different Directives together with the different national laws give shape to the legal framework within which agent-mediated electronic commerce must be placed. Current research projects take into account this framework in the specification of the management of data by agents.

A completely different question is the legality of contracts that are a result of interactions between agents. Another question is who is liable for the obligations following from these contracts. A project giving legal assistance to agent development projects is ECLIP (Electronic Commerce Legal Issue Platform) which studies the legal implications and limitations of personalised communication over Internet.

4   Research and Development Perspectives

As can be deduced from the previous section, we are witnessing the use of agents in the first stages of commerce, that is product and merchant brokering. This is why agent mediated electronic commerce has been closely related to information gathering. The short term development of the field will move a step forward and involve moving into real trading, that is, negotiating deals and making purchases. In order to facilitate this development the researchers and developers are facing a series of challenges:

- Relate ideal and actual agent behaviour with respect to aspects such as rationality, autonomy, situatedness and optimality.
- Relate roles of agents and their inherent qualities: identity, delegability, liability, and reliability (be they software representatives or mediators).
- Generate ontologies, interaction standards and social conventions: market institutions; insurance, financial and certification instruments; acceptable interactions and trading conventions.
- Generate new products, services and practices: market-specific agent shells vs. more generic trading tools; payment and contracting methods; risk-assesment and coverage; quality, prestige and performance certification.

4.1   Interaction

In order to give an answer to all these challenges researchers are looking at different fields that have faced the basic problem of interaction: game theory, economy, sociology. It is commonly believed that economic models will be useful for agents in e-commerce scenarios. And when the restrictions of a game theoretic or economic model are met, we will be better off by following the recommendations given by these fields. However, most theoretical models from economics are not valid for multiple-encounter types of interaction, which is a more than probable scenario for agent-mediated electronic commerce. There is thus a view that useful techniques will also come from other fields, such as the social sciences.

It can be argued that the real impact of electronic commerce will be on a dramatic change of supply chains. If a consumer can directly contact the producer instead of a reseller it might produce an increase in efficiency of the overall distribution chain. This increase in efficiency will obviously produce a decrease in customer's prices and then an increase of electronic commerce as a whole. These changes are still to come in many cases, we have only witnessed the creation of electronic versions of resellers on books and CDs. The direct relation between customers and producers will be permitted by the massive use of agent technology. These changes in the supply chains will permit new markets to appear, and old markets to change and permit the participation of new players.

Clear areas, where we will see many applications in the short term, will be those where the traded goods are commodities whose consumption cannot be well estimated in advance and for which trade must be done very often (e.g. power, telephone, bandwidth). The amounts traded at each occasion are very small and it is impossible to imagine a manual trade for them. Software agents will be mandatory here. In order for these applications to bloom, research results for very fast markets are still necessary.

Auctions. In the very near future we may expect, similarly to what happened over internet, an expansion of agent-mediated auctions. The four main types of auctions will be made available as protocols for agents to interact with the auction house, and the agents will come equipped with a series of parametric bidding strategies. The agent technology available now is sufficient to permit the deployment of such agent-mediated auction houses. Academic examples of them are Auctionbot [3] and FM [23]. Different European projects will deliver products supporting agent-mediated auctions during the year 2000.

Negotiation. The use of auctions is limited to certain types of products. More flexible interaction will be necessary as general types of interaction. Negotiation, understood in its more wide form as a process by which groups of agents communicate with one another to try and come with mutually acceptable agreements on some matter, is still to be wittnessed in real applications. Second generation eCommerce tools are going to provide this possibility.

We can envisage that agents will initially be used to explore the set of possible agreements, but will not be authorized to sign the contract. Agents will then pass this information (which could be a number of possible final contracts the agent was able to provisionally agree with its counterpart) to the user, who will then make the decision.

The first application domains, where we will see agent-mediated electronic commerce applications with fully automated negotiation, will have some of the following characteristics:

- *Interactions are very fast.* For instance for bandwidth trade. There is no time to go back to the user between trading rounds.

- *Interactions are repeated* with either (a) high communication overheads, or (b) the domain is limited, hence learning by the agent about the user behaviour is effective. Many B2B areas fall within this category.
- *Each trade is of relative small value.* If each transaction is of relatively small value it is possible to monitor the process and stop the automatic trade after some time without significant losses. It is important to stress the importance of *relatively* here. A small value for a company is completely different from a small value for a private consumer. This implies that most likely we will first see AMEC in business to business settings.
- *The process is repeated over long times.* The reason for this is two-fold:
  - There must be a significant gain in order to justify investments in software, hardware, and/or training.
  - Automatic agent learning of customer preferences is highly desirable as explicit preference elicitation is a very time consuming business.
- *The product is relatively easy to specify.* A number of traditional difficult computer science problems pose major difficulties to negotiations over complex objects. Such problems are mainly related to semantics of the communication. This is also related to preference elicitation. It is simply too time consuming to tune huge numbers of different parameters.

The challenges in the near future for agent mediated negotiation are:

- **Trust**
  Many aspects that will require the attention of the researchers for the next generation of systems refer to a reliable communication channel between participants in trade, mainly confidentiality, integrity, authentication and non-repudiation. Also, safe payment and delivery will be a foccus of attention.
  The first generation of agent-mediated electronic commerce systems covering the negotiation phase will be most probably a brokered service, where the contact between buyers and sellers will be supervised, following a very strict protocol and with a total control by the institution acting as broker. Later on, as robust trust mechanisms become available, direct contacts between buyer and sellers, with less structured transactions, will be possible.
  Reputation could also be achieved via external reviewers [46], or generated by peer rating, as is done at eBay and Amazon auctions. However, these systems are very vulnerable to manipulation. Reviews must be substantiated in some way to avoid false reviews. In open markets, agents must know as much about trust issues as about actual buying and selling.
  We see an important role to be played by chambers of commerce in this issue. The concept of an agent-based electronic chamber of commerce has been explored by Software Technology Group (Cambridge Consultants Limited [8]). Chambers of commerce will play an increasingly important role in mediation. They have a tremendous experience with it and will use their tradition of trust guarants to act as catalyst of electronic commerce, mainly in b2b scenarios.

– **Protocol Engineering**
We (scientists and industry) must agree on conventions of communications
at the strategic level. For example, agents will have to signal to each other
the type of negotiation problem they think they are facing (known/unknown
size of pie, etc.), and agree on the most appropriate negotiation protocol to
follow.
– **Preference models**
The modelling of preferences is essential to give an agent the capability of
acting according to a user model when negotiating. The challenges we are
facing correspond not only to the way of modelling preferences, but also
models which indicate the preferences of the opponent, as this may reveal
important aspects of its strategy. Different lines of research will help with
this task: data mining, fuzzy logic and learning, to cite just a few. Re-using of
profiles through case based reasoning techniques seems a promising approach
as well.
Near future challenges include:

- *Dynamics of preferences.* Interests and preferences of consumers change
  over time. AI approaches like learning, induction algorithms, believe re-
  vision techniques, or modal logic will become increasingly poignant in
  dealing with this challenge.
- *Different ontologies.* Providers and customers will probably use different ontologies to characterize products and interests. Different reasoning
  techniques and models to match providers and customers are necessary
  to move away from the requirement of a common ontology.
- *Fuzziness.* Preferences are by no means clear cut but fuzzy (uninteresting,
  interesting, very interesting). The use of fuzzy logic and statistics to
  model users' preferences is one of the techniques to explore.
- *Learning.* In order to construct a model of the user preferences without
  direct query it is necessary to develop appropriate techniques to observe
  the user behaviour to, for instance, present products in appropriate ways,
  or make appropriate suggestions.

– **Argumentation** Many problems cannot be solved by a simple offer/counter
offer negotiation protocol. In order to persuade an acquaintance it is necessary to use arguments to support our proposals. Protocols permitting
critiques to these arguments are hence necessary. Reasoning models to generate arguments, rebut and undercut them, and models of preference for
arguments adapted to the area of electronic commerce are also needed.

Protocols. The question of further investigating the 'rules for dialogues' in
different settings and establishing a right balance between fixed protocols and
free dialogues remains open. Again, we envisage a smooth transition from fixed,
supervised types of protocol, that will very soon be happening, to completely
free types of interaction in the mid to long term range.

We will see agents negotiating about the protocol of the interaction. In order
to do so, we'll have to study ways of formalising protocol definition, knowledge

about the goodness and badness of particular protocols and argumentative means to convince our acquaintances about which protocol to follow. As we all know from economics literature, the choice of a particular protocol can be of fundamental importance to get the right deal at the end. Arguing about protocols, or seeking advice to a specialist agent on what protocol to follow is a challenging research line.

4.2 Applications

Travel agencies and retailing industry will be the primary application domains benefiting from agent technology.

In the retail industry it is necessary to obtain a new model for on-line shopping, especially when compared to present mailer order business (catalogue based). We need to answer questions like: How to efficiently browse a large catalogue. How to present products (a tree structure aisle/shelf/range ?). How to find the product(s) the user is looking for (search tools) and how to guide the user through the site.

Agents can help on answering these questions: with search functions, guiding the customer, or helping in navigation. An example of this is SmartClient [52], specially when the products are configurable, as in travel planning. The technology used in SmartClient is Constraint Satisfaction algorithms over the product configuration constraints and the user preferences.

There is a number of applications to be developed during the year 2000. Among them an agent mediated auction house for general trading [54] and a negotiation house for travel packages [26]. Also several applications for retailing using agents are under development by J. Sainsbury in the UK and Otto Versand in Germany.

Of special interest will be the use of agents for the interaction with Public administrations. The European Union has a long tradition on helping citizens on the interaction with Public Administrations. For instance, the IDA (Interchange of Data between Administrations) programme aimed to enable EU agencies to interchange administrative documentation, or SIMAP, an electronic procurement programme. Projects like SUPPLYPOINT propose building virtual supply chains to help SME's to participate in public procurement. Inter-mediation by means of autonomous agents is one of the elements to be supported within the fifth Framework Programme. The use of agents for (public or private) procurement will be a way of decreasing the costs of procurement by automatising the reception of offers and the decision process. As an example, all of the Mexican government's procurement is achieved via the web with plans to move into agent-mediated procurement in the near future. The Mexican procurement system won the 1999 Bangeman's challenge for the Information Society.

4.3 Engineering

From the practical point of view, there is a common agreement in that agents will necessarily have to be adaptive. Mobility will be, also, in the long term, an essential issue. The modelling of trust, the creation of virtual enterprises and the enormous variety of legal issues that the community has to face will become crucial in the upcoming years.

From the point of view of engineering the crucial point of agent markets is whether the markets will be open or not. By an open market we mean one that allows interactions between agents that are not specifically designed by the owners of the market. An open market might not even have an owner. It might simply be the result of an interaction protocol that allows agents to locate each other and exchange information and offers. The first developments will be based on closed markets and then, once issues about security, privacy and trust are fixed, we will quickly move to the engineering of agent servers implementing open markets. Full autonomy will be linked, most probably, to the openness of markets. Buyers will be reluctant to permit their agents to sign up contracts when the agents are not under their complete control, even less if the market is under the control of the vendor they want to do business with.

Research on institutions will also have an impact on agent technology. According to North [38], human interactions are guided by institutions, which provide a structure for everyday life. Institutions represent the rules of the game in a society, including any (formal or informal) form of constraint that human beings devise to shape human interaction. Consequently, establishing a stable structure for human interaction appears as the core issue of institutions.

Considering agent societies, it would also be desirable to have similar mechanisms that help us shape agent interaction. Therefore, when designing infrastructures for open agent societies, we can adopt a mimetic strategy by trying to borrow and adapt well-known social mechanisms that have proven valuable when employed for articulating human societies. There are four characteristics desirable to be modelled in any agent society: Heterogeneity, Trust and scalability, Exception handling and Societal change. Human societies deal with these issues by deploying institutions that determine forbidden and permitted individual action, and the severity of the punishment to be enacted, and which evolve and are altered by human beings. It is therefore evident that the contact between Sociology and Computer Science [25,11] is currently becoming more and more important in the specification and development of multi-agent systems.

4.4   Products

The systems generated up to now are stand-alone applications used for product or merchant brokering. The new products (market places and agent servers) to appear soon will incorporate the necessary negotiation capabilities and will offer integrated services such as electronic payment, banking possibilities and transfer and storage of products.

4.5   Standards

The need for standards is crucial for the engineering of systems. There will be clear advances in the near future in this direction. For instance, W3C [59] committee is studying an update of P3P [40] profiling standard in order to incorporate some of the ideas covered by the European directives on privacy. Also, software customers will require the agent-based software be compliant with respect to those de facto standards appearing in scene. For instance, the recent incorporation of big players like SUN or IBM into FIPA, makes this a natural focus of attention for all agent developers. Also, FIPA and OMG (defining MASIF) recently agreed on a liaison in order to harmonise their standardisation efforts.

4.6   Security

Up to now most of the electronic commerce transactions over the Internet refer to low-value commodities (books, CD's, ...). As security guarantees increase high value goods will become object of trade through electronic means. Its automated trade through agents will depend on the security that software providers will include in the strategies embedded in agents. In the meantime, agents will perform tentative agreements ratified by humans.

Keeping preferences private seems a very important issue in order to increase trust on trading platforms. Protocols will have to guarantee this. P3P is the most outstanding ongoing innitiative in this direction.

There are several challenges concerning security:

- Definition of security levels and interaction protocols to negotiate security levels.
- Public key server and signature assignment managed by the agent management systems.
- A trusted broker agent architecture to guarantee anonymous customer access to company agents.

4.7   Legal Issues and Privacy

Markets use information about participants. This information must be protected. All developments of agent-mediated electronic commerce will have to satisfy the requirements established by the EU directive 95/46 [16] concerning privacy. Some international standards are being revised to become compliant with this directive.

5   Vision

We expect to face a basic re-organisation challenge for businesses: *to put the customer at the heart of the business* (sharing information on the customer from different departments, — marketing, sales, ...) in order to carry out agent-enabled personalisation. In the area of B2B We will witness the outsourcing of what is not at the heart of the business (such as delivery in the retail business, ...).

Also, a series of technological developments and economical changes will produce a dramatic impact on the use of agents for electronic commerce during the next decade:

- **Mobile devices** The computer industry is slowly bringing the computation devices to the individual. In the beginning of this century we'll witness many different low-weight devices to be worn by individuals. Electronic commerce has to be adapted to that. For instance by having agents knowing our preferences that warn us when we are close to a specialised shop in a city, or asking for instructions to close urgent deals while having dinner. Agent technology will be central to permit these new functionalities.

- **Context perception**

  One of the big challenges for technology is the detection of the context where a human being is placed. This information will be the necessary complement to the profile of a user. Knowing a user's context will permit more intelligent interaction between trading agents and human beings. For instance, we'd like our mobile devices to detect that we are in a restaurant and automatically switch into a mode where we are not going to receive messages unless they are very urgent (that is, we will not like to be interrupted by our PDA (or whatever mobile device we are wearing) to be offered a new tomato sauce from our usual eSupermarket in such a context, but we might be interested in being asked to close a deal of several millions.) When moving out of the restaurant we can then receive those that were less important. Learning of behaviours in different contexts will be an essential technique.

- **Deregulation**

  The deregulation process that we are facing at the end of the century, in most areas of trade, opens enormous possibilities for interaction with new players. In many occasions, areas being recently monopolistic are now populated with many different companies. We'll need to develop new mechanisms to establish the interaction rules among them. In some of these areas the negotiation characteristics mentioned in this paper fully apply: telecommunications and power. We expect to see lots of agent-based markets to permit the interaction among the participants in such markets.

- **Disappearing computer**

  Voice recognition, emotion detection, movement and mood detection mechanisms will be essential in the improvement of the perception capabilities of the computing devices we will have in a few years. These sensing capabilities will be placed in a computer infrastructure more and more distributed around us. The use of networking in house building and the possibility of having cheap computing devices associated to electric appliances and good items will open a new world of potential applications for agent-mediated electronic commerce. For instance, devices that will be able to connect the self-stock aware fridge with the local retailer to satisfy the needs of the owners of a flat, or negotiations between the different appliances on when to consume power after negotiation with the different power providers in order to minimize the power bill.

6   Conclusions

In this roadmap we have tried to give both an overview of current developments in agent mediated electronic commerce as well as some perspective on future research in this area.

Just like ordinary people have many different roles and need different capacities in transacting business, agents will also play many different roles and need different capacities in transacting electronic commerce. They range from information seeking and filtering to negotiation and actually conducting transactions. It is difficult to place all developments that are going on in both agent research as well as in EC research in this one overview. Therefore we have chosen to limit ourselves to the developments currently taking place in Europe.

We believe that this roadmap gives a clear view of the developments in Europe. The rest of the papers in this volume will concentrate on some particular aspects of this roadmap, indicating both results already obtained as well as interesting (and urgent) questions to be answered for future development of this area. Of course, any overview cannot pretend to be complete, but we hope that this roadmap is challenging enough for those people that feel that their area is not represented in this roadmap to actively participate in future developments in AgentLink and other international platforms.

Acknowledgements. This roadmap has been built using opinions and ideas given by the participants of the AMEC SIG meetings in Brussels, London and Barcelona during the first year of the AgentLink network of excellence. Any potential mistake or error is the sole responsibility of the author. I'm specially grateful to those that have contributed written material in the form of emails, papers, or position papers: Nir Vulkan, Lars Rasmusson, Jannilla Liden, Markus Schwehm, Mehdi Dastani, Vania Conan, Fredrik Ygge, Walter Van de Velde.

References

1. Aimedia project url. http://www.aimedia.com.
2. L. Ardissono, A. Goy, G. Petrone, M. Segnan, L. Console, L. Lesmo, C. Simone, and P. Torasso. Agent technologies for the development of adaptive web stores. In F. Dignum and C. Sierra, editors, *This volume.* Springer-Verlag, 2000.
3. Auctionbot url. http://auction.eecs.umich.edu.
4. University of Bath url. http://www.maths.bath.ac.uk/.
5. BBBonline url. http://www.bbbonline.com/.
6. BT Labs url. http://www.labs.bt.com/people/nwanah/index.htm.
7. Casba project url. http://www.casba-market.org/.
8. Cambridge consultants limited url. http://www.camcon.co.uk.
9. J. Collis and C. L. Lee. Building electronic marketplaces with the zeus agent toolkit. In Pablo Noriega and Carles Sierra, editors, *Agent Mediated Electronic Commerce*, number 1571 in LNAI, pages 1–24. Springer Verlag, 1999.
10. ConsumerInfo url. http://www.consumerinfo.com/.
11. R. Conte, R. Hegselmann, and R. Terna, editors. *Studies in Social Simulation.* Springer, Berlin, 1997.

12. CORDIS URL. http://www.cordis.lu/.
13. B. Crabtree and N. R. Jennings, editors. *The Practical Application of Intelligent Agents and Multi-Agent Technology*. London, UK, 1996.
14. M. Dastani, N. Jacobs, C. Jonker, and J. Treur. Modeling user preferences and mediating agents in electronic commerce. In F. Dignum and C. Sierra, editors, *This volume*. Springer-Verlag, 2000.
15. F. Dignum. Agents, markets, institutions and protocols. In F. Dignum and C. Sierra, editors, *This volume*. Springer-Verlag, 2000.
16. Directive 95/46/ec of the european parliament and of the council of 24 october 1995 on the protection of individuals with regard to the processing of personal data and on the free movement of such data. Published in the OJEC of 23 Nov 1995, L281,p.31.
17. J. Domingo and J. Herrera. A scheme for anonymous electronic commerce using secure intelligent trade agents. In *First Catalan Conference on AI*, pages 119–124, 1998.
18. Enersearch AB url. http://www.enersearch.se/ ygge.
19. J. Eriksson, N. Finne, and S. Janson. Sics marketspace —an agent-based market infrastructure. In Pablo Noriega and Carles Sierra, editors, *Agent Mediated Electronic Commerce*, number 1571 in LNAI, pages 41–53. Springer Verlag, 1999.
20. Yahoo Escrow url. http://dir.yahoo.com/Business_and_Economy/ Companies/Retail_Management_Supplies_and_Services/Electronic_Commerce/ Online_Escrow_Services/.
21. M. Esteva, J. A. Rodriguez, C. Sierra, P. Garcia, and J. Arcos. On the formal specifications of electronic institutions. In F. Dignum and C. Sierra, editors, *This volume*. Springer-Verlag, 2000.
22. P. Faratin, C. Sierra, and N. R. Jennings. Negotiation decision functions for autonomous agents. *Robotics and Autonomous Systems*, 24(3–4):159–182, 1998.
23. Fishmarket url. http://www.iiia.csic.es/projects/fishmarket.
24. A. Gehmeyr, L. Mueller, and A. Schappert. *Mobile Information Agents on the Web*, volume 1435 of *LNAI*. Springer, 1998.
25. N. G. Gilbert and R. Conte, editors. *Artificial Societies: The computer simulation of social life*. UCL Press, London, 1995.
26. HexMac url. http://www.hexmac.com/.
27. HP Labs url. http://www-uk.hpl.hp.com/.
28. Iescrow url. http://www.iescrow.com/.
29. IIIA url. http://www.iiia.csic.es.
30. Grasshopper version 2 url. http://www.ikv.de/products/grasshopper2.
31. Imperial college url. http://www.doc.ic.sc.uk.
32. N. R. Jennigs, P. Faratin, M. J. Johnson, P. O'Brien, and M. E. Wiegand. *Using intelligent agents to manage business processes*, volume 1435, pages 345–360. 1996.
33. J.-L. Koning. Designing and testing negotiation protocols for electronic commerce applications. In F. Dignum and C. Sierra, editors, *This volume*. Springer-Verlag, 2000.
34. A. Lomuscio, M. Wooldridge, and N. Jennings. A classification scheme for negotiation in electronic commerce. In F. Dignum and C. Sierra, editors, *This volume*. Springer-Verlag, 2000.
35. N. Matos, C. Sierra, and N. R. Jennings. Negotiation strategies: An evolutionary approach. In *Proceedings of ICMAS-98*, pages 182–189, 1998.
36. Mole url. http://www.informatik.uni-stuttgart.de.
37. H. J. Mueller. *Negotiation Principles*, pages 211–229. John Wiley, New York, 1996.

38. D. H. North, editor. *Institutions, Institutional Change and Economic Performance.* Cambridge Univ. Press, Cambridge, U.K, 1990.
39. E. Oliveira and A. P. Rocha. Agents advanced features for negotiation in electronic commerce and virtual organisations formation process. In F. Dignum and C. Sierra, editors, *This volume.* Springer-Verlag, 2000.
40. P3P url. http://www.w3.org/P3P/.
41. J. Padget and R. Bradford. A π-calculus model of a spanish fish market — preliminary report. In Pablo Noriega and Carles Sierra, editors, *Agent Mediated Electronic Commerce*, number 1571 in LNAI, pages 166–188. Springer Verlag, 1999.
42. S. Parsons, C. Sierra, and N. R. Jennings. Agents that reason and negotiate by arguing. *Journal of Logic and Computation*, 8(3):261–292, 1998.
43. S. Paurobally and J. Cunningham. Specifying the processes and states of negotiation. In F. Dignum and C. Sierra, editors, *This volume.* Springer-Verlag, 2000.
44. PersonaLogic URL. http://www.personalogic.com/.
45. D. G. Pruitt, editor. *Negotiation Behavior.* Academic Press, 1981.
46. Yahoo Reputation url.
    http://dir.yahoo.com/Business_and_Economy/Electronic_Commerce/   Consumer_Information/.
47. J. A. Rodriguez, F. J. Martin, P. Noriega, P. Garcia, and C. Sierra. Towards a test-bed for trading agents in electronic auction markets. *AI Communications*, 11:5–19, 1998.
48. V. Roth and V. Conan. Encripting java archives and its application to mobile agent security. In F. Dignum and C. Sierra, editors, *This volume.* Springer-Verlag, 2000.
49. SICS url. http://www.sics.se/.
50. C. Sierra, P. Faratin, and N. R. Jennigs. A service-oriented negotiation model between autonomous agents. In *MAAMAW'97*, number 1237 in LNAI, pages 17–35. Springer Verlag, 1997.
51. Universita di torino. http://www.di.unito.it.
52. M. Torrens and B. Faltings. Constraint satisfaction for modelling scalable electronic catalogs. In F. Dignum and C. Sierra, editors, *This volume.* Springer-Verlag, 2000.
53. Trade Direct url. http://www.trade-direct.com/.
54. TradeZone url. http://www.tradezone.onyx.net/.
55. TRUSTe url. http://www.truste.com/.
56. M. Vetter and S. Pitsch. Towards a flexible trading process over the internet. In F. Dignum and C. Sierra, editors, *This volume.* Springer-Verlag, 2000.
57. M.J. Viamonte and C. Ramos. A model for an electronic market place. In F. Dignum and C. Sierra, editors, *This volume.* Springer-Verlag, 2000.
58. Vrije Universiteit Amsterdam url. http://www.cs.vu.nl/ treur.
59. W3C url. http://www.w3.org/.
60. WAB url. http://www.wabureau.com/.

A Classification Scheme for Negotiation in Electronic Commerce*

Alessio R. Lomuscio[1], Michael Wooldridge[2], and Nicholas R. Jennings[3]

[1] Department of Computing
Imperial College of Science, Technology and Medicine
London SW7 2BZ, United Kingdom
A.Lomuscio@doc.ic.ac.uk
[2] Department of Computer Science
University of Liverpool
Liverpool L69 7ZF, United Kingdom
M.J.Wooldridge@csc.liv.ac.uk
[3] Department of Electronics and Computer Science
University of Southampton
Southampton SO17 1BJ, United Kingdom
nrj@ecs.soton.ac.uk

Abstract. In the last few years we have witnessed a surge of business-to-consumer and business-to-business commerce operated on the Internet. However many of these systems are often nothing more than electronic catalogues on which the user can choose a product which is made available for a fixed price. This modus operandi is clearly failing to exploit the full potential of electronic commerce. Against this background, we argue here that in the next few years we will see a new generation of systems emerge, based on *automatic negotiation*. In this paper we identify the main parameters on which any automatic negotiation depends. This classification schema is then used to categorise the subsequent papers in this book that focus on automatic negotiation.

1 Introduction

The term "electronic commerce" (e-commerce) generally denotes an advanced step of modern commerce in which the figures of buyer and seller are replaced by electronic entities [1]. It is widely believed that e-commerce will reduce costs for enterprises and provide customers with better bargaining tools. For example, automation can exploit short-terms contracts in combinatorially complex settings [31] and allow extensive comparisons to be performed between a wide variety of goods. Recent estimates put revenues of e-commerce at US$95 billion for the year 1999 with a forecast of US$1.3 trillion by 2003 [28].

Given the nature of the tasks involved in e-commerce, it has been suggested that agent technology [38] will play an important role in its development (see [11] for a survey). In such settings, agents will play the roles of buyer, seller, mediator

---

* This research was supported by the EPSRC under grant GR/M07076.

F. Dignum and C. Sierra (Eds.): Agent Mediated Elec. Commerce, LNAI 1991, pp. 19–33, 2001.
© Springer-Verlag Berlin Heidelberg 2001

[29], facilitator, and information provider. In so doing, agents will automate part or all the business tasks involved in e-commerce.

Most current e-commerce applications (servers and clients) may be classified as *first-generation* systems. That is, servers are connected to the Internet and they let the user browse through catalogues containing well-defined commodities (e.g., flights, books, compact discs, computer components, etc.) and make purchases typically by means of a credit card transaction. In this case the system's client can be any basic Internet browser and therefore the users' actions, being reduced to select/accept choices, are somewhat limited. However several more advanced forms of first generation clients, such as Jango [14] and Bargainfinder [3], have also been introduced. The main feature of these clients, frequently called *shopping assistants*, is the ability to perform *merchant brokering* on behalf of the user. Merchant brokering is the stage in the consumer buying behaviour where the buyer has chosen the product and is looking for the best deal to purchase it[1].

Other shopping assistants (e.g., PersonaLogic [26], Firefly [8]) offer their services earlier in the transaction by helping the buyer in the *product brokering* stage. This is the stage in the consumer buying behaviour where a decision is made about what product the buyer needs. Yet more advanced shopping agents, notably Tete-a-Tete [34], attempt to follow the buyer in more than one phase of the transaction by performing both product brokering, merchant brokering, and even some primitive forms of negotiation.

A key problem with all of these first-generation systems, however, is that they are too focused on one aspect of the transaction: price. Although price is clearly important, it is very often the case that neither customers nor enterprises have price as their only concern. Enterprises usually aim to acquire or maintain regular customers, whilst these customers are, in turn, often interested in non-price aspects of the purchase (such as warranty, delivery time, and past-record of the company). To cope with this need, more advanced forms of shopping assistant are required. Such software will have to deal with (interact over) the complete range of issues that are relevant to their user.

When faced with the need to reach agreement on a variety of issues, humans make use of *negotiation*. Similarly, we believe that automated negotiation will become the dominant mode of operation for shopping assistant agents. This *automation* of negotiation can significantly reduce negotiation time (making large volumes of transactions possible in small amounts of time) and can also remove some of the reticence of humans to engage in negotiation (e.g., because of embarrassment, personality, etc.). For these reasons, the formalisation of negotiation has received a great deal of attention from the multi-agent systems community throughout the past two decades [5,16,17,30]. Through such endeavours, it is becoming possible to develop practical automated negotiators. This will, in turn,

---

[1] The six main stages of consumer buying behaviour can be broadly thought of as: need identification, product brokering, merchant brokering, negotiation, payment and delivery, and service and evaluation. See [20,13,6,2] for more details on consumer buying behaviour.

facilitate the development of fully-fledged shopping assistants that are able to perform negotiation on behalf of users.

Negotiation strategies and their corresponding properties depend heavily on the specific characteristics of the scenarios under consideration. For example, economists and game theorists distinguish between scenarios in which the value of a good is common to all the agents (for example a typical shrink-wrapped good such as a CD), and those in which it is a private characteristic, which differs from agent to agent (such as a painting, which different agents may value differently) [23]. Whether a good has a common value, or whether its value differs from agent to agent, the valuations themselves may be common knowledge or private. These are but two illustrations of parameters upon which any negotiation mechanism crucially depends. However, as we shall see, many other parameters also play a key role in shaping the negotiation. Against this background, the principle aim of this paper is to define (for the first time) the *negotiation space* for electronic commerce. That is, we aim to identify the possible parameters that can be used to classify any negotiation mechanism for electronic commerce. Such a classification is an important step for the development of more sophisticated shopping assistants because it *defines* and *delimits* the design space for agent interactions. Thus, the classification in this paper should be seen from an analytical point of view. It does not offer any immediate practical application, but, instead, it aims at providing a conceptual framework on which protocols and strategies for negotiation can be classified and reasoned about. We argue that the components of the negotiation space that we identify constitute a complex space of possible games; indeed, we have so far been unable to find two distinct negotiation scenarios that would be described in the same manner in the classification. We illustrate our taxonomy by classifying the other papers in this volume that deal with negotiation.

The remainder of this paper is structured as follows. In section 2 we discuss and classify the main variables upon which a negotiation for electronic commerce depends. In section 3 we classify the papers in this volume according to our taxonomy. We conclude in section 4 with some discussion on the future direction of automated negotiation in e-commerce.

2 Negotiation Space

In its broadest sense, automated negotiation involves the design of the high-level protocols for agent interaction. The theme of negotiation is present in many different fields and, as a result, several definitions have been proposed in the literature [30,19]. It is not within the scope of this paper to discuss the merits of these definitions, and so we simply adopt the following definition:

> Negotiation is the process by which group of agents communicate with one another to try and come to a mutually acceptable agreement on some matter.

Two basic components are important when designing an automatic negotiation system: the *negotiation protocol* and the *negotiation strategies*. The former specifies the "rules of encounter" between the negotiation participants. That is, the protocol defines the circumstances under which the interaction between the agents takes place: what deals can be made and what sequences of offers are allowed. In general, agents must reach agreement on the negotiation protocol to use before negotiation proper begins. Reaching agreement on a negotiation strategy may itself be done by *meta-level* negotiation, but we do not consider this process here.

An agent's negotiation *strategy* is the specification of the sequence of actions (usually offers or responses) the agent plans to make during the negotiation. There will usually be very many strategies that are compatible with a particular protocol, each of which may produce a very different outcome. For example, an agent could concede at the first round or bargain very hard throughout the negotiation until its private timeout is reached. It follows that the negotiation strategy that an agent employs is crucial with respect to the outcome of the negotiation. It should also be clear that strategies which perform well with certain protocols will not necessarily do so with others: the choice of strategy to use is thus a function not just of the specifics of the negotiation scenario, but also of the protocol in use.

A *negotiation mechanism* consists of a negotiation protocol together with the negotiation strategies for the agents involved. There are some properties that are generally considered desirable for a negotiation mechanism (cf. [31, pp12–14] and [30, pp20–22]).

Computational efficiency: Ideally we seek a negotiation mechanism that is computationally efficient. Although users constantly have at their disposal faster machines, there will be little scope for negotiation algorithms that are, say, EXPTIME-complete[2].

Communication efficiency: All things being equal, we would rather have a mechanism that handles communication among the agents in an efficient way. Broadcasting to all the agents in the system, for example, may not be ideal with this respect.

Individual rationality: A mechanism should be individually rational for all the agents involved. In other words, it should be in an agent's independent interest to participate in negotiation — otherwise, a rational agent will not. If considerations of group utility need to be taken into account, they can be made a component of each agent's private utility.

Distribution of computation: Mechanisms that distribute the computation over the agents involved are preferable to ones in which one server is performing all the computation for the whole system. This is preferred for many

---

[2] One should be careful not to confuse the computational complexity associated with *designing* a negotiation strategy compared to the complexity of *executing* a strategy. The former can usefully be carried out offline beforehand, thereby reducing the computational costs of the agents. The latter obviously needs to be carried out at run-time and must therefore be manageable.

reasons, including the desire to avoid the disruptive effects of a single point of failure, and performance bottlenecks.

Pareto efficiency: An outcome is Pareto efficient if there is no other outcome that improves the lot of one agent without making another agent worse off. All other things being equal, Pareto efficient solutions are preferred over those that are not.

Symmetry: Generally in e-commerce settings, no one agent has complete control of the game. Therefore we prefer mechanisms that guarantee symmetry in terms of power of the agents.

Even with these broad guidelines in mind, many different mechanisms can be designed. These mechanisms very much depend on the specific characteristics of the negotiation space, i.e., the set of all possible negotiation games. In the next section we investigate this space in more detail in order to try and separate out the key orthogonal components.

2.1 Parameters of the Negotiation Space

As already noted, the design of an appropriate negotiation scenario crucially depends on a number of parameters, which can be seen to generate a space of possible negotiation scenarios. A preliminary attempt to classify this space has already been proposed by Wurman *et al.* [39]. In particular, they identify variables upon which auction servers can be designed. Some of the parameters introduced there are also present in our classification; but since we are not only concerned with auctions, our classification is more general.

We divide the parameters on which the negotiation can take place into the following broad characteristics:

- cardinality of the negotiation;
- agent characteristics;
- environment and goods characteristics;
- event parameters;
- information parameters; and
- allocation parameters.

Under this characterisation, an agent's negotiation strategy is simply one of its characteristics. We structure the characteristics of the protocol by analysing in more detail some key parameters such as events, information parameters, and allocation. The protocol as a whole results from the definition of all these.

Cardinality of the negotiation. We can distinguish between the cardinalities of the negotiation domain itself, and of the interactions that take place, as follows:

- negotiation domain: single-issue or multiple-issue; and
- interactions: one-to-one, many-to-one, many-to-many.

The domain of negotiation can be thought of as simply the set of tuples over which the agents negotiate. These tuples represent the issues on which an agreement is to be made. Elements of these tuples correspond to issues such as price, quality, warranties, delivery time, and so on (see for example [10]). In the case of single-issue negotiation (for example where the only issue is price) the tuples are singletons. In the case of multiple-issue negotiation, the different issues might be related by some publicly agreed utility function. This makes the process of bid formulation easier because each agent is then able to compute the utility function of each agent involved in the negotiation [36].

Interactions between agents can be classified in terms of the number of agents participating in the negotiation. *One-to-one* negotiation (where one agent is negotiating with exactly one other agent) is important for both theoretical and practical reasons. Theoretically, it is important because of the technical difficulties that this apparently simple setting provides; for example most games that result from one-to-one negotiation can be proven to have multiple equilibria [23], and a naive application of game-theoretical tools is therefore not possible. Practically, it is important because of the emerging role of one-to-one relations associated with business-to-business e-commerce scenarios.

Many-to-one negotiation (where many agents negotiate with just one agent) is the standard setting of auctions, which have been popular on the Internet for some time now [27,7]. In this setting one agent plays the role of the seller, while the many play the role of the buyers.

Finally, *many-to-many* negotiation (where many agents negotiate with many other agents) constitutes the most complex scenario. The continuous double-auction is the most complex of these scenarios that is actually in use [9].

Note that whether a given negotiation is one-to-one, one-to-many, or many-to-many is not determined simply by the number of agents. For example, it is conceivable to have a large set of agents, but arrange them such that any negotiation takes place on a one-to-one basis.

Agents characteristics. Agents are the computational entities that participate in the negotiation process. Each agent is assumed to be capable of rating its preferences, so that it can evaluate and choose between different deals. We can further characterise agents depending on their:

– role;
– rationality;
– knowledge;
– commitment;
– social behaviour; and
– bidding strategy.

Agents can interact in the negotiation as buyers, sellers, or both (as in a continuous double-action). This is their type: the role they play in the negotiation. For most negotiation domains, buyers and sellers are obviously the leading figures, but in other scenarios, (auctions for example), intermediaries can have an important role.

Rationality can be *perfect* or *bounded* [23]. The assumption of perfect rationality generally amounts to the agents being able to perform arbitrarily large computations in constant time. In all practical scenarios agents do not have the computational power (or the ability) to perform such calculations, and they are forced to bid or withdraw on the basis of finite computations. Thus, negotiation models that assume perfect rationality (e.g., many of those coming from game theory) have to use approximations in practice, whereas models that explicitly assume bounded rationality are more realistic in this sense.

Agents have knowledge about the goods they bid for, and possibly some knowledge about how other agents value the same and other goods. Depending on how such knowledge is distributed, agents may choose different bidding strategies. Whether or not agents hold private information is crucially important to design the agent's bidding strategy. For example, internal deadlines, and the valuation of the opponent's utility functions can be important parameters of an agent strategy.

Various levels of commitment can be present. For example, after having made an offer, agents might be obliged to stop bidding for similar goods until an acceptance or counter offer is received. Alternatively, agents can have the mechanism and process for reneging upon contracts built into the original negotiation (e.g., [31,10]).

Agents can act as individually self-interested entities, as altruistic units of a society, or they can strike a balance somewhere in between. Furthermore, whatever their attitude, they can play as distinct entities or effectively pursue team-formation in order to get better deals when convenient [36]. Another possibility is for agents to form coalitions — such coalitions can be a powerful tool for obtaining better deals in some domains.

An agent's bidding strategy is ultimately the component that decides about placing or accepting offers, making counter offers or withdrawing from negotiation. Although conceptually independent from the other parameters, it is reasonable to imagine the bidding strategy to be somehow related to the commitment, the knowledge, the rationality, and the social behaviour of an agent [10]. A standard assumption is that agents are individually rational, in that their bidding strategy would be against accepting deals that result in making them worse off.

Environments and goods characteristics. The negotiation environment can either be static or dynamic. A static environment is one whose variables (e.g., prices of important commodities) are constant over time; a dynamic environment is one in which these change over time. Clearly, there are various degrees of how static or dynamic environments can be, and this is only a simplification. Even so, the dynamicity of the environment might affect the design of the utility function of the agents in a subtle way. The utility functions of the agents reflect their preferences; so, while in a static environment one can imagine an agent that does not learn during the process and maintains a fixed utility function, this behaviour would be less likely to produce a positive payoff in a very dynamic environment.

The characteristics of the goods also crucially define the negotiation protocol:

- private/public value of the goods; and
- nature of the goods.

Agents can value the good differently depending on whether it is intended for private use (e.g., a cake) or whether its value depends on how the other agents value it (e.g., bonds). Frequently, both private and public valuations play a part. For example, when buying a car one has to consider both one's own preferences and how the car will preserve its value over time in case one should be interested in selling it.

The object of the negotiation can either be a discrete or continuous set (of goods). For example, a negotiation over a deadline (delivery dates, completion of contracts, etc.) is a negotiation over an uncountable set because time is intrinsically continuous. Usually, a simplification is made with respect to the granularity of the domain, and countable or even finite sets are used. For example, with a deadline one could use, days, hours, or minutes, depending on how fine the model needs to be. This simplification considerably reduces the size of the negotiation space. The simplest case arises when the set is a singleton.

Events parameters. The negotiation protocol is mainly influenced by the ways in which the offers and other events that take place during the negotiation are regulated. Indeed, what follows forms an important part of the specification of the protocol of the negotiation. We can distinguish between:

- bid validity;
- bid visibility;
- clearing schedule and timeouts; and
- quotes schedule.

The first item specifies an important part of the protocol: the criteria for validity of the bids. To be valid, bids often have to be offered at an appropriate time and must satisfy some constraints on their value. For example, in an English auction bids can be made when the auctioneer is calling for bids and must be progressively higher in value. Similarly, procedures for placing bids might be present during a negotiation.

The visibility of the bids is only relevant in the case of many-to-one or many-to-many negotiations. At the extremes, bids can be private messages passed between buyer and seller, or broadcast to all agents. Alternatively, we can have configurations in which only subsets of agents see some selected messages (especially useful if coalition formation is permissible).

A "clear" is the event producing a (temporary) allocation between buyer and seller. Clears can be scheduled at random times or following some other events (such as the first offer matching the buyer's request). For example, during the bidding phase of an English auction each round terminates with a temporary allocation of the good being auctioned to the prospective buyer that meets the auctioneer's call.

Timeouts determine the closing of the negotiation, therefore they transform clears into "final clears", i.e., a final agreement between buyer and seller about the transaction. Clears and timeouts also depend on the allocation parameters (see below).

If third-party quotes are generated during the negotiation process, their number and frequency are also part of the events and they need to be regulated. Intuitively, an excessive number of request for quotes can significantly slow down the negotiation mechanism.

Information parameters. Both before and during negotiation, information other than bids may pass between the negotiation participants. These messages are either information that can help buyers and sellers reach agreements, or information that can help limit the noise produced by agents trying to buy and sell goods. Such messages can be beneficial in order to save computational time of the agents.

Among the many possible useful messages, we can distinguish between:

− price quotes; and
− transaction history.

Quotes generated by prospective buyers requesting an indicative price from a seller before starting a negotiation can be useful to all parties, as they can reduce negotiation time.

The history of similar transactions can also be requested, or unilaterally provided, by a seller agent in order to give credibility to the information it is offering to potential buyer agents. It can be guaranteed by trusted third-parties. Together with third-party quotes, transaction histories can form the basis for argumentation-based negotiation. Such protocols [33,18] aim to bridge the gap between how negotiation is performed in human and artificial societies. In the former, expert human negotiators often focus on the reasons why an offer is not acceptable and try and persuade their counterpart of the characteristics that an agreement will have to include. In the latter, artificial negotiators traditionally are only able to propose offers to the counterpart without being explicitly able to motivate an agreement. This is often seen as a severe limitation and can limit the flexibility of the negotiation.

Allocation parameters. The allocation parameters only apply in many-to-one and many-to-many scenarios. They govern the winner of an auction when more than one agent has shown an interest in the good.

Allocation is studied in auction theory [35]. The Mth and $(M + 1)$-th price allocation policies cover most scenarios, where M is the number of received bids. Note that if the negotiation is multi-issue, in order for this mechanism to work there has to be a commonly agreed function that "weights" the different issues producing a value of utility. Without this, it would not be possible to order the offers as required by the allocation policy.

3   Papers in This Volume

This section briefly reviews the papers contained in this volume in terms of the conceptual schema we have developed.

Paurobally and Cunningham [25]

Paurobally and Cunningham [25] present a formal model of e-commerce systems in which a phase of automatic negotiation is present. The model uses the machinery of dynamic logic [12] to represent the states and processes of a negotiation system.

   Dynamic logic has the advantage of providing a precise and unambiguous language for representing and reasoning about actions and states. For this reason, the framework presented in [25] is very general and can be applied to a variety of different settings. The contribution of the paper, therefore, does not lie in a new negotiation strategy for a certain protocol, but, rather, it provides a language for performing inconsistency checks in the specification and in investigating issues such as concurrency.

   Nevertheless, the framework does commit itself to a particular subset of all the negotiation games: it deals with one-to-one negotiation and it focuses on a single issue of negotiation.

Vetter and Pitsch [37]

Vetter and Pitsch [37] present CASBA [4], a project devoted to designing and implementing a flexible and highly automated electronic marketplace. Technically the CASBA system consists of a server and three applets, all written in JAVA. The client-server communication is implemented in CORBA and XML.

   Vetter and Pitsch recognise that current e-commerce systems do not address all the stages of consumer buying behaviour (see above), and their proposal should be seen as a preliminary attempt to bridge this gap. As previously mentioned, one of the stages of consumer buying behaviour that is not usually covered is that of negotiation.

   - The negotiation protocol described in [37] is one of alternating offers. CASBA allows full parallel many-to-many negotiations over multiple attributes.
   - Agents' roles are defined in advance (buyers or sellers) and the agents are assumed to be able to evaluate an offer by computing its value in terms of a given (private) utility function. Agents have private information in the sense that their utility function is not necessarily known to other negotiation participants. Agents' commitment is total; the protocol guarantees that a

deal that has been agreed upon by two parties can no longer be negotiated upon. A feature of the CASBA system is that the agents' bidding strategy can be programmed via an expert-system shell, or chosen in advance from a set of pre-programmed strategies.
- The environment is static; indeed, the utility functions are not assumed to change during the negotiation process. This reflects the fact that the value of the attributes of the goods being traded is constant. The value of the goods, which are multi-attribute, is private.
- No timeouts or requests for information are present and bids are private.

Oliveira and Rocha [24]

Oliveira and Rocha [24] present an e-commerce architecture in which special attention is reserved for the negotiation phase. The architecture focuses on a multi-agent system in which a designed agent, called *market agent*, plays the role of the market coordinator. The other entities are either buyers or sellers.

What is particularly interesting in this work is that the decision making apparatus of the agents is built on a reinforcement learning algorithm. This approach builds upon previous work by the authors [22,21] in which Q-Learning algorithms [32] are developed and tested in market scenarios. The main contribution of [24] is to lay the foundation for a Q-Learning mechanism suitable for multi-attribute negotiations in e-commerce settings.

The protocol of negotiation can succinctly be described as turn-based alternating offer, in which the market agent initiates the negotiation by announcing the need for a product together with a deadline. In response to this announcement, agents can submit bids to the market agent. Bids are computed by the agent's reinforcement learning mechanism, and are private. Upon receipt of the bids, the market mechanism computes the most valuable and sends feedback to the agents on how to improve their bids. This process continues until the deadline is reached or a bid has been judged as acceptable.

In terms of our schema:

- The negotiation domain is multiple, as any offer consists of a variety of issues. Agents interact on a many-to-one basis. One agent is offering a good, through the market agent, and the others bid for it.
- The role of the agents can be of three different types: buyer, seller, or market agent. Agents have bounded rationality and they have private information (each agent's utility function is private). The agents are self-interested and bid according to a Q-Learning algorithm described in the paper. The commitment of the agents to follow the agreement is ensured by the protocol.
- The environment is constant, i.e., the value of the goods does not depend on external time dependent factors.
- Goods have private value. They can be discrete or continuous in nature. In general, they have more than a single attribute.
- The validity of the bids produced by the agents is guaranteed by the market agent. When bids are put forward, they are visible only to the market agent.

Timeouts for completion of a negotiation are public and announced by the market agent at the beginning of the negotiation. Clears are produced and sent to the appropriate agent.

4   Conclusions

The last few years have witnessed an unprecedented expansion of business carried out online. While these systems perform automatic transactions, thereby reducing costs, it is often the case that they amount to little more than electronic catalogues on which credit card payments can be arranged online. However a new, more flexible, class of e-commerce systems are starting to emerge. In such systems, automated software agents participate in trading activities on behalf of their user. A key aspect of these systems is the richness and flexibility of the inter-agent interactions. Here we focused specifically on automated negotiation since we consider this to be the key type of interaction in such systems. Automated negotiation, like its human analogue, is a very broad and encompassing discipline. For this reason, it is important to understand the dimensions and range of options that are available. As a preliminary step in this direction, we have developed a classification scheme that is specifically targeted at automated negotiation for e-commerce settings. This classification scheme was illustrated on the papers contained in this volume and the results are summarised in Table 1.

Having specified the negotiation design space, the next step is to identify the tools and techniques that are appropriate for specific regions of this space. Thus, we believe that no one technique or method of approach will come to dominate in this field [15]. Rather, there will be a range of alternatives that may be selected according to domain circumstances. The act of mapping the negotiation space in this manner will produce a design repository for interactions in agent-mediated electronic commerce. This repository will then constitute a valuable resource that will enable design expertise and know-how to be shared between developers.

References

1. J. P. Bailey and Y. Bakos. An exploratory study of the emerging role of electronic intermediaries. *International Journal of Electronic Commerce*, 1(3):7–20, 1997.
2. J. Bettman. *An information processing theory to consumer choice*. Addison-Wessley, 1979.
3. http://bf.cstar.ac.com/.
4. http://www.casba-market.org/.
5. R. Davies and R. G. Smith. Negotiation as a metaphor for distributed problem solving. *Artificial Intelligence*, 20(1):63–109, 1983.
6. J. Engel and R. Blackwell. *Consumer behavior*. PCBS college publishing, 4th edition, 1982.
7. http://www.ebay.com/.
8. http://www.firefly.com/.
9. D. Friedman and J. Rust, editors. *The double auction market: Institutions, theories and evidence*. Addison-Wesley, Reading, MA, 1993.

Work	Cardinality	Agent Characteristics	Goods	Events parameters	Info parameters
[25]	Negotiation issues: 1 Interactions: one-to-one	Agent roles: Buyer/Seller Bidding strategy: N/A Rationality: N/A Commitment: N/A Behaviour: N/A	Value: N/A Nature: N/A	Bids validity: N/A Bidding: N/A Clearing: N/A Quotes-sched: N/A	Price-quotes: N/A trans hist: N/A
[37]	Negotiation issues: Multi-issue Interactions: many-to-many	Agent roles: Buyer/Seller Bidding strategy: via an expert system Rationality: Bounded Commitment: total Behaviour: self-interested	Value: Private Nature: discrete	Bids validity: N/A Bidding: private Clearing: N/A Quotes-sched: N/A	Price-quotes: no trans hist: no
[24]	Negotiation issues: Multi-issue Interactions: many-to-one	Agent roles: Buyer/Seller/Market-Agent Bidding strategy: Q-Learning Rationality: Bounded Commitment: total Behaviour: self-interested	Value: Private Nature: discrete	Bids validity: N/A Bidding: private Clearing: Yes Quotes-sched: N/A	Price-quotes: no trans hist: no

Table 1. A table summarising the works analysed in section 3

10. P. Faratin, C. Sierra, and N. R. Jennings. Negotiation decision functions for autonomous agents. *Int. Journal of Robotics and Autonomous Systems*, 24(3-4):159–182, 1998.
11. R. Guttman, A. Moukas, and P. Maes. Agent-mediated electronic commerce: A survey. *Knowledge Engineering Review*, 13(2):147–159, 1998.
12. R. Goldblatt. *Logics of Time and Computation, Second Edition, Revised and Expanded*, volume 7 of *CSLI Lecture Notes*. CSLI, Stanford, 1992. Distributed by University of Chicago Press.
13. J. Howard and J. Sheth. *The theory of buyer behavior*. Wiley, 1969.
14. http://www.jango.com/.
15. N. R. Jennings, S. Parsons, C. Sierra, and P. Faratin. Automated negotiation. In *Proceedings of the 5th International Conference on Practical Application of Intelligent Agents and Multi-Agent Systems (PAAM-2000)*, Manchester, UK, 2000.
16. K. Kuwabara and V. R. Lesser. Extended protocol for multi-stage negotiation. In *Proceedings of the Ninth Workshop on Distributed Artificial Intelligence*, Rosario, Washington, September 1989.
17. T. Kreifelts and F. von Martial. A negotiation framework for autonomous agents. In *Proceedings of the Second European Workshop on Modeling Autonomous Agents and Multi Agent Worlds*, Paris, France, August 1990.
18. S. Kraus, K. Sycara, and A. Evenchik. Reaching agreements through argumentation: a logical model and implementation. *Artificial Intelligence*, 1-2(104):1–69, October 1998.
19. L. Chi-Hang Lee. *Negotation Strategies and their Effect in a Model of Multi-Agent Negotiation*. PhD thesis, Department of Computer Science, University of Essex, July 1996.
20. F. Nicosia. *Consumer Decision processes: marketing and advertising implications*. Prentice Hall, 1966.
21. E. Oliveira, J. M. Fonseca, and N. Jennings. Learing to be competitive in the market. In *Proceedings of the AAAI Workshop on negotiation*, Orlando, USA, July 1999.
22. E. Oliveira, J. M. Fonseca, and A. S. Steiger-Garção. Multi-criteria negotiation on multi-agent systems. In *Proceedings of the First International Workshop of Central and Eastern Europe on Multi-Agent Systems*, St. Petersburg, Russia, June 1999.
23. M. J. Osborne and A. Rubinstein. *A Course in Game Theory*. MIT Press, Cambridge, Massachusetts, 1994.
24. E. Oliveira and A.-P. Rocha. Agents advanced features for negotiation in electronic commerce and virtual organisation formation process. In C. Sierra and F. Dignum, editors, *This book*. Springer Verlag, June 2000.
25. S. Paurobally and J. Cunningham. Formal models for negotiation using dynamic logic. In C. Sierra and F. Dignum, editors, *This book*. Springer Verlag, June 2000.
26. http://www.personalogic.com/.
27. http://www.qxl.com/.
28. ActivMedia Research. Real numbers behind net profits 1999. Sixth annual study, New Hampshire, June 1999.
29. J. Rodriguez, P. Noriega, C. Sierra, and J. Padget. FM96.5 A Java-based Electronic Auction House. In *Proceedings of 2nd Conference on Practical Applications of Intelligent Agents and MultiAgent Technology (PAAM)*, pages 207–224, London, UK, April 1997.
30. J. S. Rosenschein and G. Zlotkin. *Rules of Encounter: Designing Conventions for Automated Negotiation among Computers*. The MIT Press, Cambridge, MA, 1994.

31. T. Sandholm. Distributed rational decision making. In G. Weiss, editor, *Multiagent Systems: A Modern Introduction to Distributed Artificial Intelligence*, pages 201–258. MIT Press, 1999.
32. R. S. Sutton and A. G. Barto. *Reinforcement Learning – An Introduction*. MIT Press, 1998.
33. Carles Sierra, Nick R. Jennings, Pablo Noriega, and Simon Parsons. A framework for argumentation-based negotiation. In M. P. Singh, A. Rao, and M. J. Wooldridge, editors, *Intelligent Agents IV (LNAI Volume 1365)*, pages 177–192. Springer-Verlag: Berlin, Germany, 1998.
34. http://ecommerce.media.mit.edu/Tete-a-Tete/.
35. W. Vickrey. Counterspeculation, auctions, and competitive sealed tenders. *Journal of Finance*, 16:8–37, 1961.
36. N. Vulkan and N. R. Jennings. Efficient mechanisms for the supply of services in multi-agent environments. *Interanational Journal of Decision Support Systems*, 28(1-2):5–19, 2000.
37. M. Vetter and S. Pitsch. Towards a flexible trading process over the internet. In C. Sierra and F. Dignum, editors, *This book*. Springer Verlag, June 2000.
38. M. Wooldridge and N. R. Jennings. Intelligent agents: theory and practice. *Knowledge Engineering Review*, 2(10):115–152, 1995.
39. P. R. Wurman, M. P. Wellman, and W. E. Walsh. The Michigan Internet AuctionBot: A configurable auction server for human and software agents. In K. P. Sycara and M. J. Wooldridge, editors, *Proceedings of the 2nd International Conference on Autonomous Agents (Agents'98)*, pages 301–308, New York, May 9–13, 1998. ACM Press.

Designing and Testing Negotiation Protocols for Electronic Commerce Applications*

Jean-Luc Koning

Leibniz-Esisar
50, rue Laffemas
26902 Valence cedex 9, France
Jean-Luc.Koning@esisar.inpg.fr

1 Negotiation Protocols for Electronic Commerce

1.1 Introduction

The most widespread and studied approach for managing negotiation between agents in a setting like electronic commerce relies on negotiation protocols. They are a set of guidelines that the agents of the system have to follow and that structure message passing. This enables agents to communicate knowing the types of messages they can receive, the types of messages they can send and at what time. Given their knowledge bases, what they perceive from the outside world, and the possible messages they receive from the other agents, they communicate among them through message passing according to a pre-established sequencing that has been possibly (and hopefully) validated. In this article, negotiation is exclusively tackled from the angle of protocols as they can be found in electronic commerce applications.

As recalled in the chapter entitled *Formal Models for Negotiation Using Dynamic Logic* by S. Paurobally and J. Cunningham, *"For electronic commerce to flourish we need to expedite negotiations and provide standardized protocols and methods for the automation or partial automation of negotiation. Negotiation can arise in several cases during a shopping process, such as negotiating on price and availability, on the payment method or on the after-sales services. A negotiation process is a joint process between a number of agents and there are various negotiation states that represent the degrees of co-operation, commitment and agreement."*

Such electronic commerce transactions may take place in electronic marketplaces where agents can buy or sell goods such as the Fishmarket (see the chapter entitled *On the Formal Specification of Electronic Institutions*), and more generally in virtual organizations such as Kraft (see the chapter entitled *KRAFT: Supporting Virtual Organizations through Knowledge Fusion* by A. Preece, K. Hui and P. Gray). As stated in F. Dignum's chapter entitled *Agents, Markets, Institutions and Protocols*, *"the institution determines the way that the parties can conduct the transaction and provides an infrastructure to do it"*. Such an infrastructure facilitates the negotiation process. The issue raised in that chapter is about the development of institutions and agents to make the

---

* Parts of this article are reproduced with permission from the Proceedings of the 13th European Conference on Artificial Intelligence, H.Prade editor, 1998. ©John Wiley & Sons Limited

F. Dignum and C. Sierra (Eds.): Agent Mediated Elec. Commerce, LNAI 1991, pp. 34–60, 2001.
© Springer-Verlag Berlin Heidelberg 2001

electronic marketplace really work. In the present chapter we only tackle one aspect of this question, i.e., the building of possible interaction protocols that can be used within the negotiation phase.

1.2   Negotiation Protocols

In electronic institutions a negotiation process translates into interactions among agents. Interaction is more than an exchange of messages. Issues associated with it, are: *models of agents* (beliefs, goals, representation and reasoning), *interaction protocols* (an interaction regime that guides the agents) and *interaction languages* (languages that introduce standard message types that all agents interpret identically). One way to structure message passing during agent communication is through protocols. By protocol, one may envision various stages.

- It can be a synonymous with etiquette, i.e. rules related to an agent's behavior. For instance, depending on a particular agent's role s/he is first—or is not—granted the right to speak. We will not consider this as actual protocols.
- It can deal with a recurring high level communication type. Thus, it better corresponds to the description of a communication phase. For instance, during negotiation, agents may first propose assertions in order to make their respective situation known, then they may discuss the various assertions, and finally the last phase would be to reach a consensus.
- It can also be a classical protocol of distributed artificial intelligence [26,5] (often called an interaction protocol), a speech acts sequence, conveyed by low level message passing. For instance, after a *request*-type message comes a message of type *answer* or *counter-request*.

We will deal with these two protocol levels: simple and rather constrained protocols, where a request awaits an answer or another request for instance; and, protocols of a higher level corresponding more to negotiation phases.

As in Paurobally and Cunningham's Chapter, negotiation protocols are viewed here as a *set of public rules that dictate the conduct of an agent towards other agents when carrying out some negotiation. Agents involved in the same negotiation need to comply to a common negotiation protocol to ensure that they and all other participants following the same rule will coordinate meaningfully.* In their chapter they present some models which show the relationship between the states of a negotiation process and permitted transitions between states. Here in the present chapter one is placed a step before, when the electronic institution's designer is building the negotiation protocol.

1.3   Outline of the Chapter

In the remainder of this paper, we will provide a detailed four-step approach leading to the building of a state transition diagram of a negotiation protocol. Such a work can be compared to the four layers given by [3] that distinguishes (1) the structure/syntax of messages, (2) the message types, (3) the procedures for preparing messages to send and for processing received messages, (4) the protocols as frameworks for dialogue. Actually that approach is completely different in its scope compared to ours since it discusses low level communication issues (layer 1 and 3), that we do not touch since we start with a given interaction language (see section 2.2). That article is more concerned with interaction (i.e., with the sending and processing of messages) than communication (i.e., the various states the agents can reach while communicating).

Throughout this article, we will show by means of an example how our four steps unfold and follow from each other. In the final section of the paper we discuss the critical phases of this procedure and present some future work.

First, this paper provides some help for the design of a protocol once its specifications have been defined. It proposes an integrated fashion to test the protocol.

The remaining of this article is divided as follows. The design and testing stages are presented according to a negotiation protocol perspective for electronic commerce. We attempt to provide an operational answer to both stages. In conclusion, limits of the approach are discussed and general perspectives applied to the context of electronic commerce are given.

2 The Design Stage

2.1 Phases in the Design of Protocols

In the context of electronic institutions dedicated to electronic commerce it is of good practice to follow a method for designing interaction protocols based on four phases going from the definition of message types all the way to the production of a protocol represented by means of a state transition diagram. Such a method lies within the scope of an agent centered approach where the electronic institution's designer chooses the agents architecture prior to the definition of its interaction module. In contrast, an interaction centered approach first of all defines the interaction and then the agents [27].

The advertised procedure for properly designing interaction protocols — once the agents have been defined (phase 0) — consists in (1) identifying the message types that are going to be handled, (2) explaining the possible message sequences between agents and defining the groups of agents that are going to receive those messages, (3) identifying the various agents' internal conversational states, and (4) making out the corresponding state transition diagram of the protocol.

2.2 Some Definitions and Notations

First of all, let us see some definitions. Each agent involved in a negotiation has their own *target objective*—or that which one would like to see ideally accomplished—as well as a *cushion* around the objective in which we would still be "on target" with the project. The purpose of this cushion is to give *room to maneuver* in our negotiations. Negotiation processes aim at building a compromise, an agreement between agents. Through such interactions, the ultimate goal is to identify (or find) solutions agreeable to all parties and lying within the target or cushion areas.

As shown in the Chapter *Formal Models for Negotiation Using Dynamic Logic*, the "*bilateral negotiation model defines the protocol followed by two parties looking for an agreement concerning a subject of negotiation. The negotiation is over one issue called the negotiation subject. In bilateral negotiation, we can think of a world inhabited by two negotiating agents, a negotiation process in a particular state, a model of negotiation and a subject of negotiation. There are a number of possible worlds that are accessible from the current world and some of these possible worlds have a successful negotiation state.*

A typical negotiation progress may encompass the following steps. First, each agent advocates an initial proposal which usually corresponds to their own objective. Then, this proposal is being discussed and new ones crop up. Finally, the best of all is accepted. If it lies within all the agents' cushion area, negotiation has succeeded. On the other hand, if this proposal does not suit some agent, one is faced with partial or total failure.

Let us see now, some notations. O_i, the ith agent's objective, is a particular proposal. From the agent's standpoint this is the ideal solution to the problem being discussed in the negotiation. C_i, the ith agent's cushion area, is a set of proposals that are close to O_i to some degree. It represents the agent's accepted tolerance as far as the distance between the final solution of the negotiation and the objective. Such distance may be defined as a fuzzy measure. S_i is the set of still possible proposals for the ith agent, that is C_i minus the subset of proposals already put forward during the negotiation process.

Phase 0: Specification of the Agents Interaction Module. In an agent centered design approach, the preliminary phase for a protocol life cycle consists in specifying the interaction part of the agents that will be brought to play in the system. Let us recall that one supposes an open electronic institution. This means it is very important to carefully list the characteristics the agents should own in order to fully communicate by means of interaction protocols. That is, external agents might interfere during the course of the problem solving. Furthermore, agents need to be of cognitive type, i.e., agents capable of a representation of themselves and others and endowed with reasoning mechanisms. A typical case for the building of such protocols is that of negotiation protocols.

Any agent should be capable of handling the interaction protocol(s) the system is to follow. After receiving a message an agent must be able to supply the types of answers the current protocol permits. Among other things this means that the agent's knowledge base must allow for storing the various proposals exchanged by the agents during the negotiation process as well as storing the agents' point of view. An agent's knowledge base KB_i must be able to keep track of the list of proposals previously sent by all the agents during the negotiation process and some related pieces of information such as their author, the other agents' standpoint as far as each of the proposals, and their intrinsic quality. Such quality may first assess (function *eval1*) the degree to which a proposal is compatible with all the objectives of the agents altogether. For example, this can be the percentage of agents whose proposals fit in the cushion area around the objective. Second, it could assess (function *eval2*) the degree of adequacy with the ith agent's objective.

As an example, let us see part of an agent's knowledge base in a negotiation process between three agents A_1 to A_3. At a given time, KB_2 may look like in table 1.

This table provides a list of the various agents' opinion for each proposal. For instance, P_0 has been put forward by agent A_2, accepted by A_1, and A_3 has put forward proposal

Table 1. Example of agent A_2's knowledge base.

GU	SA		eval2	1	0	0	1	0	1	
			eval1	.66	.66	.33	.66	.33	.33	
GU	**SA**			P_0	P_1	P_2	P_3	P_4	P_5	...
		A_1	accept	accept	propose	refuse	accept	?	
		A_2	propose	refuse	P_3	modify	refuse	propose	
X		A_3	P_1	modify	P_4	accept	modify	?	

P_1 that stems from P_0. P_5 has been put forward by A_2, and A_1 has not given any opinion about it yet. Furthermore, one notices that agent A_3 gave up negotiating after proposal P_4 was put forward. This is mentioned in row *GU* (set of agents who have quit the negotiation table), and of course no opinion is recorded thereafter for A_3. Apart from that, no agent reported a break in their putting forward proposals (row *SA*: set of stopped agents).

Functions *eval1* and *eval2* assess the quality of the proposals. *Eval1* tells the rate of agents whose proposals fit in the cushion area around the objective. *Eval2* assesses the degree to which the proposal matches the first agent's objective since we deal with KB_1. If P lies within the first agent's cushion area then $eval2(P) = 1$, if not then $eval2(P) = 0$.

Because of its knowledge base an agent is capable of providing other services such as searching for the best proposals recorded in the negotiation history.

Insofar as one is interested in the taking into account of a protocol by an agent, this phase may have deep consequences on the very capabilities of the agent's reasoning module. Indeed, depending on the expression power of the protocol to be handled, the agent's interaction capabilities will have to be more or less advanced.

Phase 1: Identification of the Possible Message Types. While negotiating, agents need to put forward new candidate proposals for solving the problem discussed during the current negotiation. Likewise, they must be able to accept, refuse or modify the proposals. They also need to point out whenever they do not have anymore proposal to put forward, or whenever they decide for some reason to give up negotiating. Finally, in order to drive the negotiation process to a close, agents must be able to tell whether they have detected an agreement on a proposal, or a failure according to some criteria which need to be defined when describing the agent's behavior.

Here are various messages we chose for our negotiation process example:

Propose(P): An agent wants to put forward proposal P that suits them.
Accept(P): An agent wants to accept proposal P.
Refuse(P): An agent wants to refuse proposal P.
Modify(P,Q): An agent wants to change proposal P into proposal Q that suits him. This is equivalent to *Refuse(P) & Propose(Q)* where Q is build from P.
No-Proposal: An agent wants to indicate he has no new proposal to put forward.
Abort: An agent quits negotiating.
Report-Agreement(P): An agent has detected a general agreement on proposal P.

Report-Failure(SBP): An agent has detected the negotiation broke down. SBP is the Set of the Best Proposals—according to function *eval1*—encountered prior to negotiation brake down.

In order to support such interaction between agents, one makes use of a language traditionally based on message passing, like ACL for instance [17]. This aspect being out of this article's scope, it is not detailed here (see [8] for example).

This technique has been developed both at a formal and applied level for quite some time in the MAGMA team (see [11] and [10] for a detailed review on this). In a few words, let us say that a message is divided into three general fields, one dealing with communication technicalities (<sender>, <receiver>, message <id>, communication <mode>), one dealing with multiagent interaction issues related to speech acts theory [24] (message <type>, message <force>, message <nature>, current <protocol>, <position> within that protocol), and one dealing with the application domain (<matter>, <proposal>).

Several of those sub-fields can be readily instantiated for all messages (see table 2). The sender is the sending agent. Since it is a broadcast, all the other agents are receivers. The type of message is *inform*, meaning no answer will be awaited (unlike *request*). The involved protocol will be the one currently under development.

Some features are also characteristic of each message. A message *force* can be seen as a type of priority [4], where *warning* conveys a higher message force than *expressing* which is itself higher than *information-seeking*. With the above basic forces all types of primitive messages that are used in protocols can be described. However, one could also have relied on illocutionnary types [25] as it is used in [6] or [13].

Table 2. Partial instantiation of message fields.

Message types	<force>	<matter>	<proposal>
Propose	information-seeking	propose	P
Modify	information-seeking	modify	P, Q
Accept	expressing	accept	P
Refuse	expressing	refuse	P
No-Proposal	expressing	no-proposal	none
Abort	expressing	abort	none
Report-Agreement	warning	report-agreement	P
Report-Failure	warning	report-failure	SBP

The message sub-field <position> indicates the internal state of the receiving agent after the message has been received. We have not detailed the various states an agent can take yet. This will take place when modeling the negotiation protocol as a state transition diagram.

In a way, this phase makes an inventory the notions to be handled by the protocol and thus allows for preparing the coming phase that aims at establishing their possible sequencing in time.

Agent's Behavior. Let us first outline the behavior of the agents that will be part of the negotiation protocol one wants to infer.

In case of distributed/decentralized negotiation, agents are distant from one another and work asynchronously. Let us precisely detail the behavior of an agent through a realistic negotiation example.

At the beginning of a negotiation process, agents decide whether or not they quit or keep on negotiating. If they do so they check their mailbox for new messages. When empty, they send a *Propose(P)* type of message, where P is a proposal belonging to S_i (their set of possible proposals) that is the closest to O_i (i.e., to the first objective of the agent). If on the other hand, their mailbox contains one or more messages, they choose whatever message with the highest force degree. They then derive the answer. The agent refers to the negotiation protocol by looking up the <position> field in the message. From this field the agent derives the various possible sorts of answers. According to their own criteria, agents choose one of the possible answers and fill out the <proposal> field according to their criteria as well. The now complete message can be sent allowing agents to check their mailbox again, and so on.

Figure 1 exemplifies the quite complex corresponding flow chart along with the criteria an agent makes use of in order to select among several possibilities as well as the way they build their proposal. Updates of the knowledge base are left implicit.

In figure 1, boxes labeled SELECT, PROPOSE, and MODIFY(Q) as well as agreement and failure criteria are not made explicit. Although it is not too complicated to define, for space reasons we will not deal with this in the paper.

Phase 2: Explaining All Possible Message Sequences. Now the design of the negotiation protocol really takes place. Let us begin with conveying possible message sequences according to the agents' behavior and messages that are to be used. This is the first step toward a complete protocol description although it is not mandatory for designing an interaction protocol. But it enables to view the message exchanges at a macroscopic level.

It is difficult to convey all possible message series that start at the negotiation process beginning and that lead to its ending, all at once. Indeed, such series must take into account how agents process the various proposals. However, agents process messages (embodying the proposals) they receive in whatever order that suits them. This thus leads to a combinatoric explosion with regard to the number of possible series.

But, if one deals with possible message sequences related to a given proposal, then expressing all of them becomes feasible. Such sequences start when a new proposal appears and end when agents run out of (outgoing) messages related to this proposal. Needless to say that during a negotiation process, several such sequences take place in parallel. Indeed, several proposals are discussed by the agents at the same time.

As a matter of fact, any messages series starting at the beginning of the negotiation process and reaching its end, is the result of overlapping smaller messages sequences each related to some proposal that appeared in the process. This overlapping depends on the order messages are dealt with by agents.

As an example, let us consider three agents A_1, A_2 and A_3 that are part of a negotiation process where two proposals P_1 and P_2 crop up. P_1 is put forward by A_1, refused by

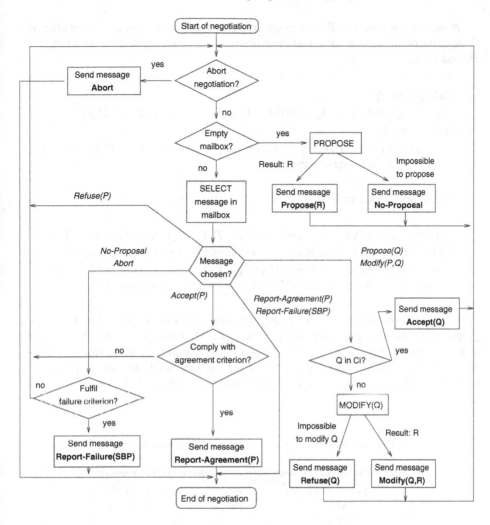

Fig. 1. Simplified behavior of agents.

A_3 and modified by A_2 into P_2. P_2 is then agreed upon by all three agents. The possible message sequences dealing with P_1 and P_2 could be for instance:

- dealing with P_1:
    1. $[A_1:$ propose(P_1), $A_2:$ modify$(P_1,\ P_2)$, $A_3:$ refuse$(P_1)]$ or
    2. $[A_1:$ propose(P_1), $A_2:$ refuse(P_1), $A_3:$ modify$(P_1,\ P_2)]$
- dealing with P_2:
    1. $[A_2:$ modify$(P_1,\ P_2)$, $A_3:$ accept(P_2), $A_1:$ accept(P_2), $(A_1,$ A_2 or $A_3):$ report-agreement$(P_2)]$ or
    2. $[A_2:$ modify$(P_1,\ P_2)$, $A_1:$ accept(P_2), $A_3:$ accept(P_2), $(A_1,$ A_2 or $A_3):$ report-agreement$(P_2)]$ or

Now, what are the possible message series that start at the process beginning and close at the end? Let us assume that the real message sequences dealing with proposals P_1 and P_2 are:

- dealing with P_1:
  [A_1: propose(P_1), A_2: modify(P_1, P_2), A_3: refuse(P_1)]
- dealing with P_2:
  [A_2: modify(P_1, P_2), A_3: accept(P_2), A_1: accept(P_2), (A_1, A_2 or A_3): report-agreement(P_2)]

The possible series are:

1. [A_1: propose(P_1), A_2: modify(P_1, P_2), A_3: accept(P_2), A_3: refuse(P_1), A_1: accept(P_2), A_3: report-agreement(P_2)]
2. [A_1: propose(P_1), A_2: modify(P_1, P_2), A_3: refuse(P_1), A_3: accept(P_2), A_1: accept(P_2), A_3: report-agreement(P_2)]

In figure 1, one easily notices that any sequence of messages related to a particular proposal (any sequence encompassing *Propose(P)*, *Modify(P,Q)*, *Accept(P)*, *Refuse(P)* or *Report-Agreement(P)*) starts with a "Propose" or "Modify" message since the agents deal with brand new proposals. For following up, one needs to look at the agent's behavior for the particular message selected from the mailbox. Table 3 shows this in an array format.

Table 3. Sequence of messages used in the negotiation protocol.

After selecting this message…	…an agent sends that message
"Propose" or "Modify"	"Accept", "Refuse" or "Modify"
"Accept"	"Report-Agreement" or none
"Refuse"	none
"Report-Agreement"	none

Figure 2 is a graph description of possible message sequences for proposal Q. It is a macroscopic view of the various message exchanges in the electronic institution. It is meant for all agents without any specification of the sender or receiver.

Any occurrence of message *Modify(Q,?)* triggers another message sequence related to a new proposal (proposal '?').

One may notice in figure 1 that any sequence of messages that is not related to a proposal (sequence encompassing *No-Proposal*, *Abort* or *Report-Failure(SBP)*) starts with a "No-Proposal" or "Abort" message. Then, agents send a "Report-Failure(SBP)" message and end the sequence or do not send any message at all. Figure 3 shows a corresponding graph of possible message sequences.

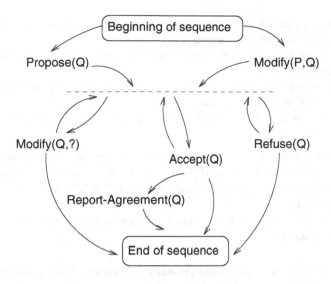

Fig. 2. Possible sequences of messages dealing with proposal Q.

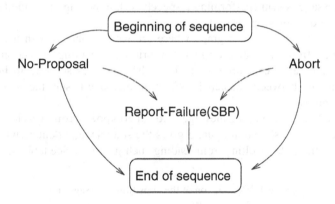

Fig. 3. Possible sequences of messages dealing with no specific proposal.

Phase 3: Identification of the Agent's Internal Conversational States. Prior to making out the state transition diagram of a protocol, one needs to know the states it will be composed of. Those states form a subset of the set of the various conversational states the agents can be in, and which were derived in the preceding phase. They are the agent's internal states. For example, by looking at the agent's behavior that comes from the graphs of the possible message series found (only one has been given above) one can identify five separate activities linked together by the messages sent or the external messages read. Here are those activities:

- The *initial* activity is triggered when negotiation starts and also whenever no other activities are triggered.

- The activity of *putting forward an opinion* on a new proposal is triggered as soon as a "Propose" or "Modify" message is read.
- The activity of *searching for a sign of agreement* is triggered after reading an "Accept" message.
- Similarly, the activity of *searching for a sign of failure* is triggered after reading a "No-Proposal" or "Abort" message.
- The *final* activity is triggered after reading a "Report-Agreement" or "Report-Failure" message.

Deriving an agent's internal states boils down to naming the state the agent enters when a particular activity is triggered. Therefore, the five activities just seen correspond to five internal states which can respectively be called: "init", "opinion?", "agreement?", "failure?", and "end".

Figure 4 shows the flow chart of figure 1 with divisions into activities which directly identify the five states.

Phase 4: Building the Protocol State Transition Diagram. Now let us establish a state transition diagram that exemplifies the agent's behavior. In order to do so one needs to find which actions allow for going from one state to the other. There are three types of actions: a message is sent (performing a speech act), a message is read after checking the mailbox, and no message is sent.

Figure 5 shows such a state graph where arrows are labeled with the name of an action. They go from the state the agent is in prior to executing the action to the state the agent reaches after executing the action. The messages sent are in **bold** and the messages read are between brackets []. When no message is sent the action is written between parentheses ().

In section 2.2, the remaining message field called <position> was left uninstantiated. Now the diagram shown in figure 5 gives the state an agent enters when receiving a message, i.e. the state resulting from reading such message. See table 4.

Table 4. Instantiation of the "position" message field.

Message types	<position>
Propose	state "opinion?"
Modify	state "opinion?"
Accept	state "agreement?"
Refuse	state "init"
No-Proposal	state "failure?"
Abort	state "failure?"
Report-Agreement	state "end"
Report-Failure	state "end"

Let us represent the resulting protocol by means of a state transition diagram where states represent an agent's internal state, and transitions represent the sending of a message by an agent. It is important to point out that in such a graph arrows go from the

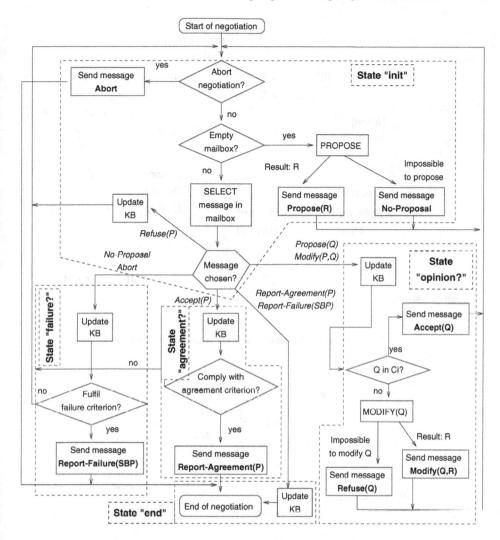

Fig. 4. Identification of an agent's internal states out of the representation of its behavior.

sending agent's state prior to sending a message and end on a state the addressed agent(s) reach after receiving the message (in other words, this is the state indicated in the message <position> field). The obtained state transition diagram of the protocol is given in figure 6.

This concludes the interaction protocol design stage.

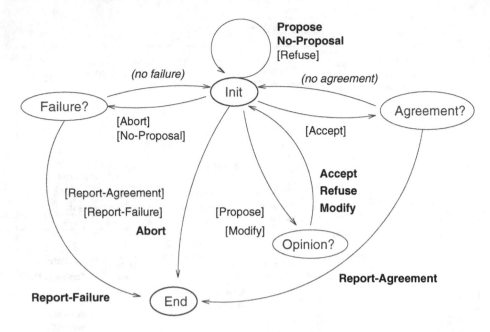

Fig. 5. State graph that exemplifies an agent's behavior.

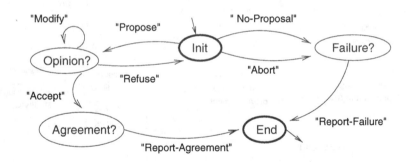

Fig. 6. State transition diagram of our negotiation protocol.

3   The Test Stage

Now that the design of a negotiation protocol for an electronic institution has been tackled, we will take up validation techniques used so far in the domain of communication protocols in networks [12] and prototyping of distributed systems [15]. We will adapt a similar method for the pre-validation of negotiation protocols in electronic institutions. The phrase *pre-validity* is used in this chapter instead of validity since one is not interested in proving a complete validity of the negotiation protocol but rather a partial one, i.e., checking the satisfaction of some elementary properties.

First of all, we will rely on Petri nets in order to model such protocols. For lack of space we will briefly introduce related work both in the domain of communication networks and the domain of electronic institutions.

Second, we will move to a protocol validation stage through the analysis of a Petri net model. We will also give a very brief presentation of a software tool that enabled us on one hand to run the analysis, and on the other hand to simulate the unfolding of typical scenarios for sequences of exchanged messages.

Finally, we will extract the global protocol properties and we will infer consequences on its (pre-)validity.

In the field of electronic commerce a similar approach has recently been taken in [20] which presents how to design and simulate a trade procedure and check the properties of such a protocol.

3.1   Petri Nets and Their Use in Multiagent Systems

Modeling an interaction between two agents of a multiagent systems comes down to building a per-agent Petri sub-net as well as a sub-net for the virtual medium, i.e., modeling the overall service that enable to rout messages between agents.

In [16], Ferber discusses a Petri net modeling of an interaction between two agents. It shows how agent A can ask agent B to provide a service. There are at least two reasons for criticizing that approach.

- The protocol that is described only deals with two agents that cannot play a symmetric role. Their statute is different; one requests and the other answers the request.
- The exchanged messages modeled by tokens in the Petri net represent hypotheses or proposals. When a hypothesis is modified by an agent the original one is lost even though its processing by the agents is not over. This stems from the fact that there is a given number of tokens that circulate in the net: one per agent which conveys its internal state and one and only one for the message that is being processed. As a consequence, this Petri net does not model a simultaneous processing of several proposals derived from one initial hypothesis.

A real interaction protocol provides a detailed description of the possible interactions between n (more than two) agents. But there is no clear approach in the DAI literature for modeling interactions that take place between more than two agents at one time. This is probably due to the fact that interaction between agents in DAI are rather grounded on Speech Acts theory than on distributed systems, which constitutes a serious bias in our point of view. As an example, the cooperative learning protocol given in [26] only deals with interactions among two agents.

Other uses of Petri nets in Distributed Artificial Intelligence include planning. In [14] a formalization of concurrent plans is proposed based on recursive Petri nets which is a suitable formalism for distributed planning. They also tackle there the management of potentially shared and conflicting resources through a recursive model.

In the field of electronic commerce, Petri nets have also been tried. [20] makes use of documentary Petri nets to describe international trade procedures.

3.2   Petri Nets for Representing Negotiation Protocols

This section addresses the modeling of interactions between agents in a multiagent system by building a Petri sub-net per agent and a Petri sub-net that represents the virtual medium.

Models of Virtual Mediums Linking Communicating Entities. Let us first model a perfect virtual medium linking n communicating entities. In a perfect virtual medium the possible loss of messages is not modeled and the transmission capacity is infinite. Such medium must offer the n entities the capability to send and receive several sorts of messages. Figure 7 exemplifies the modeling of such a medium for 3 entities A, B and C that allows each of them to receive and send two different types of messages.

In a similarmedium linking n entities and capable of exchanging m different sorts of messages, the number of links would be $n \cdot (n-1) \cdot m$. Clearly this modeling technique is not suitable for a great many entities. The virtual medium's complexity should not depend on the number of communicating entities or at least not be proportional to its square. One could also rely on the bus communication principle, where there is a bus type line of transmission for any kind of message. Figure 8 shows a bus type virtual medium that links three communication entities and enables the exchange of two types of messages.

Box (i, j) carries out the following functions:

- collect j-type messages sent by entity i and propagate them on line j in both directions, i.e., toward box $(i-1, j)$ and box $(i+1, j)$.
- transmit j-type messages coming from box $(i-1, j)$ to box $(i+1, j)$ and vice versa, while duplicating them for entity i.

Figure 9 details box (i, j).

Such a virtual medium liking n entities that is capable of exchanging m different sorts of messages, consists of m lines like those shown in figure 8. Hence, the medium's complexity does not depend on the number of communicating entities. The drawback with such a medium is that receivers of a message do not get it simultaneously. However, this is no problem when modeling asynchronous interactions.

As a summary, there are two techniques for modeling communication mediums that link n entities and support m different sorts of messages. One provides a loosely structured model whose complexity is $O(m \cdot n^2)$ links. The other provides a structured one whose complexity is $O(m)$ links (or $O(m \cdot n)$ boxes).

Petri Net Models for Assistant Agents. In a Petri sub-net that models a communicating entity [16], places represent internal states of those entities, transitions correspond to either the synchronizing of the reception of messages or actions agents perform, e.g., sending a message as a speech act.

In our framework [10], the agents' internal states and the actions the agents can accomplish are gathered in a state transition graph that describe their behavior. While Ferber's approach focuses on internal states we focus on behavioral states. See for

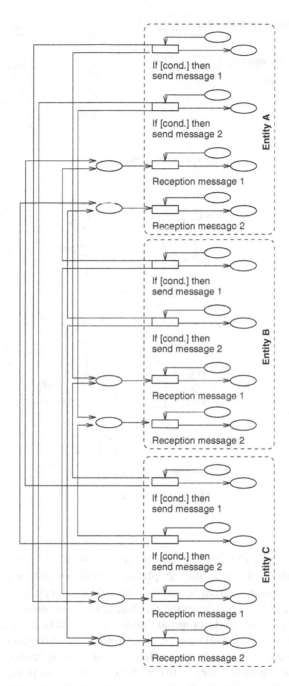

Fig. 7. Perfect virtual medium linking three communicating entities, and allowing the exchange of two types of messages.

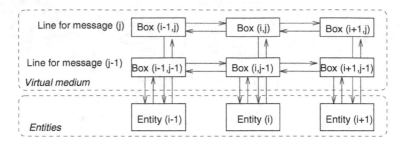

Fig. 8. Bus type virtual medium.

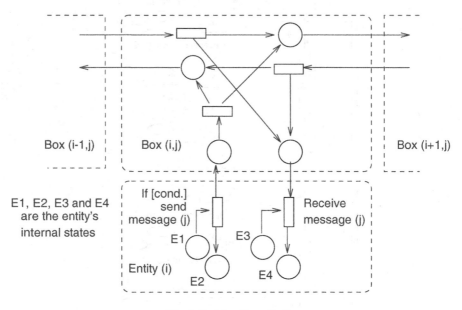

Fig. 9. Inside of box (i, j).

a detailed approach on the designing of interaction protocols in multiagent systems. Figure 6 exemplifies a state transition graph for a simple negotiation protocol.

In this graph arrows go from the sending agent's state prior to sending a message and end on a state the addressed agent(s) reach after receiving the message. In its initial ("Init") state an agent can send a proposal ("propose") which makes the receiving agent enter state "Opinion?". When an agent receives an modification (respectively acceptance) of proposal from another agent that is in state "Opinion" (respectively "Agreement?"), then it enters state "Opinion?" (respectively "Agreement?") too. In the "Opinion?" state an agent can also "refuse" a proposal which makes the receiving agent go to state "Agreement?". When the agents come to an agreement or want to abort the current negotiation they can stop negotiating ("report end") which makes the receiving agent enter state "End".

Let us see now the Petri sub-net model for agents whose behavior corresponds to the use of such a negotiation protocol.

Places are as follows:

- For internal states: P:init, P:opinion?, and P:end (for the sake of simplicity of figure 10 we have merged states "Init" in state "Agreement?").
- For the receiving and storing of messages: P:S-propose, P:S-accept, P:S-refuse, P:S-modify, and P:S-report-end.

Transitions are:

- For the sending messages: T:propose, T:accept, T:refuse, T:modify, and T:report-end.
- For the reading of a received message: T:R-propose, T:R-accept, T:R-refuse, T:R-modify, and T:R-report-end.

An agent is in state *s* if the place that corresponds to this state holds a mark (token). This mark that is unique to each agent will be called a *state-mark*. It can only go to places denoting the agent's internal state.

The other kind of mark that is present denotes the messages sent. They are only located in places where messages can be received. Hence, in such a place there is as many marks as messages of that type received and not yet read by the agent.

At this point, places, transitions and marks are identified. A Petri sub-net modeling the agent can be built. Places and transitions need to be linked by an arc so that a change of internal state caused by various actions matches the description of an agent's behavior (figure 7). Figure 10 shows the corresponding Petri sub-net.

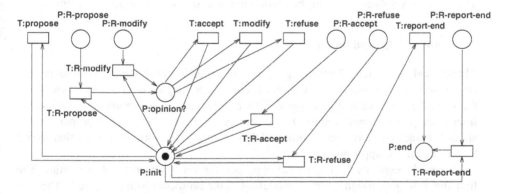

Fig. 10. Petri sub-net modeling an agent that makes use of the negotiation protocol.

There must be one token in the P:init agent's place—the state mark. This indicates the agent is in its initial state. From there, the agent is able to choose which action to perform and which transition to fire. This current Petri sub-net does not specify the way the transition to fire is chosen. As a matter of fact, interaction protocols do not provide this kind of information since this is the concern of the agent's decision. It falls within the application domain.

Complete Negotiation Protocol Model. A global Petri net can now be built in order to model our negotiation protocol. Petri sub-nets that correspond to agents have been defined. The virtual medium still needs to be chosen. Modeling the protocol and performing validation tests on a real application (with more than two agents) does not depend on the type of virtual medium. When there are very few communicating entities the loosely structured model whose complexity is $O(m \cdot n^2)$ links is bearable (see figure 7). On the other hand, for simulation reasons, when agents are complex and numerous there is a need for the simplest possible medium (i.e., bus type medium).

For space reason, no example of a final Petri net is shown here. But let us just mention that with a perfect virtual medium (the loosely structured one) places for getting and storing messages prior to their reading and storing by the agent, like P:S-propose, P:S-modify, etc. (see figure 10) belong in fact to the medium. Indeed, as shown in figure 7, the medium contains one place per agent and per type of message received. With a bus type medium, those places also belong to the medium and are duplicated in each of its boxes (see figure 8 and 9).

What is the theoretical significance of this complete negotiation protocol modeling? A protocol is a language L whose vocabulary V is the set of possible messages. V^* denotes the set of V's elements combinations, i.e., the set of all message sequences. The language L associated with the protocol is a sub-set of V^*. Given these definitions, we are building an automata A_1 by means of a Petri net, and whose language $L(A)$ is such that $L(A) \subseteq L$. In fact $L(A)$ is the restriction of L to a special case where n communicating entities are concerned. However, $L(A)$ can be viewed as a good approximation for L. The protocol validation can thus be carried out with the n communicating entities.

3.3   Protocol Pre-validation

Theoretical Approach. Performing a protocol validation boils down to conveying expected services and then check whether there is adequacy between those services and the ones the protocol really supplies. This article narrows to *elementary services* an interaction protocol must supply. Those services correspond to general properties that should characterize any "good" protocol. They are not semantic properties that would be attached to the application domain.

Figure 11 explains the theoretical approach for verifying protocol properties. The first step is to go through a formal modeling of the protocol given in figure 6. This has been done in the previous section. Let us now convey the expected elementary services as far as our negotiation protocol. This amounts to check whether it satisfies general properties necessary to any protocol [12,7].

- The first property one may wish is that the global protocol model, represented as a Petri net, be *bounded*. Indeed, a not bounded model means the protocol leads to a process with an infinite number of states.

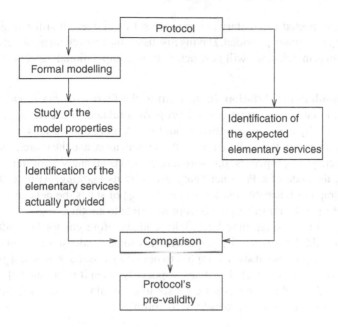

Fig. 11. Principle of protocol validation.

- The second property is that the global protocol model be *quasi-livable*. If such a property is satisfied, all the model's transitions are fireable starting from the initial marking. This ensures all protocol's messages are used.
- Thirdly, it is important to know whether the protocol leads to deadlocks and if so what they are. Obviously in case of a negotiation protocol, all markings associated with a model's deadlock[1] (or *sink state*) must contain a token in each of the agents' "End" state.
- The last property one may wish to see satisfied is that the protocol's model must enable ending with the desired sink state situations. In other words, the negotiation process inferred by the protocol must end.

This analysis being done let us express the expected elementary services:

(a) The negotiation process leads to a finite number of states.
(b) Every kind of protocol message is used.
(c) Every kind of sink state inferred by the protocol corresponds to the end of the negotiation process.
(d) The negotiation process always reaches one of these sink states situations.

A number of other properties can be subjected to verification. However, these are specific to negotiation.

---

[1] A *deadlock* is a marking such that no transition is enabled.

Once the expected elementary services are set forth, there it still remains to check whether they are actually provided. Having discussed the theoretical issues of a protocol's pre-validation principles, we will now detail more computational aspects

Use of a Simulation/Validation Tool. Editing the Petri nets that model negotiation protocols and analyzing certain general properties related to the net's structure have been carried out by means of a software tool [22]. Among other things, this tool allows for a graphical representation of Petri nets, their simulation, and the search for properties. In order to verify the properties, this software conducts an analysis of the net by means of its states; the state of a Petri net being given by its marking. At first, the software sets up the graph of reachable markings, i.e., the list of states the net can reach and the sequences of fireable transitions to go from one state to another.

The graph of markings may be infinite and therefore cannot be built. It is thus necessary to build the coverability graph which is some condensed version of the graph of markings. The purpose of such a graph is to obtain a sub-set of states that gives enough information on the set of reachable states, especially when it is infinite [9].

Subsequently, seeking properties consists in examining the coverability graph according to a procedure specific to each of the properties.

Properties and Validity. Properties of the Petri net that model our negotiation protocol are given in the appendix of this article. In this section we discuss the properties found and infer the elementary services actually provided by the protocol.

1. The net is bounded. This implies that **(1) this Petri net leads to a finite number of states**. In other words, the negotiation process thus modeled has a finite number of states. Furthermore, there is no infinite sequence of transitions in this net. This does not help us identify the final states of these sequences. On the other hand, it implies that **(2) the negotiation process does not enter cyclic or infinite sequences but always reach a terminal state**.

2. In the final Petri net that model our negotiation protocol with three agents, we have made several hypotheses in order to restrict the number of reachable states (for a simulation purpose): agent 1 is the only one to send a proposal (agents 2 and 3 cannot "propose": T:propose-2, T:propose-3), agents 2 and 3 can only send modifications (agent 1 do not "modify": T:modify-1), and agent 1 is the only agent allowed to end the negotiation process (agents 2 and 3 do not "report end": T:report-end-1, T:report-end-2). Consequently, agent 1 does not receive and therefore read any "propose" message (T:R-propose). Indeed, messages are not sent to the sending agent even when in *broadcast* mode.

   Thus, the only non quasi-live transitions are those six transitions. In particular, to each forbidden transition in an agent there corresponds an equivalent transition in a neighbor agent that is not forbidden and quasi-live. Had we not precluded some transitions on purpose, all would have been quasi-live. Thus, **(3) the protocol leads to negotiation processes in which no message is unused**.

3. The expression of the terminal states with the coverability graph shows that the terminal markings have a common feature: none have a mark in place P:init-x

and all have a mark in place P:end-x. In other words, the three agents reach their internal state "end" when the net is in a terminal state. Thus, **(4) all the net's terminal states correspond to the end of the negotiation process**.

4. Places P:init-x, P:opinion?-x and P:end-x are in mutual exclusion (i.e, it is impossible to have more than one mark in those places) and actually, there is always one mark in either of these places. Thus, **(5) at one time, agents (modeled in figure 10) have a unique internal state, and are never in a state different from "init", "opinion?" and "end"**.

All four expected elementary services (given in section 3.3) are achieved: conclusion (1) implies service (a) is achieved, conclusions (2) and (4) implies services (c) and (d) are achieved, and conclusion (3) implies service (b) is achieved.

4 Discussion : A Formal Description Language Alternative to Designing and Testing

It is relevant to model the interaction process inferred by the user defined protocol with formal description techniques [21]. In [19] we have worked with Lotos which is a specification language built upon a process algebra as defined for CCS or CSP [1]. The use of abstract types provides an even higher degree of abstraction. This language's formal definition has been recognized as a standard ISO8807.

Lotos enables to model multiprocess systems. Each process has synchronization gates through which sending or receiving messages is possible. Lotos is thus composed of a data part (typed messages) and a control part (processes). The distinctive feature of this language is that it can easily be transformed into a finite state automaton. It is then possible to make use of verification tools in order to validate certain properties based on the automaton's diagram.

[19] details how this translating of an interaction protocol into Lotos could be automated. First of all, a logical model for the interaction protocols has been put forward. Such a model allows to identify the various protocol components. Then, based on a prototypical Lotos code that a protocol description should end up in, this code is divided into five portions (specification of the set of Lotos gates, instantiation of the agent processes, instantiation of the medium processes, definition of the medium processes, definition of the agent processes) in order to facilitate the translation stage. Finally, for each of these identified pieces of code an algorithm is devised in order to transform each of the protocol characteristics into a piece of Lotos code. Once these five algorithms have been defined, the complete translation of a protocol into a Lotos description can be undertaken by successively calling each of them. We have given the whole procedure and detailed the functions for transforming a logical system representing an interaction protocol into a Lotos specification.

A lot of powerful tools are available and allow to verify all sorts of properties on a Lotos specification. The CADP tool box [18] has been used for this purpose. Thanks to its embedded compilers it is capable of transforming Lotos specifications into a finite state automaton. It also enables to verify that the Lotos formal description of the protocol is correct.

Such tools bear out the use of formal description languages such as Lotos to model interaction protocols in multiagent systems, all the more since it has been thoroughly tried and tested with communication protocols in the field of distributed systems.

5   Summary and Future Work

This chapter details two stages in the negotiation protocol life cycle: design and tests. The design stage studied in section 2 puts forward a division into four phases that allow an electronic institution designer to define a negotiation protocol and thus resulting in a state transition diagram. The test stage studied in section 3 presents what the validation of a negotiation protocol consists of.

As far as future development, several areas need further work. The first one deals with the nature of properties to be verified. We have only touched on rather general properties that one wants to find in any negotiation protocol. Those properties do not depend on the application. We are interested now in expressing and verifying semantic properties that are proper to the protocol given an application.

The second one deals with automating the protocol design process in order to end up at an implementable protocol that an electronic institution can actually run among its agents. Obviously step 0 is to be defined by hand by the electronic institution's designer. We are currently developing a tool that will help infer the last four steps.

This general tool helps design a negotiation protocol through a graphical user interface and generates a formal description of the protocol whose structure complies with the *protocol description language* (PDL) introduced in [23] and extended in [2]. Such language expounds a universal language that can be used to describe a set of protocols. It has been shown to be generic enough to describe a number of protocols that have been presented in the literature. The PDL allows the coexistence of different versions of the same protocol. This introduces dynamics to the protocols used in the society, since they can be improved.

This formal description is then translated by a code generator into primitives the agents will use in order to exploit the protocol. With such a general tool settling a negotiation protocol comes down to executing the following algorithm:

```
BEGIN
  REPEAT
    . designing the protocol by means of the graphical interface;
    . generation its formal description;
    . validation of the protocol;
  UNTIL all expected properties be verified;
  Generate the agents' primitives for handling the protocol;
END
```

Acknowledgments. The author would like to thank G. François and E. Vialle who contributed ideas to this chapter.

Appendix

Here is the file produced by PAPetri software for the seeking of properties in the Petri net modeling our interaction protocol.

```
+=========================================+
          COVERING GRAPH
        P. FRAISSE and C.JOHNEN
+=========================================+
 1 - Diagnosis
 2 - Unbounded places
 3 - Non quasi-live transitions
 4 - Home states
 5 - Live transitions
 6 - Termination
 7 - Fireable sequence from initial state
 8 - Reachable state
 9 - Expression of a state
10 - Mutual exclusion
11 - Print the net
12 - End of program
****************************************
Your choice: 1

The net admits 9000 states
It is bounded.
It does not admit infinite firing sequences.
****************************************
Your choice: 2
All the places are bounded.
****************************************
Your choice: 3

Non quasi-live transitions:
T:modify-1    T:report-end-1    T:R-propose-1
T:propose-2   T:report-end-2
T:propose-3   T:R-report-end-3
****************************************
No home state.
****************************************
Your choice: 5
No live transition.
****************************************
Your choice: 6
There are 1194 terminal components.

Component 1
 States 18

   (...)
```

```
Component 1194
 States 8977
******************************************
Your choice: 10
Enter groups of place names separated by a comma,
Enter a semicolon to end.

P:init-1,P:opinion?-1,P:end-1;

There is mutual exclusion and a group is always marked
******************************************
Your choice: 10
Enter groups of place names separated by a comma,
Enter a semicolon to end.
P:init-2,P:opinion?-2,P:end-2;

There is mutual exclusion and a group is always marked
******************************************
Your choice: 10
Enter groups of place names separated by a comma,
Enter a semicolon to end.

P:init-3,P:opinion?-3,P:end-3;

There is mutual exclusion and a group is always marked
+========================================+
            INITIAL MARKING
+========================================+
Place P:init-1, color black:       1
Place P:init-2, color black:       1
Place P:init-3, color black:       1
```

References

[1] A formal description technique based on the temporal ordering of observational behavior. International Organization for Standardization, September 1988. Geneva.

[2] Rafael Heitor Bordini and John A. Campbell. Towards an anthropological approach to agent adaptation. In *International Workshop on Decentralized Intelligent and Multi-Agent Systems (DIMAS-95)*, pages 74–83, Krakow, Poland, November 1995.

[3] Birgit Burmeister, Afsaneh Haddadi, and Kurt Sundermeyer. Generic, configurable, cooperation protocols for multi-agent systems. In C. Castelfranchi and Jean-Pierre Muller, editors, *From Reaction to Cognition*, volume 957 of *Lecture notes in AI*, pages 157–171, Berlin, Germany, 1995. Springer Verlag. Appeared also in MAAMAW-93, Neuchatel.

[4] J. Campbell and M. d'Inverno. Knowledge interchange protocol. In Yves Demazeau and Jean-Pierre Müller, editors, *Decentralized AI*, volume I, pages 63–80, Amsterdam, The Netherlands, 1990. Elsevier Science Publishers B.V.

[5] Man Kit Chang and Carson C. Woo. SANP: A communication level protocol for negotiations. In Eric Werner and Yves Demazeau, editors, *Decentralized AI*, volume III, pages 31–54, Amsterdam, The Netherlands, 1992. Elsevier Science Publishers B.V.

[6] Man Kit Chang and Carson C. Woo. A speech act based negotiation protocol: Design, implementation and test use. *ACM Transactions on Information Systems*, 12(4):360–382, 1994.

[7] J.-P. Courtiat, J.-M. Ayache, and B. Algayres. Petri nets are good for protocols. In *Symp. on Communications Architectures and Protocols*, Montréal, June 1984. Sigcomm'84.

[8] Michael A. Covington. Speech acts, electronic commerce, and KQML. *Decision Support Systems*, 22(3):203–211, 1998. Elsevier Science B.V.

[9] René David and Hassane Alla. *Petri Nets and Grafcet: Tools for Modelling Discrete Event Systems*. Prentice Hall Int., Hertfordshire, UK, 1992.

[10] Yves Demazeau. From interactions to collective behaviour in agent-based systems. In *First European Conference on Cognitive Science*, Saint-Malo, France, April 1995.

[11] Yves Demazeau, Olivier Boissier, and Jean-Luc Koning. Using interaction protocols to control vision systems. In *Proceedings of the IEEE International Conference on System, Man and Cybernetics*, San Antonio, October 1994.

[12] M. Diaz. Modelling and analysis of communication and cooperation protocols using petri net based models. In C. Sunshine, editor, *2nd International Workshop on Protocol Specification, Testing and Verification*, Idyllwild, CA, May 1982. Proc. of the IFIP WG 6.1, North-Holland.

[13] Frank Dignum and H. Weigand. Communication and deontic logic. In *Information Systems, Correctness and Reusability*, pages 242–260. World Scientific, Singapore, 1995.

[14] Amal El Fallah Seghrouchni and Serge Haddad. A framework for agent coordination oriented distributed planning and resource sharing managment. In *Eighth European Workshop on Modelling Autonomous Agents and Multi-Agent World (MAAMAW-97)*, pages 35–, Sweden, May 1997.

[15] Philippe Estrailler and C. Girault. Applying petri net theory to the modelling analysis and prototyping of distributed systems. In *Proceedings of the IEEE International Workshop on Emerging Technologies and Factory Automation*, Cairns, Australia, 1992.

[16] Jacques Ferber. *Les Systèmes Multi-Agents, vers une Intelligence Collective*. InterEditions, Paris, France, 1995.

[17] FIPA. *Specification: Agent Communication Language*. Foundation for Intelligent Physical Agents, http://www.fipa.org/spec/fipa99spec.htm, September 1999. Draft-2.

[18] Hubert Garavel. An overview of the eucalyptus toolbox. In Z. Vrezocnik and T. Kapus, editors, *Proceedings of the COST247 International Workshop and Applied Formal Methods in System Design*, University of Maribor, Slovenia, June 1996.

[19] Jean-Luc Koning. Algorithms for translating interaction protocols into a formal description. In Koji Ito, editor, *IEEE International Conference on Systems, Man, and Cybernetics Conference (SMC-99)*, Tokyo, Japan, October 1999.

[20] R. Lee. Distributed electronic trade scenarios: representation, design, prototyping. *International Journal of Electronic Commerce*, 3(2):105–136, 1999.

[21] Siegfried Löffler and Ahmed Serhrouchni. Protocol design: from specification to implementation. In *5th Open Workshop for High-Speed Networks*, March 1996.

[22] PAPetri. Institut d'informatique et d'entreprise. ftp://ftp.cnam.fr/. public domain software.

[23] P. Populaire, Y. Demazeau, O. Boissier, and J. Sichman. Description et implémentation de protocoles de communication en univers multi-agents. In *1ères Journées Francophones sur l'Intelligence Artificielle Distribuée et les Systèmes Multi-Agents (JFIADSMA-93)*, Toulouse, April 1993. Afcet & Afia.

[24] J. Searle. *Speech Acts: An Essay in the Philosophy of Language*. Cambridge University Press, Cambridge, 1969.

[25] J. Searle and D. Vanderveken. *Foundations of Illocutionary Logic*. Cambridge University Press, 1985.

[26] Sati Singh Sian. Adaptation based on cooperative learning in multi-agent systems. In Yves Demazeau and Jean-Pierre Müller, editors, *Decentralized AI*, volume II, pages 257–272, Amsterdam, The Netherlands, 1991. Elsevier Science Publishers B.V.

[27] Munindar P. Singh. Developing formal specification to coordinate heterogeneous autonomous agents. In Yves Demazeau, editor, *International Conference on Multiagent Systems (ICMAS-98)*, Paris, France, July 1998.

Specifying the Processes and States of Negotiation

Shamimabi Paurobally and Jim Cunningham

Imperial College of Science and Technology, London
{spl, rjc}@doc.ic.ac.uk

Abstract. *Negotiation can be considered to be an important aspect of commerce. It is part of those wider dynamic processes whereby commercial goals are achieved by the parties to a contract. Overt negotiation, as deal making, is often suppressed by agreed rules of encounter, but it is rarely absent altogether. In this paper, while recognising the need for more complete logics to represent both states and processes with abstraction, we start to build a more formal link between negotiation and Artificial Intelligence. We illustrate the use of dynamic logic to specify a shopping scenario between a retailer and a customer agent. The negotiation that arises in such a scenario can follow one of the negotiation models described. From a given negotiation model we obtain the corresponding negotiation protocol. These formulations have allowed us to remove inconsistencies and ambiguities in less formal models and to suppress issues such as concurrency. Finally, we discuss how an agent, given that it has mental states and a library of plans, can find a path for negotiation that will not only be successful in achieving its goal but also be optimal.*

Keywords: negotiation, electronic commerce, goals, dynamic logic.

1 Introduction

Studies in various sectors indicate technical features needed for successful interactive electronic commerce: security, privacy, payment, auditing and notary services, negotiation, brokering as well as human expertise (Cunningham et al 1998). Current on-line trading systems do not support all of these features, although there tends to be provision for security and payment. Users, providers and software developers also need interoperability protocols so that systems can interact with components in different domains and enable service providers and customers to coordinate and converge towards mutually satisfactory deals. In an open market, customers have to be able to inspect service offers regardless of the specific tool used to publish them. Standardised access to catalogues must be coupled with complete, up-to-date distribution and inspection of information to allow greater choices, wider user access, on-line enrolment and compatibility with other catalogues. Then, with each party having their own model of what makes a good deal and a bad deal, negotiation mechanisms can allow interaction between consumers and providers towards the

F. Dignum and C. Sierra (Eds.): Agent Mediated Elec. Commerce, LNAI 1991, pp. 61-77, 2001.
© Springer-Verlag Berlin Heidelberg 2001

resolution of an agreement. An agreement between parties must be established, drafted as a contract and subsequently engaged. A contract is a conceptually shared structure that binds parties together in a set of mutual obligations such as the exchange of commercial services. Finally, customer retention, service quality and competitiveness of on-line service delivery are key aspects of relationship management, involving long term interaction between provider and customer.

So for electronic commerce to flourish we need to expedite negotiations and provide standardised protocols and methods for the automation or partial automation of negotiation as a step towards agreement resolution. For example, negotiation can arise in several cases during a shopping process, when negotiating on price and availability, on the payment method or on the after-sales services. A negotiation process is a joint process between a number of agents, where there are various negotiation states that represent the degrees of co-operation, commitment and agreement. In this paper, we present a shopping scenario between a retailer and a customer agent and its representation in a dynamic logic. From the shopping scenario we can see where negotiation processes arise and that these negotiations may comply with a negotiation model. We also provide an abstract theory of the states involved in the shopping scenario and derive the paths leading to a particular shopping state. We then give several negotiation models that can be followed by agents engaged in a negotiation process. The possible paths of a negotiation are derived from the diagrammatic specification of the negotiation models using dynamic logic. A negotiation can follow a possible set of paths to reach a goal state. Finally we discuss the question of how an agent can find a successful negotiation path given it has mental states and it complies with the negotiation model.

2 Representing States and Processes

It is difficult to find notation where processes and states are given equal status, let alone form the basis for a simple and rational calculus for an executable system. Traditional imperative programming languages, such a C and Pascal leave reasoning about programs to external axiomizations which impose complexity and incompleteness. Object oriented languages provide otherwise missing capacity for data abstraction, but without solving the problems of the need for a rational calculus. Process calculi like CCS (Milner 1989) do not consider state, while specification languages like Z are removed from executable systems. In logic programming, we see demonstration of the practical capacity of predicate logic to define and combine data to give more abstract properties through which one can reason about machine state, but at some cost in confusing state transition processes with inference itself. Dynamic logic (Pratt 1976) is rare in providing reasoning about the effect of processes on states of affairs, but in its primitive form it lacks process abstraction, and has no seriously executable form as a programming system.

Thus there is no established notation to even represent both the states and processes of an active agent, let alone a calculus for deciding why a particular negotiation should achieve the mutual goals. Instead we shall improvise, conceptually treating an agent as capable of atomic actions, each constituting a primitive process which may be combined in more complex ones. Dynamic logics of action fit naturally with a multi-modal theory of agent beliefs, goals and intentions. A suitably rich first order logic with action terms and variables appears capable of a practical reasoning system which can relate processes to goal states.

Informal Syntax of the Logic
Our syntax is an adaption of the program logic described in (Goldblatt 1987). We associate an agent with processes by prefixing the process with an agent in the same way an object is suffixed by its methods. So the party executing a process and the process itself are separated with a full stop, e.g., *r:retailer.display* means retailer *r* executes the *display* process. Usually we omit the agent category and denote a joint process between two parties with ' ' as in *(c   r).shopping*. A process, whether joint or not, may be decomposed into a sequence of sub-processes each coupled with the agent or agents executing that sub-process. An action is an atomic process. The process denoted by *a;b* is composed of *a* followed by *b* in sequence, *a** denotes zero or more iterations and *a⁺*, one or more iterations e.g. {*r   c* }. *shopping =* *r:retailer.display ; c:customer.browse⁺; c:customer .choose**
A state test operator ? allows sequential composition to follow only if successful. For example *c.browse*? ; *c.choose* is the process *c.choose* if *c.browse* is true, otherwise it fails. We remark at this stage that conventional program-like *if ... then..., repeat ... until ...* commands could be more intuitive than the primitive test, union and iteration operators, ?,   , *, ⁺, borrowed from dynamic logic for task composition, but we reserve judgement on notation because there are tougher criteria in relating successful task composition to the goals and constraints of the agents.

When we specify the informal models of negotiation presented in section 4 we introduce additional connectives to give a logic that applies to a list of propositions. We use the prolog style for denoting lists, so that an empty list is [ ], a singleton list is [*X*] and a list containing at least one proposition is [*X*|*T*]. Thus *'none_of'* is a connective that takes a list of propositions and returns true if all the propositions are false, *'one_of'* takes a list of propositions and returns true if exactly one of the propositions is true. Formally,
none_of ([ ])   *true*, *none_of* ([*H* | *T*])   *H   none_of* (*T*).
one_of ([ ])   *false* , *one_of* ([*H*|*T*])   (*H   none_of* (*T*))   (¬ *H   one_of* (*T*)).
For example *none_of* ([*A, B, C*])   ¬*A   ¬B   ¬C*, while
one_of ([*A, B, C*])   (*A   ¬B   ¬C*)   (¬*A   B   ¬C*)   (¬*A   ¬B   C*).

3 Tasks of a Shopping Scenario

Consider the interaction between a retailer and a consumer, familiar to all as shopping. One can envisage a simple retail agent as seeking to maximise a long term profitability goal by wise buying, efficient distribution and stock management, and successful sales. In contrast, the goals of a retail customer are more subtle, involving, say maintenance of a personally adequate supply of garments, foods, or other consumables, through purchase within a fixed budget. The joint shopping process is illustrated in Figure 1 by an incomplete hierarchical JSD diagram (Jackson 1975), where task sequencing is left to right, iteration is loosely indicated by the symbol *, and shading distinguishes the activities of different or joint agents. Note that at the lowest level each task is attributed to a single agent, but it is not yet necessarily atomic.

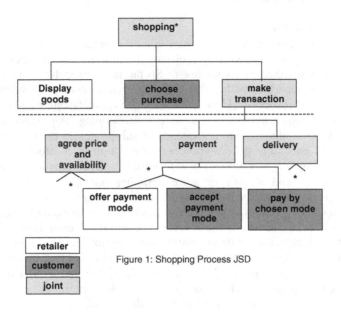

Figure 1: Shopping Process JSD

The shopping process is a joint process which can be decomposed into abstract parts done by either one agent or both agents at a time. First the retail agent displays the goods being offered, perhaps in the form of a catalogue or an event sent on an event channel to broadcast what is proposed. The customer then browses through the offers and chooses what he/she wants to purchase. At this stage there has not been any interaction between the two agents except for the sequencing itself, and synchronising this is a suppressed detail. The process of making a transaction will embody greater interaction between the two agents. In figure 1, the *make transaction* joint process has been broken down into three joint processes. These three processes can themselves be further broken down into sequential actions done jointly by the two agents or by a single agent. The illustrated decomposition is by no means definite and is just one of many possible decompositions.

Using the process operations we can compose the hierarchical shopping task as a joint process:

$(retailer \quad customer).shopping=(r{:}retailer.display\_goods;$
$\qquad\qquad c{:}customer.choose\_purchase; \{r \quad c\}.make\_transaction)*$
$\{r : retailer \quad c : customer \}. make\_transaction = \{r \quad c\}.$
$\qquad\qquad (agree\_price\_and\_availability ; payment ; delivery)$
$\{r{:}retailer \quad c{:}customer\}.payment = (r.offer\_payment\_mode (m);$
$\qquad\qquad c.accept\_payment\_mode(m))^{+}; c.pay\_by\_mode(m)$

{*r:retailer   c:customer*}.*agree_price_and_availability* =
c.within_budget(*r.advertised_price*) ?; *r.in_stock*? *null.*

The first composition that expresses the shopping process is a joint process between the retailer and customer agents and consists of three sequential processes: the retailer *display goods*, the customer *choose purchase* and the joint *make_transaction* process. The joint process of agreeing on price and availability is composed from two sequential test conditions. If the condition that the retailer's advertised price is within the customer's budget succeeds then the next condition of the service being in stock at the retailer is tested. Although a faithful representation of the joint processes implicit in the JSD diagram, this is itself an idealisation which ignores abnormal termination, such as when the customer makes no choice.

4 Joint States of the Shopping Scenario

If we consider the effects of the actions of the agents on the states of the shopping process we can represent them in a shopping state transition diagram whose essence is a dual of the above Jackson Diagram. We use a notation similar to Harel's statechart notation (Harel and Namad 1996). Abnormal transitions can be portrayed conveniently in this notation, so it supplements the state transitions implicit in figure 1. Whereas figure 1 is portraying joint tasks and process hierarchy of the shopping process and of the agents, figure 2 is a high-level state transition model that portrays the hierarchy of joint states for the shopping process linked by the abstract *display goods, choose purchase* and *make_ transaction* tasks. We can derive the essential structure of the state transition diagrams from the coloured JSD and vice versa, provided we ignore abnormal transitions. Through a JSD to represent the process hierarchy and a collection of diagrams for the implicit state transitions, we can suppress the full complexity of potentially concurrent interaction processes.

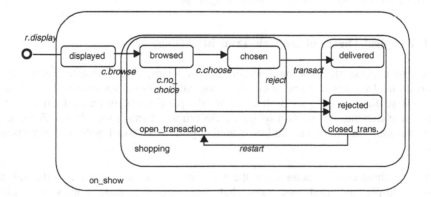

Figure 2: First Level State Transition Diagram of the Shopping Process

In figure 2, the parent state *on_show* is the overall state condition. The *shopping* substate is entered by the customer browsing. The substates of the *shopping* state are *open_transaction and closed_transaction* which themselves include other substates. *Rejected* and *delivered* are terminal substates that may be the subgoals of the agents. Possible ways for achieving these goals and subgoals are discussed in section 6. The *on_show* state is entered by the retailer making a display, leading to the *displayed* state. Then, the entrance of a customer through browsing leads to an *open_transaction*. Various state transitions change the substates of *open_transaction* and eventually terminate in the *closed_transaction* state. From the *closed_transaction* state, the customer or the retailer can restart a transaction, shown in figure 2 by the restart transition and shown in figure 1 by the iteration of the shopping process.

The high level state transition *transact* (*make_transaction* in figure 1) can be further broken down as required by the JSD to show negotiation over the price and availability, the mode of payment and the delivery. The negotiation over price may follow the state transition model of something like figure 3, leading to a *closed* state. Likewise, after the retailer has offered goods for a certain price and the customer has agreed to this offer, negotiation on the payment mode can follow the same negotiating model but be parameterised for a different issue i.e. the mode of payment. Eventually the state of negotiation on payment mode changes from *open* to *agreed*, a substate of the *closed* state.

Each state in the joint shopping model may also imply certain consequential states of affairs on each party's side. For example in the *displayed* state of the shopping process we may infer a parent state of the retailer having certain goods for sale. Similarly the *chosen* state of the shopping process may imply a need for a customer state of *has enough money*. So the state transition diagram in figure 2 represents the joint states of the shopping process but implies states of the involved agents. By speaking of joint states, we are supposing that the corresponding distinct states of the individual agents are implicitly known and controlled by lower level protocols for interaction. We do not discuss these assumptions here. In a distributed system they must be ensured by task and session management.

4.1 A Logical Theory of the State Transition Diagram

We can express the relation between parent states, their substates, and the state transitions, by using dynamic logic. The logical theory shown here is that of the high level state diagram in figure 3. It describes the relations between the high level states. The state transitions can themselves be decomposed into more detail. For example, the *transact* transition can follow some negotiation model with its corresponding theory.

The first three equivalencies show the relation between the parent and the substates. For example the first one says that the *shopping* state consists of disjoint *open_transaction* and *closed_transaction* substates, so if the current state is either *open_transaction* or the *closed_transaction* state then the *shopping* state is valid. The relation between *open_transaction* and *closed_transaction* states and their substates are similarly represented:

shopping   one_of [*open_transaction, closed_transaction*]
closed_transaction   one_of [*delivered , rejected*]
open_transaction   one_of [*browsed, chosen*]
on_show   one_of [*displayed, shopping*]

The actions performing state transitions can also be characterised by equivalences:
$\neg$ *on_show*   [*r.display*] *displayed*   (1)
displayed   [*c.browse*] *browsed*   (2)
browsed   one_of [[*c.no_choice*] *rejected*, [*c.choose*] *chosen*]   (3)
chosen   one_of [[{*r   c* }. *reject*] *rejected* , [{*r   c* }. *transact*] *delivered*]   (4)
closed_transaction   restart [*open_transaction*]   (5)

According to action condition 1, provided the retailer was not already involved in an *on_show* state, when the retailer makes a display action, the state changes to *displayed*. The entrance of the customer by browsing, in condition 2, leads to the *browsed* state which is a substate of *open_transaction* and *shopping* states.

Likewise for equivalence 3, if the current state is *browsed*, either the customer does not choose and triggers the state of the shopping to the *rejected* state or the customer invokes a choose transition to the *chosen* state. The terminal *closed_transaction* states, *rejected* and *delivered* can be entered from the *chosen* source state by the customer or the retailer making a *reject* or after a successful joint *transact* state transition.

4.2 The Paths of the Shopping Process

We can consider the shopping process as a graph whose nodes are the states and edges are the state transitions. The logical theory above represents the shopping process graph. Condition 1 gives the entry edges and conditions 2, 3, 4 and 5 the internal edges of the graph. The *delivered* node or state is the goal. We need to find paths to get from an entry node to the goal node. Here we can use the '?' notation to test whether we are able to find a path to a certain node or state and check if that state holds.

For example the paths to an *open_transaction* state are the union of the following sets of paths
- the customer entering the *open_transaction* through a *browse* action
- paths to the *closed_transaction* state in sequence with the edge of either the customer or the retailer restarting the transaction.
- paths to the *chosen* state

From our earlier presumption that an open transaction state is either a *browsed* or a *chosen* state we can infer the paths to the *closed_transaction* state and thus the paths to an agent's goal. Let p_0 be paths to *open_transaction* and p_c be paths to *closed_transaction*. Then p_0 and p_c can be derived from the above conditions.

$p_0 = p_c$; *restart*   ((*on_show*)? *r.display ; c.browse*)   (6)
$p_c = p_0$; ((*chosen* ? *transact   reject*)   (*browsed* ?; *c.choose*; (*transact   reject*)
c.no_choice))   (7)

Eliminating p_0 by substitution in (7) gives:
$p_c = (p_c$; *restart*   ((*shopping*)? *r.display ; c.browse*)) ; ((*chosen* ? *transact
reject*)   (*browsed*?; (*c.choose* ; (*transact   reject*)   *c.no_choice*))   (8)

Let *entries* = (*on_show*)? *r.display ; c.browse* and *exits* = (*chosen* ? *transact
reject*)   (*browsed* ?; *c.choose* ; (*transact   reject*)   *c.no_choice*). We thus have:
$p_c = p_c$; *restart* ; *exits   entries*; *exits*, whence: (9)
p_c = *entry_points*; *exits*   (*restart* ; *exits*) *   (10)

So a path to the *closed_transaction* state consists of entry to the *open_transaction*
state followed by *exit* paths from that state with optional reiterations by restarting the
transaction followed by *exit* paths. The recursive path equation (9) is solved as (10) in
the regular algebra of paths, when viewing the state transition diagram as a graph, by
postulating the inference rule:
$$(x = x ; A   B)   (x = B;A^*).$$
See (Backhouse and Carre 1973).

5 Bilateral Negotiation Models

Following our illustration of task analysis for the first level processes and states of the
joint shopping process, we find that details of the transaction involve a sequence of
negotiations over price, payment and delivery.   These too can have similar
representation and analysis.

A negotiation protocol is the set of public rules that dictate the conduct of an agent
towards other agents when carrying out some negotiation. Agents involved in the
same negotiation need to comply to a common negotiation protocol to ensure that
they and all other participants following the same rule will coordinate meaningfully.
The models presented here show the relationships between the states of a negotiation
process and permitted transitions between the states, so implicitly define a negotiation
protocol which is made explicit in the logical theory of the model. A group of agents
involved in a negotiation process can invoke state transitions to achieve terminal
states or goal states. If the goal state is to reach an agreement, and it is achieved, an
engagement process can be launched for achieving commitment and for setting up
contracts between the agents.   These models can form the basis for further
customisation into more specific negotiation models. Negotiation may also be on
various issues that could be a concurrent execution of single-issue models or another
compound model.
In a negotiation process, there are constraints on joining the negotiation and on the
disclosure of information. An agent who is not involved in a particular negotiation
cannot become a member or join in without authorisation. An agent may be involved
in several concurrent negotiations. In each, an agent has a task to negotiate. It

associates the negotiation process with its participants, the subject and model of negotiation.   So an agent is able to distinguish between its possibly multiple negotiations to decide the current negotiation state and in choosing the appropriate action.   Implicitly each negotiation state is characterised with a tuple (negotiation process, participants, negotiation model, negotiation subject) and each negotiation action is implicitly subscripted with the tuple (negotiation process, perpetrator of that action, negotiation model, negotiation subject).

5.1 Bilateral Negotiation Models

The bilateral negotiation model defines a protocol followed by two parties looking for an agreement. The negotiation is over one issue called the negotiation subject. In bilateral negotiation, we can think of a world inhabited by two negotiating agents, a negotiation process in a particular state, a model of negotiation and a subject of negotiation. There are a number of possible world/s that are accessible from the current world state and some of these possible states have a successful negotiation state. We describe two bilateral negotiation models, a generic one and an expanded one.

Generic Bilateral Negotiation

Abstract open states in a bilateral negotiation are:

offered: In this state, the subject of negotiation cannot be changed and can only be agreed to or rejected. The offering party is committed to the offer.

proposed: proposed is a sub-state of offered and may be agreed to, or the subject can be further changed by transition to a requested state.

requested: This state allows a respondent to change the subject of a negotiation and the other party to respond with propose, offer or suggest.

A user initiates the negotiation process in either a proposed, requested or offered state. The bilateral negotiation model, shown in figure 3, is derived from a proposal to the Object Management Group (OSM SARL 1998).   It incorporates corrections of the ambiguities emerging from our methods.

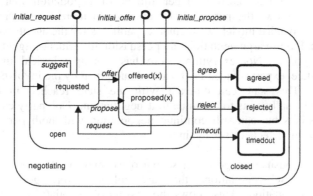

Figure 3: Generic Bilateral Negotiation Model

The logical theory of the model:
negotiating   one_of ([*open, closed*])
open   one_of ([*requested, offered*])
closed   one_of ([*agreed, rejected, timeout*])
proposed(X)   *offered*(X)

Thus the negotiating state condition holds if and only if it is an open or closed negotiation state. Similarly it is in an open state only if it is a requested or offered state. The closed state consists of the *agreed, rejected* and *timedout* substates. If agents X and Y are involved in such a bilateral negotiation, the primitive actions leading to the states are:

¬ *negotiating*   [X.*initial_request*] *requested*
¬ *negotiating*   [X.*initial_offer*] *offered*(X)   } 3 entry points
¬ *negotiating*   [X.*initial_propose*] *proposed*(X)
offered(X)   [Y.*agree*] *agreed*   (X= Y).
requested   one_of ([[Y.*offer*] *offered*(Y) , [Y.*propose*] *proposed*(Y), [Y.*suggest*] *requested*]) .
proposed(X)   [Y.*request*] *requested*   (X=Y).
open   one_of ([[(X   Y).*reject*] *rejected* , [*timeout*] *timedout* , [*offered*(X)? Y.*agree*] *agreed*])   (X=Y).

Here, for simplicity, the parameterisation is suggestive but incomplete.

On entering the negotiation, an *initial_request* action by agent X leads to the *requested* state. There are three transitions that can be performed by Y from this requested state – an *offer* leading to the *offered* state, a *propose* leading to the *proposed* state and the *suggest* leading to the *requested* state. From state *offered* triggered by X, an *agree* action by Y leads to the *agreed* state. From the open state, a *reject* by both agents or a *timeout* action may occur.

Expanded Bilateral Negotiation
In some cases we may need a richer model of negotiation that allows more interactions and allows the parties to be able to do more than restricted primary actions. In an expanded model, we include capabilities for the agents to seek answers to questions and to use argumentation and persuasion to influence agent beliefs and to achieve their goals. Not everything here has a simple logical theory. In the *investigating* state, expert advice may be asked and given by the involved agents or by third parties. This state can co-exist with the state reached in the enclosing negotiation and finally exits to continue that negotiation. One party can partly-reject an issue it dislikes but can still continue negotiating, with both parties keeping in mind not to use the rejected issue again.

In a business to business negotiation scenario we may need to be able to break a negotiation into sub-negotiations that are solved before going back to the encompassing negotiation. This allows the nesting of negotiations and the ability to change dimension in negotiating, first dealing with subgoals and subsequently negotiating about the main issue.   When one of the agents needs to delay the negotiation process, the negotiation state changes to pending. The state chart in figure 4 allows for simultaneous negotiation processes to take place, where an agent A negotiates with agent B on multiple processes giving rise to several negotiation threads in a negotiable state. An agent A may also negotiate with other agents in parallel with agent B. Agent A can then use the proceedings of its other negotiations to influence the negotiation with agent B.

This negotiation model is an attempt to show richer interactions between agents as compared to a generic bilateral negotiation.   A formal theory for this expanded negotiation model can be expressed as before but there are several open issues that still need to be clarified in this model.

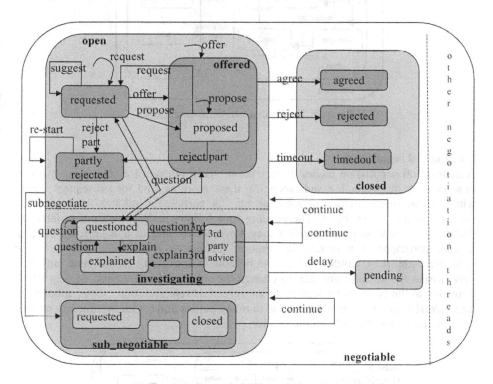

Figure 4: Expanded Bilateral Negotiation Model

5.2 Other Negotiation Models – Auction, Multi-lateral and Promissory

Auction
A popular model of negotiation for open multilateral bidding is an auction, of which there are several protocols for bidding and disclosure, including English auctions,

Dutch auctions, sealed bid auctions and Vickrey. Auctions specify the boundaries of the negotiation process and therefore are a quite simple form of negotiation to implement. There are automated, semi-automated and manual auctions currently online. The bargaining is restricted to price and the seller's strategy to assign awards is made known. Figure 5 shows a basic model for English auctions.

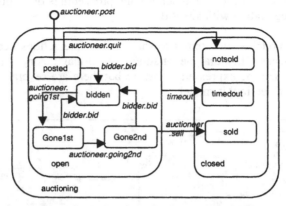

Figure 5: Simple English Auctioning Model

Multilateral Negotiation

A multilateral negotiation model defines the protocol relevant for submitting motions in a quorum, for seconding and amending these motions, and for subsequent voting within a community of two or more agents. A participant initiates the process by raising a motion on a subject. The *pending* state follows under which the initiator can withdraw the motion or the motion may time out leading to a *withdrawn* state or another participant can second the motion leading to a *seconded* state. In the *seconded* state, the countdown to a vote timeout is activated. In this state, any user may invoke the amend transition to change the subject of negotiation or may call a transition to the *voting* state leading to an *agreed* or *rejected* state. Other models for multilateral negotiation provide for one to many parties and for many-to-many parties, as in protocols for channel communication.

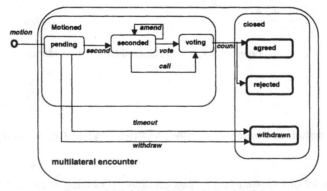

Figure 6: Multilateral Negotiation Model

Promissory Negotiation

Promissory models specify promises to execute a process, the right of one party to call on a promise and the obligation to fulfil a promise, for example by engaging into contract or by fulfilling the contract. The promissory negotiation process is initialised when a provider either makes a promise resulting in the consumer having a *right* to call upon the promise, or when the provider makes a commit which results in a *pending obligation* of the provider. In the *promised* state, the consumer can call upon the promise and request a transition for his right to be fulfilled. This leads to a *pending obligation* of the provider. The right of the consumer can timeout and lead to the terminal *expired* state. From the pending state, either the provider fulfils her/his obligation by calling the fulfil compound transition or the *pending* state times out and leads to the *overdue* sub-state. The fulfil transition launches a bilateral negotiation between the two agents and the result of the bilateral negotiation determines the result of the promissory negotiation. A waive transition may be invoked by either the consumer or the provider.

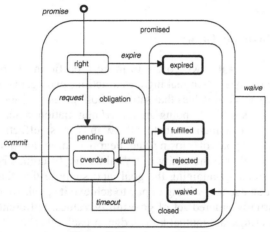

Figure 7: Promissory Model

6 Finding a Path for Negotiation

The expanded bilateral, auctioning, promissory and multilateral negotiation models can be expressed in dynamic logic in the same way as for the generic bilateral negotiation model. Negotiating agents can use the formal theories as inference engines in order to comply to a negotiation protocol. From such specification, the abstract rule of a particular negotiation protocol emerges. For example, in the bilateral negotiation, where the most abstract state is *negotiating*, the abstract process *negotiate* represents all the paths leading to a closed state of negotiation. This can be represented as: ¬ *negotiating*   [*negotiate*] *closed*

The *negotiate* process is the set of paths that the retailer and the customer can take to reach their goal state. Negotiating agents must use a subpath of the abstract path *negotiate* such that from an open state, entered by a *initial_request, initial_offer* or *initial_propose*, they seek an *agreed* state that satisfies their goal. Thus   *p:path* <*open*? *p* > *agreed* asserts that from *open*, there is a path *p* leading to *agreed*, a possible outcome of *negotiate*. The paths may themselves be represented in dynamic logic, deduced from the logical theory of the negotiation paths, or may form part of the library of an agent's plans of actions. A rational agent will seek to derive a path that will lead it to an *agreed* state. An abstract negotiating state like *agreed* has significance for an agent because the *agreed* state represents a subgoal of the agent, moving it closer to its greater goal.

Referring back to the scenario of the shopping process in section 3, the stages of offering and accepting a payment mode can follow a bilateral negotiation model. The retailer and customer will use an instance of the abstract process *negotiate*. An example of a path for {*r:retailer,c:customer*}.*negotiate_payment* is:
r.propose_mode(m); (*c.request_mode(n)* ;(*r.propose_mode(x)* ; *c.request_mode(y)*) * ; *r.offer_mode(z)*) [1] ; (*c.accept_mode(z)* | *c.reject_mode(z)*).

6.1 Gaining the Maximum Utility

Although, each agent has its own goal – to make a profit and to buy a service at a certain price respectively – when making a transaction, two agents will negotiate and converge to some final set of values that satisfies both goals. A rational agent will not only seek to achieve its goal of finding an *agreed* negotiation state. It will also try to achieve such a goal in a manner that will be most cost effective for it, so will negotiate with the subgoal of closing the negotiation in an *agreed* state at the minimum cost. If we define the utility of a goal as the difference between the worth of the goal and the cost of attaining the goal, and suppose that the worth to be the maximum cost that an agent is willing to pay to achieve its goal, we can consider each agent to have a partially ordered set of goal utility values. Different agents can have differing utility orderings and mutual knowledge of each other's utility values may be incomplete. The agent goal may be the maximum utility, but its decisions can only be based on estimates of how to achieve this.

The agent has to comply with the negotiation protocol and the external and internal constraints of the environment. As shown in section 4, an agent can infer the set of the paths leading to a particularly state when it is given the logical theory of the state transitions and conditions. Likewise, given the relations between states and substates and the primitive actions leading to these states from negotiation models, the paths towards an *agreed* state can be derived. We have seen that using the algebra of paths, a set of paths can be composed in terms of other paths and edges with   , ;, etc, but an agent has to choose its goals, utilities and thus its paths. The cost of the goal may be a fixed cost of the path to get to that goal state or some estimated cost in a heuristic or statistical scheme. In order to choose between paths, build a plan of action, and eventually make its response, an agent can use assignments of estimated utility for each element of a path, then use some computational rationale to compose utility or estimated utility. For example, for a optimal choice of single path:

- *utility(path to state_a)* is *utility(state_a)* if *path to state_a* does not consist of subpaths
- *utility(path_a ; path_b)* is *utility(path_a)* + *utility(path_b)*.
- *utility(path_a   path_b)* is *maximum (utility(path_a) , utility (path_b))*.
- *utility(   )*, the null path, is utility of value 0.
- *utility(   )*, the empty set of paths, is utility of value -   .
- *utility(a*)* is *maximum (0 , utility(a) + utility(a*))*.

In such an idealised case, we may assign a full worth to desired (goal) states and zero worth to unsuccessful terminal states such as *rejected* in the shopping process of figure 2. It may also be required that the cost of each transition to be positive in order that the utility of a loop is ultimately negative. However the actual cost of a transition such as *transact* will include the price of the chosen goods, which depends on successful choice, while the success of the transact sub-negotiation may depend on this choice and the strategy of the retailer. Thus more realistic computations must replace the third and sixth utility axioms above by probability estimates for a set of paths, for example, the estimated utility of a set of terminating paths starting with *c.browse* and ending in a closed transaction, and thus incur more complex computations for statistical estimation.

An agent must thus have a library of negotiation plans, each providing a set of paths that enable it to interact with and respond to other agents with the aim of satisfying its goals. These plans will reflect the agent's individual beliefs about utility, the common beliefs of the agents about negotiation paths and estimates of the beliefs or behaviour of other agents.

7 Related Work

Parsons, Sierra and Jennings (1998) present a formal model of argumentation-based reasoning and negotiation for autonomous agents. They show how agents can construct arguments to help guide their proposals, how agents can critique proposals and how agents can exchange arguments to help guide their problem solving behaviour towards acceptable solutions. In an article by Oliveira and Rocha (1999), multiple criteria and distributed constraint formalisms are used to construct a negotiation protocol and to select organisations to become members of a virtual organisation. Their multi-agent architecture has a coordinator agent to help in the virtual organisation formation process. The agents also use learning algorithms to adapt to changes in the environment. Negotiations in the CASBA system (Vetter and Pitsch 1999) are parallel and follow pre-defined rule-based strategies which can be adapted by the user and evolve through learning methods. Agents agree to only one offer and must notify each other if they agree to the last offer made by the other agent. Then both agents submit their agreement information to an administrator agent for checking the deal. Four types of auctions are supported in this system and agreements are implied by posting the service and by bidding. For a more game theoretic analysis see Rosenchein and Zlotkin 1994.

Noriega and Sierra (1996) also use a form of dynamic logic (CDDL) to specify multiagent systems, in their case an extension of concurrent dynamic logic. An agent has layered architectures and is represented in CDDL as a collection of formal theories in potentially different languages, and with bridge-rules to model the interactions between the formal theories. In their multi-agent system, exchanges between agents are performed according to a dialogical framework. The latter determines the set of illocutions and predicates that can be used between the agents. A set of bridge rules also models the translation between different communication languages and ontologies of the agents. As an example of their framework, the Spanish Fish market auction is specified in CDDL.

8 Conclusion

Information and communication technologies have given birth to Electronic Commerce. However, to escalate from web surfing to interactive online trading, an open architecture needs to support requirements amongst which automated negotiation is a major one. One can think of scenarios where user agents will have goals to be satisfied and will negotiate on behalf of their owners with other agents on a market-place. To do so, the agents need to have negotiation models which dictate the public protocols for effective cooperation between the agents and enable eventual convergence towards a state that satisfy the agents goals. In these models, an agent joins an instance of negotiation by establishing a member role, and interacts in the negotiation by operations to apply and invoke transitions and commands on states. Models of negotiation can be further customised following the patterns presented in this paper. Even if their private negotiation models differ, two agents must agree to a common negotiation model. This common negotiation model must form part of the belief of each agent and is a common belief. Thus the mutual beliefs of the agents include the negotiation protocol itself, the current state of the negotiation, and the goals.

From an attempt to represent a scenario of negotiation in a shopping process, we have exposed a need for notation whereby processes and states are both represented. Using dynamic logic, we have illustrated the construction of a logical theory for a shopping process and similar interactions. We have found that this theory construction process can expose errors in less formal definitions. At an abstract level, from an initial state, an agent can follow a set of execution paths to perform the negotiation process and end in a state that satisfies its goal. Stored paths form the plans of the agent. When constrained by the model of negotiation an agent should still in principle find a path leading to desirable states. The individual goals and intentions of the agent will determine the chosen paths. When a provider and a customer negotiate there is already some common knowledge that each agent has about each other. The customer knows the provider's goal is to sell his goods. This common knowledge of the other's intentions also plays some part in the choice of the optimal path. As the negotiation progresses, each agent can build up more beliefs about the other agents. With its beliefs and goals, an agent will need both logical and statistical analysis of paths to seek the best way to satisfy its goal.

Acknowledgements

This work has been done in the context of the OSM+ project (ACTS 211). We wish to acknowledge constructive comments from Stephen McConnell on an earlier draft and from reviewers of an AAAI workshop. Shamimabi Paurobally also wishes to acknowledge the support of the trustees of the Beit Fellowships.

References

Backhouse, R., Carre, B. 1975. Regular algebra applied to path-finding problems. *J. Inst. Maths Applics. 1975, Volume 15, pp. 161-186.*

Cunningham, J., Paurobally, S., Diacakis, A., Lorenzen, L., Gross, G., McConnell, M. 1998. Satisfying requirements for electronic commerce. *Proceedings of Trends in Electronic Commerce 98, Hamburg.*

Goldblatt, R. 1987. Logics of time and computation. *CSLI Lecture Notes No.7.*

Harel, D., Politi, M. 1998. Modeling reactive systems with statecharts, The Statemate approach. *McGraw-Hill.*

Jackson, M. 1975. Structured design. *Academic Press.*

Milner, R., 1989. Communication and concurrency, *Prentice Hall.*

Noriega P., Sierra C. 1996. Towards layered dialogical agents. *Proceedings of the ECAI'96 Workshop Agents Theories, Architectures and Languages, ATAL'9, Budapest, pp. 69-81.*

Oliveira, E., Rocha A. 1999. Agents advanced features for negotiation in electronic commerce and virtual organisations formation process. *this volume.*

OSM SARL. 1998. Negotiation facility. http://www.omg.org/pub/ec/99-03-01.

Parsons S., Sierra C., Jennings N. 1998. Agents that reason and negotiate by arguing. *Journal of Logic and Computation.*

Pratt, V. R. 1976. Semantical considerations on Floyd-Hoare logic. *Proceedings of 17th IEEE Symposium, Foundations of Computer Science, pp. 109-121.*

Rosenschein, J., Zlotkin, G. 1994. Rules of encounter, Designing conventions for automated negotiation among computers. *MIT Press.*

Sierra C., Godo J., López de Mántaras R., Manzano M. 1996. Descriptive dynamic logic and its applications to reflective architectures. *Future Generation Computer Systems Journal, Elsevier, Special issue on Reflection and Meta-level AI Architectures, Vol. 12, pp. 157-171.*

Vetter, M., Pitsch, S. 1999. Towards a flexible trading process over the Internet. *this volume.*

Agents Advanced Features for Negotiation in Electronic Commerce and Virtual Organisations Formation Process

Eugénio Oliveira and Ana Paula Rocha

LIACC, Faculty of Engineering, University of Porto

Abstract. Electronic Commerce technology has changed the way traditional business is being done. Transactions' complexity is increased due both to the huge amount of available information and also to the environment dynamics. Moreover, Electronic Commerce has enabled the arising of new economical structures, as it is the case of Virtual Organisations.

Our research aims at providing flexible and general-purpose systems for intelligent negotiation, both for Electronic Commerce and Virtual Organisation formation.

This paper proposes an Electronic Market architecture implemented through a Multi-Agent system. This architecture includes both a specific market agent which plays the role of market coordinator, as well as agents representing the individual business partners with their own goals and strategies. We also include a sophisticated negotiation protocol through multi-criteria and distributed constraint formalisms. An online, continuous reinforcement learning algorithm has been designed to enable agents to adapt themselves according to the changing environment, including the competitor agents.

1 Introduction

Electronic Commerce was often identified, in the recent past, with the capabilities of making available and/or searching for product information in electronic format through inter and intra nets.

Last years research efforts gave birth to new computer frameworks and platforms making it possible for electronic agents, acting as individual or business organisations delegates, to automatically negotiate through the internet. However, most of the current available systems still are inflexible under several perspectives: language, strategic behaviour, adaptability, specific purpose. Electronic commerce techniques have to be seen as enabling technologies for more advanced inter-organisational relationships leading to the effective creation of virtual organisations.

A Virtual Organisation (VO) is an aggregation of autonomous and independent organisations connected through a network (possibly a public network like WWW) and brought together to deliver a product or service in response to a customer need. Virtual Organisation management should be supported by efficient information and communication technology. This aggregation of organisations is advantageous in the sense that it will reduce complexity – today's products and services are increasingly complex and requires close coordination across many different disciplines – and most important, will enable the response to rapidly changing requirements. The Virtual

F. Dignum and C. Sierra (Eds.): Agent Mediated Elec. Commerce, LNAI 1991, pp. 78-97, 2001.
© Springer-Verlag Berlin Heidelberg 2001

Organisation will only exist for a temporary time limit, that is the time needed to satisfy its purpose.

The VO life cycle is decomposed in four phases (Faisst, 1997) (Fischer, 1996), namely:

- Identification of Needs: Description of the product or service to be delivered by the VO, which guides the conceptual design of the VO.

- Partners Selection: Rational selection of the individual organisations (partners) which will compose the VO, based in its specific knowledge, skills, resources, costs and availability.

- Operation: Control and monitoring of the partners' processes, including resolution of conflicts, and possible VO reconfiguration due to partial failures.

- Dissolution: Breaking up the VO, distribution of the obtained profits and storage of relevant information.

Our work is currently focused on the second above mentioned phase (partners selection), and our proposal concerns the development of a Multi-Agent System (MAS) architecture to model the Electronic Market that supports the automatization of the VO.

In the process of virtual organisation formation, goals representing the future virtual organisation purpose have to be described along several issues and made available to all those single organisations (enterprises) that are connected to the market. In order to compete, trying to bring their own specific competencies to the future consortium, agents representing organisations are endowed with several different possible behaviour tactics and higher level strategies for negotiating in a multi-dimensional space. In fact, price is no longer the solely characteristic of importance for the consortium.

Moreover, those negotiable issues may not be independent and mutual constraints are often attached to more than one issue the potential partners have to agree upon. Agents representing those partners (enterprises, customers, suppliers, buyers and sellers) have to be able to gradually approximate their own proposals taking into account a complex graph of inter-relationships between different variables.

Another aspect we are paying attention to is the agents' capability to automatically adapt to the market's dynamics. Static behaviours, although ingenious, can easily be beaten either by other agents constantly adapting their own behaviour, or by the rapid change of other environment factors.

An online, continuous reinforcement learning algorithm (an adaptation of Q-learning) is being tested in a number of scenarios aiming at proving that adaptive agents may easily become winners when competing with agents using fixed behaviours.

To apply these learning methods as well as multi-criteria and constraint based policies to agents representing either organisations or individuals searching for an agreement in a future action is what we intend to deliver through our multi-agent based system suitable for electronic commerce and virtual organisation formation.

In the following section, we will introduce our proposed MAS architecture to model the Electronic Market, focusing our description in the agent's structure and behaviour. A brief survey on agent-based architectures for electronic commerce can be found in (Guttman, 1998). Then we describe a negotiation protocol that includes both multi-criteria and constraint-based formalisms. We also detail the negotiation decision' making, in particular the multi-criteria evaluation function and the reinforcement learning algorithm (Q-learning) for which we include some experimental results from preliminary related work. We finalise the paper with some conclusions and directions for future work.

2 Electronic Market Architecture

Economic organisations are forced to respond to increasingly more complex and rapidly changing requirements. Virtual Organisations can satisfy these new challenges, as they combine the core competencies of several autonomous and heterogeneous organisations aggregated in a temporary network, presenting high flexibility and agility.

An Electronic Market infrastructure can efficiently support VO formation and operation. An Electronic Market (Bakos, 1998) can be seen as the virtual marketplace where business participants that are geographically distributed and possibly not known in advance can meet each other and cooperate in order to achieve a common business goal. An electronic network is used as an information and communication infrastructure, in order to link these distributed entities. In our proposed Electronic Market, autonomous organisations are the participants and the common business goal is the formation of a VO as the most favorable group of organisations that can satisfy a specific need. Besides individual organisations, other participants operate in the Electronic Market, whose role is to facilitate a set of auxiliary market functionalities like searching for goods or participants, filtering information or helping in negotiation.

Agents are autonomous or semi-autonomous entities that can perform tasks in complex and dynamically changing environments. Agent technology seems to be an appropriate paradigm for use in modelling individual organisations that participate in the Electronic Market, since they exhibit some relevant capabilities like autonomy, adaptability and ability to interact with others.

A Multi Agent System (MAS) – see (O'Hare 1996) for a general survey – consists of a group of agents that combine their specific competencies and cooperate in order to achieve a common goal. Efficient cooperation as well as coordination procedures between agents endow a MAS with a capability higher than the sum of the individual agent's capabilities.

We therefore propose a Multi-Agent System architecture to model the Electronic Market that supports the establishment of the VO (see Figure 1). This MAS includes several heterogeneous and semi-autonomous intelligent agents representing the different independent organisations, and also a special agent called **Market Agent** that helps in the VO formation process. Each one of these organisations are then represented by means of two kinds of agents: the organisation itself which is responsible for the "Identification of Needs" phase (which will not be dealt with here in this paper), and the organisation representative agent for that specific previously identified need (which is called **Organisation Agent**).

We will now describe in more detail the structure and functionality of these agents.

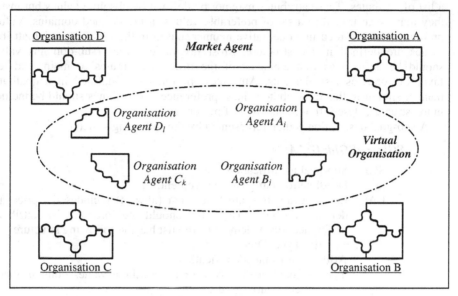

Fig. 1. Electronic Market architecture

2.1 Market Agent

When a specific consumer's need is identified (a consumer being either a human or an organisation), a new special agent, which is called **Market Agent**, is created and included in the Electronic Market system. This agent plays the role of coordinator in the Electronic Market where it is placed and its main goal is the Virtual Organisation formation. The Market Agent structure includes two principal modules: *"Goal Descriptor"* and *"Virtual Organisation Selector"* (see Figure 2).

Market Agent

Goal Descriptor
Virtual Organisation

Fig. 2. Market Agent structure

We assume, for now, that the *"Goal Descriptor"* module is instantiated by the consumer. This module includes the description of the goal to achieve, which is decomposed in a set of sub-goals.

Each sub-goal (SGD) is described by means of a deadline and price value, and also a list of attributes. These attributes may not be defined by absolute values but instead they may be restricted to a set of preferable values in pre-defined domains. Values' preference is measured in a qualitative manner, based in the order by which attribute values are defined in the structure. Most favorable values (sub-domains values) should be defined as first elements of the ordered attributes' domain, and least favorable ones as last elements. Attributes' preference is defined in a qualitative manner similar to that of attribute values' preference, so attributes should be included in the structure description by its order of preference.

A sub-goal description is then represented by the following structure:

SGD = (SGId, D, LAt)

SGId: Sub-goal identification.

D: Deadline for sub-goal achievement.

LAt: List of evaluation attributes that (always) includes the price as a default attribute. This list should be ordered by attributes' preference. Each element of the list has the following structure:

At_i = (AtId, Type, Dom)

AtId: Attribute identification.

Type: Identifies the type of the attribute values domain, that is, continuous or discrete.

Dom: Attribute values domain. These values are elements of a list ordered by preference. Each element of the list is either a single value (case of a discrete domain), or an interval of values (case of a continuous domain).

The sub-goals themselves may be related to each other through constraints attached to their attribute values. This is represented by a set of structures like the following:

constraint (SG, At, V, SG_c, At_c, V_c)

SG: Constraining sub-goal identification.

At: Constraining attribute identification.

V: Constraining attribute (domain) value(s).

The 'c' index in SG_c, At_c and V_c, refer to similar information concerning now the constrained issues.

The *"Virtual Organisation Selector"* module is responsible for the rational selection of the VO partners. In a first step, a set of invitations (one for every sub-goal described in *"Goal Descriptor"* module) is send to the Electronic Market system. The market Agent second step leads to the evaluation of the received proposals. Senders of the most favorable ones are then selected and committed as partners of the VO. VO partners selection is done through multi-criteria evaluation and constraint-based negotiation protocols described later in this paper.

2.2 Organisation Agent

In order to be competitive in today's economic markets, organisations need not only to be efficient in their business field, but also to be able to quickly react and adapt to new environments as well as to interact with other organisations. The control architecture adopted for the design of an organisation agent should meet these requirements. Figure 3 describes our proposed organisation agent structure.

Organisation Agent

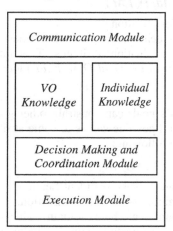

Fig. 3. Organisation Agent structure

An Organisation Agent's structure comprises three functional modules: *Communication, Decision Making and Coordination,* and *Execution* modules, plus two knowledge-based modules: *Individual Knowledge* and *Virtual Organisation Knowledge* module.

The *"Communication module"* is responsible for all processes related with messages handling. Incoming messages are filtered and the ones that are not relevant for this specific agent are ignored. The relevant messages are then ordered by degree of importance. Outcome messages are sent out only to those agents that are known to be possibly interested in that particular piece of information. Agents use KQML - Knowledge Query Manipulation Language – (Finin, 1996) to exchange messages between them.

The *"Decision Making and Coordination module"* is the most complex one. Its role is to manage local tasks and cooperative behaviour. For our current presentation, the most relevant issue of this module includes the process to formulate a bid in response to an announcement (e.g., a proposal for becoming a VO partner). The bid formulation process uses a reinforcement learning technique to (re)formulate a response in each negotiation round. The learning process is done in a continuous way along the negotiation process. A detailed explanation of this process is given later in this paper (section 4.1).

The *"Execution module"* is the intelligent system responsible for the execution of local tasks an agent is committed to.

Information related to organisational and operational rules defined by the VO, is included in *"Virtual Organisation Knowledge"*. This module contains also information concerning individual organisation's rights and duties. This module is to be filled in during the VO formation phase, and can be modified during the VO operation as new organisations join the VO and partners leave the VO.

The *"Individual Knowledge"* contains information about the agent itself: agent's own capabilities and current workload, as well as information related to other agents: other agents commitments and capabilities. Agent's own capabilities are represented by the following structures:

> **has_capability (GId, D, LAt)**
>
> GId: Goal identification.
> D: Relative deadline for goal achievement.
> LAt: List of evaluation attributes. This information is similar to that included in the *Goal Descriptor* module of the *Market Agent* (see 2.1).

Each one of the agent's goals can constrain other goals (achieved by this one or other agents) by improving possible values to some attributes. This fact is mapped in a set of structures like the following:

> **constraint (SG, At, V, SG_c, At_c, V_c)**
>
> SG: Constraining sub-goal identification.
> At: Constraining attribute identification.
> V: Constraining attribute (domain) value(s).
> The remaining parameters with 'c' index refer to similar information concerning now the constrained issues.

The Organisation Agent is a template supplied by the Electronic Market that, once being filled according to the individual organisation's specific tactics and strategies, will represent that particular organisation in the market.

Although only the VO formation issue is being discussed here, the Organisation Agent structure proposed is able to support all phases of the VO life cycle.

3 Negotiation Protocol

Several examples of intelligent agent-based systems suitable for electronic market operations already exist (Chavez, 1996) (Tsvetovatyy, 1997). Moreover, electronic market functionalities available in existing systems, vary from searching for goods to either simple purchasing or selling goods, or even to more complex negotiation of goods. It is this negotiation process between participants in an electronic market that becomes our main concern in this paper.

Auctions (Vulkan, 1998), game theory (Rosenschein, 1994) and intelligent agent technology (Jennings, 1996) are paradigms used in many automated negotiation systems. Auction mechanisms are very popular due to its simplicity and well pre-defined rules, but only involve single criteria negotiations. Game theory mechanisms can only be applied in contexts with perfect information and perfect rationality. Intelligent agents technology is a more flexible paradigm suitable for dynamic and open environments, since agents can effectively cope with the complexity and large amount of information. Intelligent agents technology seems to be an appropriate paradigm to use in our case, since VO operates in very dynamic and complex environments.

A VO combines competencies derived from several heterogeneous and independent organisations present in the Electronic Market. A negotiation protocol has to be defined in order to select the individual organisations that, based on its capabilities and availability, will become members of the VO. In VO formation process, two important issues have to be considered:

- A multi-criteria evaluation is used to select the most favorable candidates: lower cost, higher quality, higher availability, etc, have to be taken into account.
- Organisation's competencies may be inter-related by constraints attached to their attributes' values which leads to a kind of distributed constraints problem.

Attaching utility values to different criteria helps to solve the problem of multi-criteria evaluation. Generally, an evaluation formula is a linear combination of the current attributes' values weighted by their corresponding utility values (Oliveira, 1999) (Matos, 1998). However, in some cases, it can be a very difficult task to attach absolute values to attributes' utilities. A more natural and realistic situation is to simply impose a preference order over attributes' values and/or attributes itself. Contrary to the work mentioned above, we have adopted a multi-criteria evaluation based on a qualitative, not quantitative, measure.

Distributed Constraint Satisfaction Problems (Yokoo, 1992) are defined by a set of variables $(x_1, x_2, \ldots, x_n)$ which can take values from domains $D_1, D_2, \ldots, D_n$ respectively, and a set of constraints on their values. Here, in our scenario, variables are distributed among organisations in the Electronic Market and instantiations of the variables must satisfy these inter-organisation constraints.

In this paper we propose a multi-criteria negotiation protocol that uses Reinforcement Learning techniques for the selection of VO partners. We also include a simple algorithm for the resolution of constraint-based problems that can arise in this VO formation process.

Figure 4 illustrates the negotiation protocol. The Market Agent plays the role of coordinator in the VO formation process through its *"Virtual Organisation Selector"* module. This agent knows VO sub-goals that are described in the *"Goal Descriptor"* module. For each one of them, Market Agent sends out an announcement message to all organisations present in the Electronic Market. Organisations Agents reply with bid messages. Received bids are then evaluated using a multi-criteria function and the most favorable are selected. The negotiation process involves several rounds, and ends when a deadline is reached or when the *Market Agent* evaluates the current proposal(s) as acceptable. Those organisations that have sent out winning proposals become VO members and are committed to the respective goal achievement. Meanwhile, if different bids include attributes' values that are incompatible, the respective organisations' agents activate a negotiation process searching for an agreement through a set of compatible values.

3.1 Announcement

The *Market Agent* sends out an announcement message for each of the VO sub-goals that are described in its *"Goal Descriptor"* module. The announcement, made by the *Market Agent*, will initiate the negotiation process. These messages are delivered to all organisations existing in the Electronic Market, and contain the following structure:

announcement (MAg, GId, D)

MAg: Market Agent identification.
GId: Goal identification.
D: Deadline value for goal achievement.

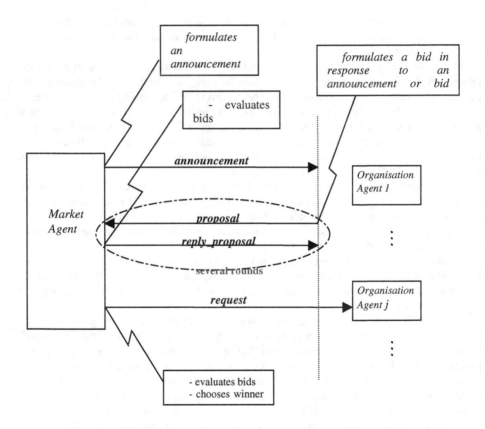

Fig. 4. Negotiation protocol

3.2 Bid Formulation

In response to an announcement message or in response to a new negotiation round, the *Organisation Agent* formulates a bid based in its own capabilities, current availability, past experience (if possible) and *Market Agent* feedback. A reinforcement learning algorithm that enables continuous learning along the current negotiation process is used to formulate an agent bid. The message with the proposal is then sent out to the *Market Agent*, using the following structure:

proposal (OAg, PId, GId, T, LAt)

OAg: Organisation Agent identification.
PId: Proposal identification.
GId: Goal identification.
T: Time due for goal achievement.
LAt: List of attributes' values. Each element of the list has the following
structure:
$At_i = (AtId, V)$, where:
AtId: Attribute identification.
V: Attribute value.

Some constraints on other sub-goals' attribute values may result from accepting a particular agent's bid. This information is sent out to the *Market Agent* in one or possibly more messages including the following structure:

constraint (OAg, PId, G, At, V, G_c, At_c, V_c)

OAg: Organisation Agent identification.
PId: Proposal identification.
G: Constraining goal identification.
At: Constraining attribute identification.
V: Constraining attribute (domain) value(s).
The remaining parameters with 'c' index refers to similar information concerning now the constrained issues.

3.3 Bids Evaluation

The *Market Agent* through its *"Virtual Organisation Selector"* module evaluates all bids received in the current negotiation round (for each one of the announced goals) based on a multi-criteria function. The organisation agent that presents the most valuable bid is informed that its bid is the selected one in the current negotiation round. A message is then sent out by the *Market Agent* to this organisation agent:

reply_proposal (PId, winning_round)

To other agents that participate in this round and are currently loosing, an advice in order to improve future proposals is also sent out:

reply_proposal (PId, loosing_round, Reason)

This message informs the respective *Organisation Agents* that *Market Agent* has received a better proposal, and their current bids are loosing the negotiation. Moreover, this message also includes the reason why this particular bid was not chosen, that is, what attributes were not considered good enough and how they can be improved.

After that, a new negotiation round begins and *Organisation Agents* will send new proposals to *Market Agent*, who will then reply accordingly. After a deadline is reached or a satisfactory proposal is received, the *Market Agent* will end the negotiation episode and organisations that have formulated the winning bids are informed that they are included in and committed to the new created VO:

request (GId, PId)

If an admissible bids set cannot be found because some attributes values are mutually incompatible, a constraint satisfaction resolution process is activated. This process is described in the following section.

3.4 Constraint Satisfaction Problem Resolution

Here, in our scenario, variables (describing attributes of goals) are distributed among organisations in the virtual marketplace and instantiations of those variables must satisfy existent inter-organisation constraints.

We propose a distributed constraint based algorithm that tries to obtain a global solution that satisfies all constraints and is optimal for the set of organisations included in it.

In response to the *Market Agent*, the *Organisation Agent* formulates a proposal in order to become a VO partner. This proposal message includes a list of attributes' values the organisation is willing to deliver according to its own self-interested objectives. If this particular proposal puts constraints on other sub-goals' attribute values, that same information is then sent to the *Market Agent*[1].

If the *Market Agent* receives proposals that include mutually incompatible attributes' values, it sends out that information to the respective constrained agents. The *Market Agent* job is to put in touch mutually constrained agents. It does not participate any more in the constraint problem resolution.

Constrained agents have to negotiate between them in order to agree in a set of admissible values for their constrained attributes. The initial proposal that a particular agent have made is its best local solution at that moment. We will call it solution $\mathbf{s}*$. In order to solve the constraint problem and reach an agreement, agents change possible local solutions. Choosing the local solution $\mathbf{s}^k$ (necessarily different from the best solution $\mathbf{s}*$) implies decreasing the agent' utility value, if compared to the best solution for the agent. We will call this difference the decreasing utility value ($\mathbf{du}^k$), which can be calculated as the difference between the evaluation values[2] of either solutions:

$$du^k = Ev(s*) - Ev(s^k)$$

Each local solution proposed by an agent to other(s) during the constraint resolution process should include the decreasing utility of that particular solution to that agent. Agents will agree in a final solution that presents the lowest global decreasing utility value (that is, the minimum sum of all constrained agents' decreasing utility). When this agreement is reached, the final solution for formulating an acceptable proposal is sent out to *Market Agent*.

Next we describe the procedure adopted in the resolution of the distributed constraint satisfaction problem:

---

[1] As a simple example, suppose that a VO has to be formed in order to deliver a specific type of car. The attribute *"dimension"* of the component *"wheel"* may restrict the values of the attribute *"material"* of the component *"screw"*.

[2] In section 4.2, we present a formula for calculating a bid (solution) evaluation value. For now, we will only refer that evaluation values are defined in the domain [0,1].

(1)   An agent receives a set of bids that are the most favorable for the senders. These sender agents also indicate the decreasing utility value of the proposed solutions. Among the solutions proposed, the receiver agent then selects the most favorable one according to its own objectives, and calculates its decreasing utility value. The receiver agent also calculates the decreasing utility values for the proposed solutions received, and send out this information to sender agents.

(2)   Receiver agent selects, within the solution space, the most favorable solution that has not been proposed yet. The local agent decreasing utility value for participating in this new solution is also calculated.

(3)   Receiver agent chooses between solution obtained in (1), solution obtained in (2) and the better solution already proposed in the past. The solution that presents lower decreasing utility value is selected. Notice that we are comparing different decreasing utility values: total decreasing utility for solution (1) and local agent decreasing utility for solution (2). If the solution selected is the one already presented in the past or the one obtained in (1), then this is the final solution (the proposal that is mutually acceptable in accordance to the constraints). If the solution selected is the one obtained in (2), then it is sent out to constrained agent(s) participating in the negotiation and the constraint resolution process continues.

Usually, an organisation does not want to reveal its private information. In the procedure described above, not all possible variable domain values are made available since the beginning to other organisations in the system. Instead, this variable domain values is made available to others only when necessary, in order to reach an agreement, as the negotiation continues. Another aspect that we want to emphasise is the fact that solution utilities values, exchanged between organisations during the negotiation process, does not represent the real utility. Instead, agents exchange just utilities deviations (offset values).

Figure 5 illustrates how the distributed constraint based procedure is executed.

Suppose the existence of two organisations O_1 and O_2 and a VO objective described by means of goals G_x (with attributes A_{x1}, A_{x2}, ..., A_{xn}) and G_y (with attributes A_{y1}, A_{y2}, ..., A_{ym}). Organisation O_1 knows how to achieve goal G_x and Organisation O_2 knows how to achieve goal G_y. Possible values for attribute A_{x1} are represented as x_1, x_2, ..., x_5 (by O_1's order of preference). Possible values for attribute A_{y2} are represented as y_1, y_2, ..., y_6 (by O_2's order of preference). Attributes A_{x1} and A_{y2} are mutually constrained, as illustrated by the closed lines in figure 5. The evaluation value associated with particular solutions is enclosed in brackets.

Organisations O_1 and O_2 establish the following set of conversations:

• O_1 proposes

  ($A_1 = x_1$, $A_2 = y_3$) , O_1 du $= 0$

  ($A_1 = x_1$, $A_2 = y_6$) , O_1 du $= 0$

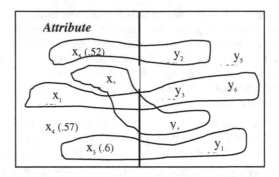

Fig. 5. Constraint space solution

- O_2 evaluates solutions proposed by O_1, and sent out that information as a bid to O_1

  ($A_1=x_1$, $A_2=y_3$) , total du = 0.04   (0.04=0.66-0.62)

  ($A_1=x_1$, $A_2=y_6$) , total du = 0.1

  O_2 proposes

  ($A_2=y_1$, $A_1=x_3$) , O_2 du = 0

- O_1 evaluates solution proposed by O_2, and sent out that information as a bid to O_2

  ($A_2=y_1$, $A_1=x_3$) , total du = 0.08

  O_1 proposes

  ($A_1=x_2$, $A_2=y_4$) , O_1 du = 0.03

- O_2 evaluates solution proposed by O_1, and send that information as a bid to O_1

  ($A_1=x_2$, $A_2=y_4$) , total du = 0.09

  O_2 proposes

  ($A_2=y_2$, $A_1=x_5$) , O_2 du = 0.02

- O_1 evaluates solution proposed by O_2, and send that information as a bid to O_2

- ($A_2=y_2$, $A_1=x_5$) , total du = 0.18

  O_1 accepts the solution already proposed in the past

  ($A_1=x_1$, $A_2=y_3$) , total du = 0.04

The final solution is the last proposal, which besides being in accordance with mutual constraints has the lowest total decreasing utility value.

4 Decision Making for Negotiation

4.1 Bid Formulation

Organisation Agents formulate bids for the goal satisfaction in response to an announcement message (or feedback messages from previous bids) sent by the *Market Agent*. The bid formulation process uses a Q-learning algorithm endowing the agent with the capability to learn on-line along the negotiation process. After each negotiation round, the *Market Agent* will reply to individual organisation agents by telling them how their bids could be improved in next rounds.

Reinforcement learning (RL) systems learn how to behave through trial-and-error interactions with its environment. Unlike supervised learning, no samples input-output pairs from the function to be learned are required, but instead the system receives a scalar evaluation from the environment for each action selected in a specific situation. RL is based in the idea of rewarding actions that produce good results and punishing those that produce bad results.

Q-learning is a reinforcement learning algorithm that maps state-action pairs to values, called Q-values. When an agent in current state s, performs action a, receives reward r and arrives at next state s', the correspondent Q-value is updated as follows (Sutton, 1998):

$$Q(s,a) \; = \; Q(s,a) + \quad r + \; \max_{b} Q(s',b) \quad Q(s,a)$$

where   0   1 (learning rate) and 0   1 (discount factor).

The discount factor is used to decrease the weight of reinforcements received in the future. It causes immediate reinforcements to have more importance than future reinforcements.

An agent is faced with a dilemma in order to choose what action to perform in each specific situation. Should it choose the most promising one? Or should it try to explore new states? If no exploration is made, the agent although using a greedy strategy, may miss the dynamics of the market. If too much exploration is made, the agent can make a lot of poor choices. It is necessary to ensure that sufficient exploration is made while choosing actions with high known Q-values (*Boltzmann exploration*):

$$p(a) \quad = \quad \frac{e^{Q(s,a)/t}}{e^{Q(s,a')/t}}$$
$$a' \; A$$

where   t   0 (temperature)

p(a) is the probability of choosing action a and t is a parameter that controls the amount of exploration (it is usually decreased over time to decrease exploration). When a high temperature value is used, all actions are chosen with approximately equal probability. When a low temperature value is used, more highly evaluated actions are chosen.

We have adapted the Boltzmann exploration formula to our application domain, by not exploring all the possible actions but reducing the exploration to set A of those actions which are constrained by means of the *Market Agent* feedback to past bids.

In our application domain, a state is defined by the n-uple:

$$s = (V_1, V_2, \ldots V_n) \qquad\qquad , V_i \text{ is the value for attribute i}$$

The state will also represent the bid sent to the *Market Agent*.
We define an action by the n-uple:

$$a = (A_1, A_2, \ldots, A_n), \qquad\qquad , A_i \quad \{\text{increase, decrease, maintain}\}$$

Continuous attributes' values can be increased (decreased) by pre-defined amount steps. Discrete attributes' values can be increased (decreased) by moving to the next (previous) element in the enumerated domain.

When an *Organisation Agent* receives a feedback message from the *Market Agent* to its previous bid (this bid represents the state s that results from performing action a_p in state s_p), it tries to formulate a new bid following the procedure:

(1) Calculate a reward value for the previous bid (that also defines the current state s). This reward value is calculated using the qualitative evaluation included in the received feedback message:

$$r = n \qquad\qquad\qquad , \text{if winner}$$
$$= n \quad penalty^i \quad , \text{if not winner} \qquad\qquad , 0 \quad penalty \quad 1$$

In the above formula, penalty is a parameter that decreases the reward value for bids with low evaluated values (remember that bids were evaluated by the *Market Agent*). This parameter should be defined by each organisation agent according to its own criteria and its value increases with the evaluations' category: low/high, very_low/very_lhigh, extremely_low/extremely_high. In this formula, attributes should appear in the same order they apper in the feedback message sent by the *Market Agent* (in this feedback message, attributes are ordered by *Market Agent*'s order of importance).

(2) Update the pair state/action Q-value ($Q(s_p, a_p)$) using the Q-learning formula presented above.

(3) Store the current sate s, and its associated reward value r.

(4) Derive all **new** promising actions a' taking into account that specific feedback message. For instance if the feedback message evaluates *attribute_2* as *too_low*, one possible promising action is to increase *attribute_2* and maintain all the others.
Store pairs s/a' with a default Q-value ($Q(s,a') = default$).

(5) Move to the state $s*$ with greatest reward value.

(6) Choose the action $a*$ with greatest probability value, according to the Boltzmann exploration formula, (note that actions not ever tried are stored in that state $s*$ with Q-value=*default*).

(7) Perform action $a*$ and send the new bid (state) out to the *Market Agent*.

4.2 Bids Evaluation

In order to select the most promising partners in the VO formation (or, in a more general electronic market environment, the most favorable buyers/sellers for a business transaction) a negotiation process is started by the Market Agent. This negotiation process comprises several rounds, starting when the *Market Agent* sends an announcement for all agents registered in the electronic market. The negotiation ends when a deadline is reached or a satisfactory proposal is received. At each negotiation round bids are evaluated, and the one with the greatest evaluation value is considered the winner in current round. Received bids comprise a solution to a specific needed goal, and includes proposed values for multiple issues.

Bid evaluation is done through a multi-criteria function that encodes the attributes' and attributes values' preferences initially stipulated by the *Market Agent* and defined in its *"Goal Descriptor"* module. This multi-criteria evaluation function is defined by the following formula:

$$Ev = \frac{1}{Deviation}$$

$$Deviation = \frac{1}{n} * \sum_{i=1}^{n} dif(\text{PrefV}_i, V_i)^i$$

where   n = number of attributes for a specific goal.

In the formula above, each parcel should be presented in increasing order of preference. Attribute identified by number 1 ($i=1$) is the one that *Market Agent* classifies as the least important, and attribute identified by number n ($i=n$) is the most important.

The function $dif(PrefV_i, V_i)$ quantifies for an attribute i, the degree of acceptability of the current value (V_i) proposed by a specific organisation agent when compared to its preferable value *(PrefVi)* for the *Market Agent*. If the attribute values domain is of continuous values, this quantification simply is a normalised difference between the two values V_i and $PrefV_i$. If the attribute values domain is of discrete values, the result of the $dif(PrefV_i, V_i)$ function is now calculated as a normalised difference between the preference attached to V_i and $PrefV_i$, which can be calculated as the difference between the relative position of the two values in the enumerate domain values specification[3].

The winner bid in the current round is selected as the one that presents the highest evaluation value, since it is the solution that contains attributes values closer to the preferable values. The winner bid in this current round is compared with the winner bid in all past rounds, and the best one is selected.

All other bids are compared to the winner bid in order to inform the respective agents about the reason why their bids were not selected. A comparison is made for the values proposed for the most important attributes (from *Market Agent* point of view, of course). These values are then classified in a qualitative way: low/high, very_low/very_high, extremely_low /extremely_high.

---

[3] In the *"Goal Descriptor"* module of the *Market Agent*, the domain values of a discrete attribute are defined in a list ordered by preference (see 2.1).

Let us suppose that $_i$ (i=1,2) splits the domain into the three mentioned regions, and w is the winner bid.

> For all bids k w, do
>> For all most important attributes i, do
>>> $_{i,k}$ = dif($V_{i,k}$,$V_{i,w}$)
>>> If $_{i,k}$ < $_1$ then **Evaluation** = low (high)
>>> Else If $_{i,k}$ < $_2$ then **Evaluation** = very_low (very_high)
>>> Else **Evaluation** = extremely_low (extremely_high)

This information is included in the message that is sent out to all bidding agents except the currently winning agent, as a reason why their bids have not been selected. Such information is a list where each element is a pair (AtId, Evaluation), where AtId means the attribute identification. Agents will receive this information and will formulate new bids to send to *Market Agent* in the next negotiation round.

The negotiation process ends when:

- Market Agent receives a bid which has a satisfactory evaluation value (Ev). This bid is the winner bid.

- A deadline is reached. The winner bid is the one that presents the highest evaluation value among all bids received until then.

4.3 Preliminary Work with Q-Learning

Our previous work with Q-learning was experimented in a electronic market where different agents (sellers) try to sell their services (available time) to different buyers (announcing tasks to be executed at a particular time in the future) using a first-price sealed bid auction. Sellers can only serve one customer at a time. Our simulation scenario is inspired by a real-world application in which several physical resources such as excavators, trucks, workers, etc, compete to win tasks in an open electronic market (Oliveira, 1997).

One of the several experiments made (Oliveira, 1999b) includes adaptive agents, using different   values, and a "step changing price agent" (SCPA). We have studied the influence of parameter   on agent's adaptive behaviour. Figure 6 shows the performance of the agents using different alpha values (=0.05, 0.1, 0.25, 0.5) when compared with SCPA. As expected, a lower value for   leads to a slower reaction to market changes and a higher value for   leads to a faster reaction. However, a fast reaction does not automatically mean better results. Actually, the results of the different adaptive agents are broadly similar but the agent using   =0.25 obtains the best cash flow (utility) results. Initially, and after each SCPA change, the   =0.5 agent obtains the best results (highest slope on the cash flow curve) because it is the fastest to propose the ideal price. However in the long run, its over reaction in the face of sporadic positive or negative results leads to losses that are caused by inappropriate bids.

We are confident that using the Q-learning techniques presented in previous sections, that includes not single criteria problems (like the results presented above) but multi-criteria problems will conduct to similar results.

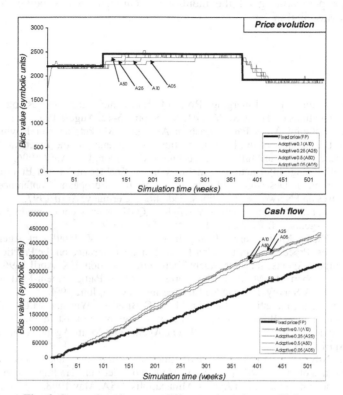

Fig. 6. Comparison between different adaptation coefficients.

5   Conclusions and Work in Progress

Virtual Organisations are of increasing importance mainly due to its flexibility, agility and efficiency. These main characteristics enable VO successful behaviour in dynamic and complex business environments.

In this paper we propose the use of intelligent agent technology for Electronic Commerce and VO formation.

In the KRAFT system (Preece, 1999) agent-based technology is also used to support VO formation and operation through a simple constraint fusion mechanism. KRAFT supports VO operation where members with heterogeneous knowledge and data models exchange information in the form of constraints. Instead, our proposal includes a more complex and powerful negotiation protocol suitable both for VO formation and Electronic Commerce in general. This new protocol includes resolution of multi-criteria and distributed constraint-based problems. We also show how agents can efficiently compete in a dynamic market by adapting themselves to market changing, due to their continuous on-line learning capabilities.

A Multi-Agent System architecture was also proposed as a support for the implementation of the Electronic Market where individual business partners meet each other, negotiate and cooperate.

A prototype featuring all the mentioned characteristics is being developed for future experimentation.

References

1. Bakos Yannis. The Emerging Role of Electronic Marketplaces on the Internet. Communications of the ACM, Vol. 41, No. 8, pp. 35-42, August 1998.
2. Chavez Anthony, Maes Pattie. Kasbah: An Agent Marketplace for Buying and Selling Goods. Proceedings of the First International Conference on the Practical Application of Intelligent Agents and Multi Agent Technology, London, UK, April 1996.
3. Faisst Wolfgang. Information Technology as an Enabler of Virtual Enterprises: A Life-Cycle-Oriented Description. Proceedings of the European Conference on Virtual Enterprises and Networked Solutions. Paderborn, Germany, April 1997.
4. Finin Tim, Labrou Yannis, James Mayfield. KQML as an agent communication language. Software Agents. Jeff Bradshaw (Ed.), MIT Press, 1997.
5. Fischer Klaus, Muller Jorg, Heimig Ingo, Scheer A-W. Intelligent Agents in Virtual Enterprises. Proceedings of the First International Conference on the Practical Application of Intelligent Agents and Multi Agent Technology. London, UK, April 1996.
6. Guttman Robert H., Moukas Alexandros G., Maes Pattie. Agent-Mediated Electronic Commerce: A Survey. Knowledge Engineering Review, June 1998.
7. Jennings N. R., Farantin P., Johnson M. J., O'Brien P., Wiegand M.E. Using Intelligent Agents to manage Business Processes. Proceedings of the First International Conference on the Practical Application of Intelligent Agents and Multi Agent Technology. London, UK, April 1996.
8. Matos Noyda, Sierra Carles. Evolutionary Computing and Negotiating Agents. Proceedings of the Workshop on Agent Mediated Electronic Trading, Second International Conference on Autonomous Agents. Minneapolis, USA, May 1998.
9. O'Hare G. M. P., Jennings N. R., Foundations of Distributed Artificial Intelligence, John Wiley & Sons, 1996
10. Oliveira E., Fonseca J. M., Garçã, A. S. MACIV - A DAI Based Resource Management System. International Journal on Applied Artificial Intelligence, Vol. 11, pp. 525-550, 1997.
11. Oliveira Eugénio, Fonseca José M, Steiger-Garção A. Multi-criteria negotiation on Multi-Agent Systems. Proceedings of the First International Workshop of Central and Eastern Europe on Multi-Agent Systems, St. Petersburg, Russia, June 1999.
12. Oliveira Eugénio, Fonseca José M, Jennings Nick. Learning to be competitive in the Market. American Association of Artificial Intelligence Workshop on Negotiation, Orlando, USA, July 1999b.
13. Preece Alun, Hui Kit, Gray Peter. KRAFT: Supporting Virtual Organisations through Knowledge Fusion. (in this same volume)
14. Rosenschein Jeffrey S., Zlotkin Gilad. Rules of Encounter. MIT Press, 1994.
15. Sutton R. S., Barto A. G. Reinforcement Learning: An Introduction. MIT Press, Cambridge, MA, 1998.
16. Tsvetovatyy Maksim, Gini Maria, Mobasher Bamshad, Wieckowski Zbigniew. MAGMA: An Agent-Base Virtual Market for Electronic Commerce. Journal of Applied Artificial Intelligence, Special issue on Intelligent Agents, Vol. 11, No. 6, 1997.

17. Vulkan Nir, Jennings Nick R. Efficient Mechanisms for the Supply of Services in Multi-Agent Environments. Proceedings of the First International Conference on Information and Computation Economics. Charleston, South Carolina, October 1998.
18. Yokoo Makoto, Durfee Edmund, Ishida Toru, Kuwabara Kazuhiro. Distributed Constraint Satisfaction for Formalizing Distributed Problem Solving. Proceedings of the Twelfth IEEE International Conference on Distributed Computing systems, June 1992.

Agents, Markets, Institutions, and Protocols

Frank Dignum
Faculty of Mathematics & Computing Science
Eindhoven University of Technology
P.O.Box 513, Eindhoven,
The Netherlands
email: dignum@win.tue.nl
tel: +31-40-2473705, fax:+31-40-2463992

1 Introduction

Thinking about agent mediated electronic commerce usually two situations come to one's mind. The first is agents that shop on the Internet and find the best bargain (Jango (http://www.jango.com/) (Doorenbos et.al., 1996), Bargainfinder (http://bf.cstar.ac.com), etc.) and the second is that of electronic marketplaces where agents can buy and/or sell goods. Some good examples are Kasbah (Chavez & Maes 1996), the Fishmarket project (Rodriguez 1997) and AuctionBot (Wurman 1998). Although the agents in the first case play a role in electronic commerce their actual role is that of searching the Internet in an intelligent way. These types of agents are not supposed to interact with agents at the selling side and strike bargains with these agents. The scenario assumes that prices are fixed and can be found by searching the WWW.

In the scenario of the electronic marketplaces, both sides play an active role. In most cases the selling agents advertise their products in the market. They indicate a price, but this price does not have to be the final selling price. In case of an auction model the price indicated by the seller is the reserved price. It will not sell its products for less than that price.

In these electronic marketplaces the agents have the task to "bargain" about the price of the products and try to find the best deal. An easy way to organize the bargaining is by way of auctioning the products. This way of bargaining is very structured and can easily be done automatically. Of course, the strategies of the participating agents are not trivial and much work is done in trying to find so-called "dominant" strategies for certain types of auctions (see e.g. Varian 1995; Huberman & Hogg, 1995; Rosenschein & Zlotkin 1994; Sandholm 1996). These strategies are guaranteed to give the best result no matter what the other agents do. Unfortunately very little situations arise where a dominant strategy really exists.

Although auctions become increasingly popular as a means to organize electronic marketplaces, they are certainly not suitable for all types of electronic commerce transactions. They do not function very well in cases where the buyer needs a

F. Dignum and C. Sierra (Eds.): Agent Mediated Elec. Commerce, LNAI 1991, pp. 98-114, 2001.
© Springer-Verlag Berlin Heidelberg 2001

customized product or requires other conditions to be fulfilled. In these cases, the negotiation that takes place is more complex and usually is a one-on-one negotiation.

In this paper we want to discuss in a more systematic way, which types of (electronic) commerce transactions can be distinguished and what the role of agents is for these types. Depending on the role of the agents they should meet certain requirements. Specifically we will look at the requirements on the ability of the agent to communicate with its environment. In section 2 we will take a look at some theory about markets and institutions. In section 3 we will look at the interactions of the agents within these electronic institutions. In section 4 we will look at the future roles that agents can fulfil in electronic commerce transactions and which research questions are of interest in this context.

2 Markets and Institutions

In this section we will look at the role of institutions in (electronic) transactions. Although the transactions can have many different forms, in general they all follow the following pattern (see also e.g. Kalakota & Whinston, 1996)):

1. determine needs

2. exchange information on products and companies

3. negotiation / price discovery

4. establish (legal) contract

5. contract fulfillment

6. guarantee and feedback

Depending on the type of market (product and participants) there will be more emphasis on one or the other phase. The role of institutions is to facilitate the transactions. An institution only is useful if it improves the performance or quality of the transactions in some sense. In (van Heck 1997) it is argued that an (electronic) institution is only viable if the stakeholders have converging interests in using the institution. I.e. if both buyers and sellers have some advantage in using the institution and the intermediary that manages the institution also has some benefit. This can be the quick fixing of decent prices, enhancing trust in partners (through securities), opening new markets, preventing information asymmetry, etc.

In the next section we will discuss the two main transaction mechanisms and the influence of product and company characteristics on the choice of mechanism. In section 2.2. we will discuss the basic elements of institutions and the role of institutions in the market mechanisms.

2.1 Markets

Economic transactions can be organized through two mechanisms: hierarchy or market (see also (Malone 1987) for an analysis). In the hierarchical mechanism the buying and selling party have a "special" (usually longstanding) relationship. This can be because they are part of the same company or because they have a frame contract that covers the transaction. In this situation the negotiation phase (price discovery) can be skipped during the individual transaction. All negotiation is done at the time the parties enter into the frame contract. The situation is relatively static and most suitable for EDI applications. One of the big advantages of this mechanism is that it is possible to make a tight integration between the production processes of the buyer and seller. Something that is very important in just-in-time production in e.g. the car manufacturing industry. A disadvantage is the dependence on a few suppliers and/or buyers. If one of the suppliers fails to deliver (or goes bankrupt) it immediately creates a problem in the production line.

The second mechanism to organize transactions is the market mechanism. The main idea is that there are many providers of a product and many clients that want to purchase the product. The parameters of the transaction (like the price of the product) are not fixed for a long period of time, but determined for each single transaction. In general it holds that the coordination costs for this mechanism are higher than that of the hierarchy mechanism. However, because of the economy of scale and growing competition the production costs are usually lower. Tight coupling of production processes is harder using the market mechanism, because of the fact that suppliers will change regularly.

In general one could say that there is a trade-of between the coordination costs and the production costs. If a complete product is manufactured within one company the coordination costs are very small and optimal logistics can be achieved because all is under control of one party. However, the production itself is more expensive because some parts could be produced much more efficient by other parties. If on the other hand the manufacturing and assembly of all parts of a product are out-sourced then maximal efficiency can be achieved in the production processes. However, the costs of coordinating these different parties are much higher.

Some characteristics of products, companies and markets influence the decision on whether the products should be traded through a hierarchy mechanism or through a market mechanism. The first characteristic is the asset specificity of a product. For instance, if a product is very location specific (i.e. produced only at a specific place and relatively difficult to transport) then it will be more difficult to trade the product through a market mechanism because it is more difficult to choose freely between different producers (or consumers). A good example is the car manufacturing industry. Because this industry is very competitive they try to lower costs as much as possible. One way to achieve this is by reducing stocks. In order to accomplish this the factories only start manufacturing a car after it has been ordered. Moreover they only want the parts to arrive when they are needed in the production process. As a consequence the factories depend on the fact that their suppliers are located in the vicinity of the manufacturing plant such that parts can be reliably delivered just-in-time. In this situation a hierarchy mechanism is more efficient than a market mechanism. The extra costs that are incurred because the company is tied to a few suppliers are easily outweighed by the benefits of the just-in-time delivery.

Another example of asset specificity is the fact that a product can be related to a specific type of customers and/or producers. For example, if a symphony orchestra is needed for a concert than the quality of the orchestra is very dependant of the people playing in it. One cannot easily substitute one orchestra for another. On the other hand some products are completely geared towards a small market, like operation tools for surgeons. Also for these types of products a hierarchical model is usually preferable to a market model.

Also products that are difficult to specify are not so easily traded through a market mechanism, because it is hard to compare products from different producers. So, it is not about the complexity of a product but about how easy it is to specify. E.g. a car is very complex, but is relatively easy to specify, because most parts are standardized. However, a business insurance policy is very difficult to describe accurately, because there are no standards at all.

Finally, the players that are in the market for a certain type of products play a role in the choice between market or hierarchy mechanisms. If there are only a few suppliers in the market, like e.g. in rail transport, telephones or large building constructions, then a market mechanism does not work properly, because the suppliers can easily collude to manipulate the market. E.g. if the government puts out a call for offers on a large bridge and only three or four companies are able to build it, they can collude and agree not to make a bid below a certain price. They may split the difference after the project is awarded or take turns in other big projects.

To conclude, it can be said that there are products for which the market mechanism is the obvious choice. E.g. commodities like books and CD's. There are also products and markets where the hierarchical mechanism seems natural. E.g. specialized tools for industries with only a few (but large) companies. However, there is also a whole range of products and markets for which the choice is not obvious. For this area it can be said that the use of information technology reduces the coordination costs in all cases and therefore more products in these markets will be traded through some form of market mechanism. In principle this is very promising with respect to support of these transactions. It seems that the market mechanism is easier to support (and even automate) than the establishment of a hierarchical mechanism. (note that the situation is almost reversed once the hierarchy has been established. In that case EDI can be used and much of the logistics supported efficiently). If all products could be exchanged using a market mechanism then we could devise some auction mechanism to support it and fully automate the exchange. However, we do not believe that this will be feasible for all situations. The main question at this moment is what type of support can be offered (and what role do agents play) if no pure market mechanism like the auction mechanism can be used?

2.2 Institutions

In the previous section we described two main mechanisms for economic transactions between organizations. Our main interest lays in how the transactions can be supported when they are performed electronically. Especially of interest is the role of (electronic) institutions to support the transactions. In general one might say that institutions play two roles:

1.   They enhance the efficiency of the transaction between the partners

2.   They enhance the trust that the parties have in a proper performance of the transaction.

The efficiency of the transaction is enhanced by providing e.g. an efficient price discovery mechanism and a standard transaction protocol.

The role of enhancing trust in the transaction is often underestimated. In many cases though institutions have evolved from in order to remedy a lack of trust in the market. The institution can enhance trust e.g. by providing trusted information on potential partners (Like Chambers of Commerce). They can also provide regulations for the behaviour of the parties during the transactions and ways to enforce that behaviour. They can enforce for instance guarantees of the parties on payment and/or credit. Often the institutions also provide a legal back up for the contracts that are closed within the institution. E.g. in the form of standard legal contracts that cover all transactions within the institution.

The emphasis on which role is played will be different when market transactions are supported and when hierarchical transactions are supported. In case of hierarchical transactions the institution can play a role in establishing a relationship between the parties (the contracting phase), but usually the negotiation phase is far more complicated and involves much more than just price discovery. During the fulfillment phase of the contract, the role might be in monitoring the workflow and assisting in case of disputes. In case of the use of a market mechanism for the transaction the role of the institution will be to structure the way buyers and sellers can interact on the market. E.g. by providing an efficient means for price discovery (like an auction mechanism).

Institutions are determined by two things. First the infrastructure that they provide and secondly the type of interactions that are supported by the institution (see also (Tsvetovatyy 1997)). E.g. an institution might provide both an auction as well as a shopping mall.

2.2.1 Infrastructure

The infrastructure for electronic institutions should at least contain banking facilities, communication facilities and an ontology. In any transaction at some stage one party has to pay the other party. This can be done very simple by giving a credit card number or very complicated by setting up some letter of credit or other financial security. An institution should provide different ways of payment such that the parties can always find a common way to pay. It is very awkward if a whole transaction is concluded but a payment cannot be made because one side can only pay with a Visa card and the other party only accepts Digital cash. Preferably the institution has some back-up such that it can convert itself between different methods of payment.

Of course the payment should be safe and guaranteed. This means e.g. that credit cards should be checked but also that the communication of the credit card number is encrypted in a secure way.

The communication facilities have two aspects. The first is that the communication should be confidential, integrity should be guaranteed, authentication of messages possible and repudiation of messages impossible. These are all measures of security that should be taken such that parties that do business through the institution can communicate in a secure and reliable way. The second aspect of the communication facilities is the provision of protocols and languages that can be used during the (formal) interaction between the parties. A good example is an auction protocol like the descending bids protocol. Finally there should be a common ontology available for the parties in the institution. This is needed such that they can check whether they are referring to the same objects when they use specific terms. E.g. it might state that a "monitor" refers to a 14" color monitor unless specifically stated otherwise. Also it might state that a "contract" refers to a legally binding contract according to a certain statute of the law.

2.2.2 Transaction Types

The transactions that are performed between two parties can be performed either directly or through some broker. In the case that the transaction takes place through the hierarchy mechanism the transaction is almost always performed direct. This means that the contacts are between the parties themselves directly and no third party plays an intermediary role.

However, the most common example of direct trading is "shopping". Producers expose their products in some way and customers can compare by entering several shops. After the customer makes a choice the transaction is performed directly with the shopkeeper. Another good example of direct trading is the use of classified ads. Of course the cases where the parties enter into a direct negotiation without interference of an arbitrator is also an example of direct trading.

The most common example of indirect trading are the auctions. In that case the producers deliver their products at the auction house and the consumers can buy the products using some predefined auction mechanism. In this case the broker brings buyer and seller together and helps the market to set a fair price. Another way of indirect trading is through distributors, which actually buy the products themselves first and later on resell it to the customers.

Although this is not the place to present a detailed analysis of the roles of the broker in indirect trading (see e.g. (Choi 1997)), it is good to at least sketch some of its functions. Although it might seem that brokers and institutions are the same (namely intermediaries in the trading process) we want to stress that they have different functions. An institution is facilitating the trading process and is usually not seen as an extra link in the supply chain. A broker is an extra link in the chain between supplier and customer.

Brokers can have many functions. First of all they might have information about products and/or companies that are not easily available to the potential customers. In that case they can play a role in matching the interests of customers and suppliers.

Usually brokers do not actually provide a mechanism for price discovery. However, they can be involved in price discovery in at least two ways. First of all they can provide information about current (and/or fair prices) to customers and suppliers, therewith in effect influencing that price if the market is quickly changing (e.g. stock brokers) or very opaque (e.g. house brokers). Secondly, they can operate as distributor, thus first buying the products from the suppliers and later on selling them to the customers. By operating this way, the broker actually determines a price together with the suppliers and customers. This can be beneficial for both sides because of the economy of scale that a distributor can realize. Therefore it can claim a lower prize than normal customers from the supplier. The difference in price is usually large enough such that the customers also profit from the intermediary and still can get a lower price.

A third function of the broker is that of organizing the logistics more efficient. This can e.g. be done through keeping stock in a central place.

Another function of a broker is as trusted party in the contracting phase. The broker can organize the contract and validate it against industry standards. Also the broker might have specific knowledge about procedures that should be followed in the process.

In general it can be said that the function of the broker is to provide knowledge for those phases of the transaction where it is not economical for the parties to obtain that knowledge themselves and to provide economies of scale in those cases where that is profitable for both suppliers and customers. See (Moss 1998) for an economical analysis of the profitability of establishing a broker in a market.

There seem to be at least two cases in which direct trading is the most profitable way of trading. First is the case where there is a "good market". I.e. a market with many buyers and sellers, which can easily get into contact and which have enough information to compare parties and products. A good example are the commodity markets. In these markets the existence of brokers is usually not profitable. The second case where direct trading is the most profitable is where direct contact between buyer and seller is important. This can be important because the contract is complicated and very personal, but also because the product is "personalized" or feedback on the products is very important.

2.3 The Role of Institutions

The role of the (electronic) institution in direct transactions is naturally smaller than in indirect trading. Because in direct trading the contacts are directly between supplier and customer, the institution has little control over the content of the contract and the transaction. However, the institution can provide facilities to the parties to support their contact. E.g. it can provide payment methods, standard contracts, common ontology, etc. One of the main roles of an institution in direct trading will be to reduce the costs and time of the coordination during the establishment of the hierarchy. However, another important role will be to establish the necessary trust between the parties in order to conclude the transaction. This can be achieved by providing securities to the parties with respect to the information they get (e.g. through certificates on data), providing standard internationally recognized contracts, providing settlement constructions, etc.

In the indirect trading the role of the institution will be an intermediary between the two parties. In fact it will support many of the functions that were described for brokers as well. From this role it follows that the institution has more power to control the whole transaction. It can determine the protocol through which the interaction takes place. This tighter control possibilities make it easier to automate parts of these brokered transactions. For instance, an auction protocol can be implemented . It is easy to write software that can operate with the auction protocol and automatically sell or buy products. This situation is different for the direct transactions. It is more difficult to automate a free negotiation than an auction mechanism. Of course many aspects can be supported in direct transactions as well. E.g. the information exchange and even price discovery can be supported by shopping agents and shopping malls.

3 Institutions and Agents

In this section we discuss the roles that agents might have in electronic commerce and more specific how they can be combined with the use of electronic institutions. Before going into this discussion we will reiterate the key properties of agents and indicate which type of tasks agents are particularly suitable for.

3.1 Agents

A commonly used definition of intelligent agents states that they are software systems that should be autonomous, pro-active, reactive and sociable (Wooldridge 1999).

The first property (autonomousness) means that the agents should be relatively independent in executing their functions. It means that agents will not be dependent on input of the user for every decision they have to take. In the other hand an agent cannot be controlled in the way objects are controlled. When sending a message to an object this will evoke a method of the object that is executed whenever the message is of the right type and the sender had the right authority (the center of control lays with the requesting object). In the case of agents, the agent will determine itself when it receives the message whether it will respond to the message or not (the center of control lays with the receiving agent).

The last property (sociability) has as consequence that an agent should be able to communicate with its environment and is able to cooperate with it (including other agents). This means that an agent is not completely autonomous, but can be influenced by other agents and the user.

The property of pro-activeness means that agents have their own (in-built) goals that they try to achieve. Therefore they do not rely on explicit commands of a user to start operating.

Finally, the reactiveness of agents means that they can react to changes in the environment. This property balances the pro-activeness somewhat. It prevents that agents only try to achieve a certain goal without looking whether the goal is still achievable, whether the current plan is the best one, etc.

Some other properties that agents can have are mobility and learnability. The first indicates that agents might move themselves from one machine to another (instead of sending messages) and the second indicates that agents can adapt their behavior on the basis of their experiences.

Unfortunately the practical, implemented agents of today do not have all the properties sketched above. However, we will use these properties to see for what type of tasks agents can be most useful.

The first task that comes to mind is that of collecting and filtering information. Agents can move over networks to gather information, compare it and filter the best information based on the past appreciation of the user.

A second type of task that agents are good in is to negotiate in simple ways over resources and other tasks to be performed. A good example is the use of the Contract Net protocol to divide tasks among a set of agents.

A third task that agents can do very well is to distributedly solve a complex problem.

A last task that agents can perform well is to guide and monitor longterm processes that need frequent attention and have a life span of several hours to several months.

3.2 Agents and Electronic Commerce

Agents can play several roles in the (electronic) commerce transactions. At least one should distinguish a role of agents where they support one or both parties in the trading process and a role of the agent as representative of a party in the trading process. Agents will only be used as user representative if the benefits of using an agent are high and the trust that an agent will realize them are high enough. Practically this means that agents can more easily be used in this role if the value of the transaction is relatively low (and thus the loss incurred in the case of not getting an optimal deal are not very important) and when the procedure followed in the transaction is well defined. If the user knows exactly which steps are followed, the user will more easily trust that an agent will get an optimal deal.

However, even when the process steps are clear the process itself might still be vague. First of all the product might be difficult to specify. In that case the consumer or supplier might want to start with a vague (or incomplete) description and fill it in during the negotiation. This uncertainty about the actual product makes it very difficult to delegate the trading to an agent, which needs a clear goal to operate reliably. A second major problem is that the user does not always know on forehand what he will accept as a good deal. It is clear that a consumer wants the price to be as low as possible if he negotiates about price only. However, when negotiations are performed over multiple attributes, the relative importance of the attributes is usually not fixed at the start. E.g. when negotiating about price and guarantee a customer can indicate that it finds price very important and guarantee hardly (say they get an importance mark of 90 vs. 10%). However, he might find during negotiation that whenever the price drops below a certain level no guarantee can be given at all. Although it might be that the utility, calculated on the basis of the scales and relative importance he gave earlier, is maximal at that price he still wants some guarantee on the product and decides to go for a sub-optimal price. The main point here is that people usually do not foresee the consequences of their choices for the utilities of the attributes on the final outcome.

Besides the above points that prohibit an easy delegation of the trading process to agents, it might also be that the trading process itself is either not very clear or very complex and context dependent. E.g. if the negotiation is very complex with several parties at the same time or about many interrelated issues, it is not very likely that a customer will delegate this task to an agent.

The representative role is most likely to occur when market mechanisms are used for trading. For the market mechanism there are at least a number of cases where the trust needed is relatively low, the procedures are quite simple and clear and thus the advantage of delegating this task to an agent can be high.

In the other hand setting up a hierarchical relationship is a complicated process that requires the building up of trust between the parties. This will not easily be delegated to a piece of software. However, also in a hierarchy agents can have an important role. First of all the agents can be used to assist in setting up the hierarchy. In the past this was a complicated process, where many agreements had to be made. However, with the advent of "virtual enterprises" where different independent organizations form a company for a specific project or purpose, it becomes more easy to couple several organizations into a hierarchical relation. In cases where the interactions between different organizations are well defined this might be automated using agents (something that is not feasible at this moment yet, due to the fact that exactly those interactions between organizations are usually not formally defined).

Agents can also be used to support the logistics in a hierarchical relation (see Nissen 1999). Of course one could think of using a traditional ERP package like SAP or Baan, or a Work Flow Management package to streamline the logistics. However, these software packages start from the idea that all the logistics is controlled through one organization. It means that the control of the logistics process is centralized as well. In the case of a hierarchical relation between companies this is not (always) the case. Each company is at least to some extend autonomous. Therefore resource allocations as made in the traditional Work Flow Management and ERP packages cannot be made in this case. The use of autonomous agents to represent departments and organizations might solve this problem. Instead of just allocating a task to a resource, the allocation is done through a request that can be negotiated by the agents.

As said before the role of agents is most clear in case a market mechanism is used to perform the transactions. In this case agents can be used to compare products of several producers and help to find the best bargain, but they can also be used to perform the actual transaction. Only in the last case do we speak of actual agent mediated electronic commerce. If a direct trading procedure is followed, agents of producers and consumers should negotiate the deal and inform their users. In case the negotiation is very simple (or not existing as in the case of fixed price markets) this can be done without the use of an institution. E.g. an agent can buy a CD at CD-now, because the transaction is completely specified and simple. However, in most cases a certain context is needed in which the transaction can be performed. This context can be formed by an institution. In the next section we will discuss what role institutions can play when agents are used for electronic commerce.

3.3 Agents and Institutions

The institution determines the way that the parties can conduct the transaction and provides an infrastructure to do it. Good examples are Kasbah and AuctionBot, market places where agents can buy and sell goods. They give a predefined structure for specifying the product and also facilitate the negotiation process (about the price of the product).

As said before, in the case of indirect trading there exists a natural institution in the form of the broker that mediates in the transaction. In case of an auction, this is the auction house. The auction house determines the procedure through which products can be delivered at the auction as well as an auction mechanism that determines the way products can be bought.

In all cases holds that the more elements of a transaction protocol are determined by the institution the more efficient the transaction can be performed. That is, the interaction between the agents is more determined and thus the communication complexity reduced. However, it also holds that the more elements of the transaction protocol are determined by the institution the less flexibility there is to "negotiate" a deal. E.g. in an auction every item is traded separately and basically on price only. It is not possible to buy a whole package of products at once for a lower price.

Institutions that employ very rigid and well-defined protocols for the interactions are the best context for the use of agents in electronic commerce at this moment. First of all the users can trust the agents more easily if the procedures are well defined and rigid. Also the agents that enter the institution can be very simple in terms of communication. Their model of the outside world can be limited to those elements that are relevant for the protocol and also they do not have to adjust to unexpected events in the outside world (all events are determined by the rigid protocols). All the intelligence can be put in the modules that determine the best strategy under the fixed protocol for the transaction process. Therefore the trust of the user in the delegation of the task to the agent is bigger.

One of the disadvantages of institutions that employ rigid protocols for the trading procedure is that many current procedures cannot be captured in that rigid way (yet). In fact one of the few procedures that can easily be formally modeled and implemented is the auction model. For each of the auction types one can very precisely and formally define the procedure to which the participants must adhere. This is one of the main reasons why auctions became a popular form of electronic commerce.

One way of extending the use of institutions and agents is to formalize richer trading procedures such that they can also be handled in the same way as auctions. For instance, multi attribute auctions are an example, as well as multiple linked auctions. Although some first attempts are made in these directions (see e.g. Gutman 1998; Matos 1998), little formal theory is available to make adequate models for the protocols needed in these situations and especially for the strategies that should be used for the agents in these situations.

It is also possible to look at institutions that do not fix the entire transaction procedure, but only give some boundaries or support. For instance, it is well known that the negotiation process itself is very complicated. However, the institution might support (or enforce) certain types of negotiations that are still feasible for agents. The main question is, how to extend the negotiation possibilities. Which type of products are traded that need these types of negotiations? If these products are mainly traded through the hierarchy mechanism it might not be very useful to develop such a market mechanism.

Another way of extending the use of institutions is to just let them give support to the trading process without having them dictate the protocol used. E.g. in the negotiation phase the institution might keep track of all commitments that are made so far and that cannot be reneged. It can also set the boundaries in between which negotiation can take place, such that the negotiation is fair for both sides. This can be achieved by indicating the norms that both parties have to adhere to while interacting through the institution. These types of extensions are also useful in the cases where the parties are trading directly, but need a trusted third party to secure the trading process.

Two things have to be done for these types of extensions of institutions to work. First, the institutions should be described formally. Whenever institutions adhere to strict protocols like the auction mechanism, the description of the institution can be given in terms of several finite state machines that are linked. One finite state machine describes the auction itself, the others describe the payment procedure, entering the institution, etc. Finally one finite state machine describes how one gets from one "scene" to another. E.g. from registration to auction and subsequently to settlement or exit.

However, when the protocols within the institution are not that rigid, it is also not possible to define the working of the complete institution as a set of protocols anymore. What is needed is a normative description of the boundaries of the behavior of the participants within the institution and possibly the penalties incurred when those norms are violated. One way of achieving this is through the use of deontic logic as used in e.g. (Dignum 1999; Meyer & Wieringa 1993)

The second element to be adjusted are the agents that operate within these institutions. Because the protocols are not all fixed anymore, it is important that the agents know what protocol they are following when interacting with other agents. So, the agents must also have a representation of different types of protocols to be used and their abilities to follow those protocols. E.g. there might be agents that can only negotiate about prices using a common haggling protocol of alternating bids that converge to a compromise. Other agents, however, might negotiate about the price using arguments for each bid. Or agents might negotiate over many aspects of the product at the same time. There should at least be a "uniform" way to specify the abilities of the agents to handle all types of different protocols.

The next question is how to develop the institutions and agents together to make it really work. The agent should know both the protocol of the institution, which can be still very precisely specified and definite as well as the possible protocols that can be used within the different phases of the trading procedure.

The ideal situation would be an institution where all types of agents could trade their products. The "simple" agents only accept a very simple transaction protocol. They might miss the very best bargain, but could be very efficient. The "complex" agents can accept both the simple as well as the complicated protocols and can thus trade with simple agents but also try to conduct real negotiations with other complex agents. This means that the protocols for negotiation should be built in a modular version where each module can be seen as an extension of the basic module.

All of the above actually assumes that there is one institution where all agents meet. But in an open environment there will be many different institutions. So, for the future it seems important that agents are able to move to different institutions and compare the products and processes at those institutions. E.g. some auctions may use a descending bidding protocol while others use an ascending bidding protocol. How should an agent determine in which auction to participate to get the best bargain? Is it possible to participate in both auctions in parallel and use that as an advantage? Although the institutions give a context in which to perform a transaction, the existence of multiple institutions creates new possibilities and problems for agents again.

Of course, it does not seem very feasible for user agents to know how to choose the best institution and trading procedure. This requires specialized "trading" knowledge, which cannot be required from the agents at the user sites that actually just want to buy or sell a product and only have specialized product knowledge. One way to remedy this problem is through the development of specialized "trading agents" that have knowledge how best to trade in certain institutions. If an agent wants to buy a product it will give a description and a price limit to a trading agent. This trading agent will find the best institution to suit your needs and negotiate the best deal within that institution. Although there is a general tendency in electronic commerce to abolish intermediaries, it seems that this is a viable area for a new type of intermediary!

A possible architecture of such a trading agent is given in the following figure. It is based on (Tsvetovatyy, 1997; Verharen, 1997; Dignum et.al., 1997; Norman et.al., 1997).

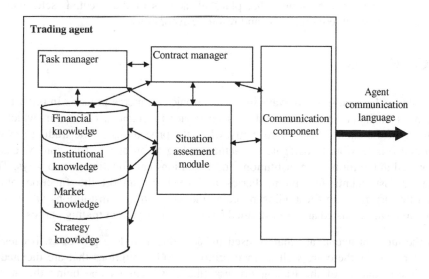

Fig. 1. Trading agent architecture

The knowledge base consists of several parts: the financial knowledge (about ways of payment), institutional knowledge (about the protocols and norms of institutions), market knowledge (about the type of market that is suitable for which type of product) and strategy knowledge (about strategies for interacting most profitable within an institution).

The communication manager takes care of all communication with other agents within and outside institutions. It also receives all messages from other agents and sends it to the most appropriate module. It incorporates some knowledge on communication protocols that it should follow (outside institutional protocols). Messages can be anything from bidding on a product, to a payment order to the bank.

The contract manager has control over the negotiation phase in the sense that it keeps track which negotiation strategy is followed, how successful it is and finally which commitments (contracts) have been made. Once a contract has been made, the contract manager keeps track of the fulfillment of the contract. I.e. it will initiate payment at the right moment, check delivery, etc.

The situation assessment module is the decision module of the agent. In this module all knowledge of the agent is consulted and a decision is made about where to sell or buy a product, when to start, when to quit negotiations, etc. This module also contains the goals of the agent as set by the clients. E.g. sell this product as quick as possible, but not below a certain price.

The task manager is a module that plans all actions of the agent. It schedules the actions based on all commitments and resource availability.

4 Conclusions

Agents can be used in many ways in the electronic commerce process. In order to use them as mediators it is almost always necessary to create a context in which the trading of the agents takes place. Only when the procedures of the trading are well defined it is feasible to delegate the actual trading to an agent. This context can be provided in the form of an institution. So, institutions can function in two ways. They can be instruments for intermediaries and used to support the function of the intermediary party in the trading process (indirect trading). Institutions can also be used to create a trusted and well-defined environment for direct trading parties.

At the moment agents are mainly used in the indirect trading processes, because in those processes there are well defined protocols and institutions that are dictated by the intermediaries of the trading process (the most famous one being the auction houses). In order to use agents in more complex trading processes, the institutions should be extended to allow more types and more flexible protocols. Only when these can be formally defined and the boundaries of the behavior of agents within the institutions is clearly defined can agents successfully be employed in these more complex trading processes.

The institutions should be flexible enough to provide different types of scenarios. Depending on the type of product and market situation a certain type of trading can be chosen. This means that agents should be able to select the proper (most efficient or profitable) trading procedure for the case in hand. If the chosen procedure allows some freedom within the interaction (e.g. negotiating in different ways) the agent should agree with the other party on a common acceptable way of interacting. One cannot expect all agents to have the same capabilities, therefore agents should be designed in such a way that they can deal with both simple and complex agents in the context of the same institution.

A new challenge will be to design trading agents that function as intermediaries for the trading procedure. They have specialized knowledge on strategies and trading protocols, such that the agents of the trading parties only have to have product and market knowledge and can leave the burden of finding the suitable trading procedure to the trading agent.

References

Chavez, A., and Maes, P. 1996. Kasbah: An agent marketplace for buying and selling goods. In *First Int. Conf. On the Practical Application of Intelligent Agents and Multi-Agent Technology,* London, UK, 1996

Choi, S-Y., Stahl D. and Whinston, A., 1997. *The economics of electronic commerce,* MacMillan , Indianapolis, USA, 1997.

Dignum, F. 1999. Autonomous agents with norms. In *AI & Law,* vol.7, pp.69-79, 1999.

Dignum, F., Verharen, E. and Bos, S. 1997. Implementation of a cooperative agent architecture based on the language-action perspective. In M. Singh et.al. (eds.) - *Proc. Of the fourth Int. workshop on Agent Theories, Architectures and Languages (ATAL-97),* Providence, USA, 1997.

Doorenbos, B., Etzioni, O. and Weld, D. 1996. A scalable comparison-shopping agent for the World Wide Web. *Technical report TR96-01-03,* University of Washington, 1996.

Heck, van E., Damme, van E., Kleijnen, J. and Ribbers, P. 1997. New entrants and the role of information technology; Case-study: the tele flower auction in the Netherlands. In *Proceedings of the thirtieth Hawaii International Conference on System Sciences (HICSS'30),* 1997.

Huberman, B. and Hogg, T. 1995. Distributed computing as an economic system. In *Journal of Economic Perspectives* 9(1): 141-152, 1995.

Kalakota, R. and Whinston, A., 1996. *Frontiers of electronic commerce,* Addison Wesley, 1996.

Malone, T., Yates, J. and Benjamin, R. 1987. Electronic markets and electronic hierarchies. In *Communications of the ACM,* vol. 30, nr. 6: 484-497, 1987.

Matos, N. and Sierra, C. 1998. Evolutionary computing and negotiating agents. In *Proceedings of the first international workshop on Agent Mediated Electronic Trading (AMET'98)*, pp. 91-112, Minneapolis, 1998.

Meyer, J.-J. and Wieringa, R. 1993. *Deontic logic in Computer Science*. John Wiley & Sons, Chichester, 1993.

Moss, S. 1998. The Cost of Rational Agency. Technical report 51 of the Centre of Policy Management, Manchester University, http://www.cpm.mmu.ac.uk/cpmrep51.html.

Nissen, M. and Mehra, A. 1999. Some intelligent software supply chain agents. In *Proceedings of the third international conference on autonomous agents (Agents'99)*, pp.374-375, Seattle, 1999.

Norman, T., Jennings, N., Faratin, P. and Mamdani, E. 1997. Designing and implementing a multi-agent architecture for business process management. In J. Müller, M. Wooldridge and N. Jennings (eds.) *Intelligent Agents III - Proc. Of the third Int. workshop on Agent Theories, Architectures and Languages (ATAL-96)*, LNAI-1193, Springer-Verlag, Heidelberg, 1997.

Rodriguez, J.A., Noriega, P., Sierra, C. and Padget, J.A. 1997. FM96.5 A Java-based Electronic Auction House. In *Second International Conference on the practical application of intelligent agents and multi-agent technology: PAAM'97*, pp. 207-226, London, 1997.

Rosenschein, J. and Zlotkin, G. 1994. Designing conventions for automated negotiation. *AI Magazine*, fall-1994, 29-46.

Sandholm, T. 1996. Limitations of the Vickrey Auction in Computational Multiagent Systems. *ICMAS-96*, Keihanna Plaza, Kyoto, Japan, December, pp. 299-306, 1996.

Tsvetovatyy, M., Gini M., Mobasher, B. and Wieckowski Z. 1997. MAGMA: An agent-based virtual market for electronic commerce. In *Journal of Applied Artificial Intelligence*, 11:501-523, 1997.

Varian, H. 1995. Economic mechanism design for computerized agents. In *USENIX workshop on Electronic Commerce*, New York, 1995.

Verharen, E. 1997. A Language-Action perspective on the design of cooperative information agents. Ph.D.thesis, KUB, Tilburg, 1997.

Wooldridge, M. 1999. Intelligent Agents. In G. Weiss (ed.) *Multiagent systems: A modern approach to distributed artificial intelligence*, pp. 27-78, MIT Press, 1999.

Wurman, P., Wellman, M. and Walsh, W. 1998. The Michigan Internet AuctionBot: a configurable auction server for human and software agents. In *Proceedings of the second international conference on autonomous agents (Agents'98)*, pp. 301-308, Minneapolis, May 1998.

A Model for an Electronic Market Place

Maria João Viamonte and Carlos Ramos

Instituto Superior de Engenharia do Porto
Departamento de Engenharia Informática,
Rua São Tomé, 4200 Porto, Portugal
{viamonte,csr}@dei.isep.ipp.pt

Abstract. The Electronic Commerce is one of the areas in which the technology of intelligent agents can be successfully applied, and maybe, the only way to allow consumers to deal with the complexity and diversity of the electronic services offered and in particular in environments like the Internet. While there are many Web services, which help users find things to buy, there are few that help buyers and sellers. The purpose of this paper is to present a model for a virtual electronic Market Place more flexible than the existing on the Web, where users create autonomous agents to buy and sell goods on their behalf. Four stages of the Consumer Buying Behaviour (CBB) model are addressed.

1 Introduction

With the increasing importance of electronic commerce across the Internet the need for agents to support both customers and suppliers in buying and selling goods or services is growing rapidly. Today there are several Web sites where people can look for a specific good or service [1][2][3][4] but most of them does not take advantage of the intelligent systems and knowledge technology to automate the process and few help buyers and sellers. The traditional electronic commerce systems on the Internet require a large effort from users and include searching for parties interested in selling or buying what users want to buy or sell, comparing prices and other features of the good or service in order to make an optimal purchase decision. Neither dynamic price according to the actual demand nor customer specific offers are possible. The customer and the supplier cannot negotiate the details of a deal. The comparison with competitors like in markets is not supported by these systems.

Agents can help people on consumption activities [5]. In the past, agents were used successfully to execute a set of tasks like information search, information selection, execution of repetitive procedures, decisions making based on a specific criterion, etc. Agents technology seems to be the best to use in electronic commerce, since agents can sell, buy and represent the interests of their owners, whether they are customers or suppliers. On Electronic Commerce agents used like intermediates are going to revolutionise this kind of commerce and we believe that the use of agents can reduce transaction costs involved in electronic commerce, in general, and in consumer-to-consumer transactions, in particular.

Most of current commerce agents like "shopping bots" only support the Product or Merchant Brokering stages, only two of the six stages of the CBB model [6] that is

F. Dignum and C. Sierra (Eds.): Agent Mediated Elec. Commerce, LNAI 1991, pp. 115-125, 2001.
© Springer-Verlag Berlin Heidelberg 2001

used to explain the different stages of a deal. Few systems go into the negotiation part and even fewer help anticipate consumer needs (Need Identification stage) and provide paths into the subsequent CBB stages. But a flexible market place needs to support more stages to be successful.

The goal of this work is to give a contribution to create a market place more flexible than the existing electronic commerce places, including four stages of the CBB model. We will present a model for a virtual market place on the Web where users create autonomous agents to buy and to sell goods or services. The intelligent agents automate the time consuming process of looking for partners (buyers and sellers) and have the ability to negotiate with other agents in order to obtain the best deal. There is the need for some *data mining* and *knowledge discovery* techniques to build customer/supplier profiles, to permit customer/seller group identification and to do forecasting.

Our model has many providers for a product or service and many clients that want to purchase the product or service. Any transaction has specific parameters and is based in items like price, available stock, delivery policies, terms of guarantee, satisfaction with certain providers, etc. Dynamic pricing according to the actual demand and customers offers is possible too.

2   Agents as Mediators in Electronic Commerce Applications

The traditional electronic commerce approach requires a direct communication between the potential buyer and seller. The buyer collects information about a product by directly accessing the information provided by the seller. If the offer satisfies his needs he negotiates directly with the seller of the product. Negotiation, delivery and payment are usually done manually.

The traditional approach has the following disadvantages:

- It requires a long time to gather the necessary amount of information about a product or service, since all information sources have to be accessed manually;
- The growing number of similar goods and services available further increases this problem. The buyer is forced to compare a number of products before he is able to make a decision to buy;
- For the seller of products or services it becomes increasingly difficult to get potential buyers to notice his products. He is forced to spend more time and money on advertising than necessary;
- Information deficits on the side of the buyer or seller can lead to pricing inefficiencies.

An agent-based architecture for electronic commerce allows the creation of a virtual market place in which a number of autonomous or semi-autonomous agents trade services and goods. This approach offers a number of new opportunities to reduce or even eliminate the disadvantages mentioned above. Agents are able to examine a large number of products before making a decision to buy or sell. This not only eliminates the need for manually collected information about products but also allows negotiating an optimal deal with the various sellers of a good.

Software agents will play an increasing variety of roles as mediators in electronic commerce. The personalised, continuously running autonomous nature of agents make them well suited for mediating the consumer behaviours involving information filtering and retrieval, personalised evaluations, complex coordinations, and time-based interactions [6]. These roles correspond to Product Brokering, Merchant Brokering and Negotiation stages of the CBB model.

2.1   Actors

We need intelligent agents to buy and sell goods or services on their behalf. Shopping agents are software agents that represent users and their goals in online shopping. Early shopping agents behave like information agents. They only were able to collect price and available information for a certain good or service [1]. Improved systems can also make recommendations [7]. Other systems introduced more sophisticated agents, which could autonomously negotiate about price in order to obtain the best deal [8]. Negotiation about price is sufficient only if there are no other properties to consider when buying or selling goods or services. But we can think in other properties that are relevant in a deal like: short delivery times; extended terms of guarantee; satisfaction with certain providers. Interestingly, simulation results have been reported, showing that well-informed shopping agents concentrating on price comparisons solely can lead to disastrous price wars [9]. Price wars force suppliers to concentrate only on goods for the mass market in order to compensate lower profit by much higher sales rates. Suppliers with more specialised range of goods or services coupled with additional terms have either to conform to the simple price-comparing process or to draw back from the online market. The customer will find a reduced number of different online suppliers and a decreasing diversity of goods and services.

We need agents that can do negotiation taking into account multiple interdependent attributes specified by the users.

"The negotiation process requires a **state space** and **utility functions** [10], the state space describes what the parameters of negotiation are and how they are measured. A buyer and seller who cannot agree on a price/delivery date combination may see things quite differently when credit terms are entered into the negotiation as an extra dimension. The utility functions determine how happy a participant is with a certain location in the state space. For example, a buyer would have higher utility for a low price, and a seller would have a utility function that works differently". The state space expands as new issues come up, and the utility functions are refined as a person has a "gut feeling" reaction to a proposed deal. This approach tries to find new points in the solution space that benefit both buyers and sellers.

When a user creates a selling agent, he gives it a correct description of the item to sell. The user needs to specify a set of attributes when creates the seller agent like:

- Description of the item;
- Desired price;
- Lowest acceptable price;
- Stock available;
- Desired date to sell the item;
- Delivery times (Physical goods);

- Terms of guarantee;
- Authorisation to do the transaction / need user approval;
- Other relevant parameters.

The user needs to specify his preferences and a range of preferred values and some measurement for the interdependencies between the attributes.

Basically, the agent goes to the market place, contacting interested parties (buying agents) and negotiating with them the best possible deal taking into account the attributes specified by the user and the corresponding preferences.

The agent goal is to sell the item in question. The user can change the initial parameters at any time. The user can check on its selling agents, see which other agents they have talked to, and what prices they have been offered. This information can imply changes like decreasing the price, if they see that the offers are lower than expected. But this agent has to take into account the different attributes and preferences specified by them (only concentrating in the price if it is the user choice).

When they obtain their objectives, they have to notify their owners. At this level two situations are possible: the agent has a previous authorisation to do the transaction and only has to notify the user; or the user has the final decision, and agents have to communicate the possibilities being considered. The agent can show his opinion, but the user has the final decision.

In contrast there are the buying agents, which job is to buy goods on behalf of users. When a user creates a buying agent, a correct description of the item that he wants to buy must be given. Basically, the agent goes to the market place, contacting interested parties (selling agents) and negotiating with them the best possible deal taking into account different users preferences. The user needs to specify a set of attributes when he creates the buyer agent like:

- Description of the item;
- Desired price;
- Highest acceptable price;
- Desired date to buy the item;
- Terms of guarantee;
- Satisfaction with certain providers;
- Delivery times acceptable (Physical goods);
- Authorisation to do the transaction / need user approval;
- Other parameters.

The user needs to specify too their preferences and a range of preferred values and some measurement for the interdependencies between the attributes.

The agent goal is the negotiation with selling agents, trying to make the best deal, taking into account the attributes specified by the user and the corresponding preferences.

When they obtain their objectives, they have to notify their owners too. At this level we also have two possible situations: the agent has a previous authorisation to do the transaction and only has to notify the user; or the user has the final decision, and agents have to communicate the possibilities being considered.

The users can specify more parameters than those mentioned above. The agents negotiate with each other by using strategies based on rule systems and utility functions defined by the individual user.

Once a buying and selling agent has a deal and their respective user approval, then the transaction can occur.

2.2 Number of Actors

The number of partners on a Market for a specific good or service can be one-to-one, one-to-many or many-to-many.

One-to-one, single seller for single buyer, negotiation between one seller and one buyer and can involve various aspects of a deal. This relation is the simplest model possible.

One-to-many, we can have a single seller for multiple buyers or we can have a single buyer for multiple sellers at any time for a certain good or service in the market place. Auctions are an example of this kind of relationship where there are negotiation between one seller and many buyers, but an auction reduces the negotiation to a single variable: the price and they do not function very well in cases where the buyer needs a customised product or service. Another problem is that bids in auctions are usually binding and therefore the user has to trust his agent.

Agents can have two different roles in to online auctions. They can participate in auctions selected by the user, being responsible for the bidding process or they can select the auctions by themselves but for this they need knowledge about what to buy.

Many-to-many, we can have many buyers for many sellers for a specific good or service at any time. This model is more complex because there are negotiations and transactions in parallel. The parameters of the transaction are not fixed for a long period of time, but determined for each single transaction. This situation increases the market competition, what can be good in order to implement dynamic pricing according to the actual demand and customers offers. Unfortunately deadlocks may occur when the demand for some resources exceeds supply.

One-to-one, one-to-many and many-to-many is not determined simply by the number of agents. We can have agents that represent buyers associations and agents that represent sellers associations. For example, some web sites offer buyers the opportunity to make grouped orders to get a better price.

The rules of the game, the used protocols, and the number of parties and players can be different but the outcome should remain the same, a negotiation deal which will satisfy the participants.

3 Market Place Objectives

Agents can be used in many ways in the electronic commerce applications and for this it will be necessary to create a scenario where they can interact with each other.

The Market Place function is to permit and facilitate the interaction between the agents. We support the idea of a Web site where users go to sell and buy things. All agents are notified by the market about existing buying agents and selling agents and about what they want sell and what they want buy. We expect that we have agents interested in buying and selling the same kind of things.

We can have at any time a variable number of partners in our Market and every transaction has specific parameters.

A language support for inter-agent communication has to be defined; we need to ensure that all the agents participating in the market use the same language, or that the languages in use can be translated.

Another objective is supporting some of the stages of CBB model:

Need Identification, "the consumer can be stimulated through product information". Although all the buyers agents are notified by the market about existing selling agents and about their products, the Market Place needs some additional functions like a database with information about last deals and users profiles. This data can be worked by *data mining* techniques to have more information available. The system can use this information to notify the users about products available based on their profiles and last deals.

Product Brokering, "the evaluation of product alternatives based on consumer-provided criteria." The agents system must be able to assist consumers in deciding which products best fit their personal criteria, they must act as recommendation agents, make predictions based on profile and "business intelligence", possibly derived by *data mining* techniques.

Merchant Brokering, "*who to buy from,* includes the evaluation of merchant alternatives based on consumer-provided criteria". The customer agent must be able to find several providers for each item, taking into account different user preferences and based in past events and users satisfaction with certain providers (this information can be available in the mentioned database).

Negotiation, "This stage is about *how* to determine the terms of the transaction". The agents negotiate with each other by using strategies based on rule systems and users criteria. Searching for an agreement on multiple goals and considering tradeoffs between the goals.

4   A Model for an Electronic Market Place

The model is going to implement two different perspectives: the one of customers and the other of suppliers. In the customer centred view, the system must act as a decision support system, helping and advising the user where and how to buy the items he or she is looking for. The customer's agent must be able to find several providers for each item taking into account different users preferences and have the ability to assist consumers in deciding which products best fit their personal criteria. They must act as recommendation agents, make predictions based on profile and "business intelligence", possibly derived by *data mining* techniques. Learning is an important characteristic of this agent, since it must remember past events and users satisfaction with certain providers.

From the provider point of view, there is the need too for some *data mining* techniques to build customer profiles and to permit customer group identification. Another important issue is the ability to "*spy*" its competitors in which concerns prices, payments, delivery policies and available products. There is the need for some *simulation techniques,* namely the well known "*what if*" simulation capability, which can be very advantageous, in order to allow to test the implications of introducing new measures like: new product prices, news products, etc.

In real physical commerce the employees of the companies selling goods have the sensibility for the business based in a long experience in the interaction with clients. When we move to the electronic commerce paradigm this sensibility is lost since we have a kind of blind negotiation (we may not keep the profile of the client). This is the reason why *data mining* and *knowledge discovery* is so important in electronic commerce in order to deal with aspects like client clustering, forecasting, etc. On the other hand in physical commerce, clients are able to learn by their own experience which companies are reliable, where to look for personalised goods or services and how to handle the negotiation process. When we pass our competencies to agents this knowledge can be lost and *data mining* is also important here. Electronic market needs much more agility than traditional market. In order to react to competitors or in order to gain advantage over them. Electronic agents will need to take decisions. However, the possible impact of decisions needs to be studied and simulation techniques are important for this purpose. Some features of *Decision Support Systems*, like *"What if"* simulation, are adequate for our agents. Figure 1 presents the architecture of the agents Market Place.

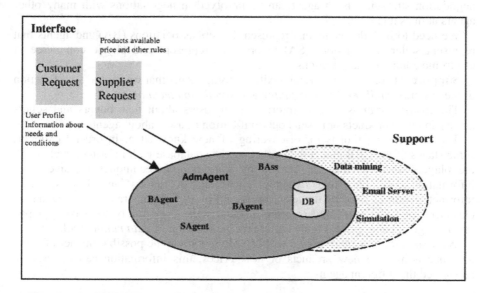

Fig. 1. Architecture of the Agents Market Place

The architecture is modularised, so that changes in one component would cause at most minimal changes to be made to the others, and comprises three primary components:

Interface: Front-end of the application, it consists of a set of Web pages located on a Web server. The combination of Multi-Agent systems and World Wide Web technologies provides the means to develop high level interfaces, being able to support process interaction among Internet users and remote Multi-Agent system applications [11]. The current WWW tools, their abilities and potentialities, give an excellent support to reduce the efforts of developing and using interfaces, to simplify interface maintenance, and to create better communication channels among distributed applications.

We need a clear set of forms because the success of our model is directly depending on the "rich" and precisely information given by the users. A clear message should explain what this data will be used for.

Back-End: The *application engine*, can be implemented in Java. Conceptually it is the place where agents "*live*" and interact with others, trying to find the best deal.

This component has a database and an administrator agent.

The database (DB) has information about registered users, users profile, users needs, last deals, customer satisfaction with certain providers, products available, running agents and other relevant information. The information about user profiles are obtained through the answers to questionnaires, from purchase history or extracted and inferred from a statistical analysis.

The administrator agent (AdmAgent) is responsible for the management of different running agents and the market place.

This component is also responsible for creating the buyers (BAgent) and sellers (SAgent) agents for a given user and responsible for the implementation of different negotiation strategies. Each agent can be involved in negotiations with many other agents at the same time.

We need to include agents that represent buyers associations (BA) and agents that represent sellers associations (SA) in order to represent real physic commerce in electronic commerce applications.

Support: There are also several auxiliary components that warrant a good function of the system: *email server*, *data mining* and *simulation technology*.

The *Email server* is used to inform system users about new buyers and sellers agents and new products or to send out notification to users about agents actions.

The *data mining* tool is for discovering of new knowledge. In order to support some stages of the CBB model the market needs a database with information about all the players, this data can be worked by *data mining* techniques to have more information available (like dynamic clustering of sellers and buyers). This information can be used by the agent users and by the administrator agent. Dynamic clustering of sellers and buyers offer to buyers the opportunity to make grouped orders to get a better price. Figure 2 presents the function of *data mining* tool.

With *Simulation technology* we will be able to known the possible impact of some new decisions, like new products or new prices, this information can be used to advertised the different agents.

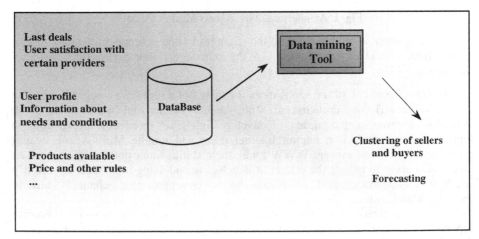

Fig. 2. Data Mining Tool

The **Interface** sends requests to the **Back-End**, the **Back-End** is the component with the responsibility to give an answer to the user, and for which it might use auxiliary components (**support**), sending back the answer to the client.

A client can be a potential seller or buyer or also a user that only wants a piece of information.

The agents can have answers to their functions on the local system or they have the ability to be mobile.

Because the architecture that we present here has agents that represent buyers and others that represent sellers, one important issue is the security of the on-line queries. In order to preserve the information about users, it is expected that agents representing the sellers have access to additional buyers information only if they are authorised, otherwise the information is inaccessible or available only to a specific seller. The system must explain clearly what will do with the information collected through a questionnaire.

In order to do their functions the agents must have some capabilities like personality, being autonomous; "smart"; sensitive; mobile; cooperative; informative; accurate; responsible.

The characteristics that we choose try to guarantee that *our* agents are able to do their functions.

Personality, agents operate on behalf of their users, and hence can be equipped with a personal profile to better reflect their owner preferences;

Autonomy, the big advantage that agents bring is their ability to automate previously manual operations. This can be used to advantage by employing agents to look for buyers or sellers and attempting to find the best deal, these autonomous agents differ from common retrieval and filtering agents, like shopping agents, in their ability to do negotiations with other agents.

"Smart" agents refers to their ability to learn as they react or interact with their environment and other agents and indicates that agents can adapt their behaviour on the basis of their experiences. An agent capable of learning should perform better over time, and in Electronic Commerce this may be equivalent to "making more money" for its user (buyer or seller).

Sensibility is the ability to act using stimulus/response type of behaviour by responding to the present state of the environment in which they are embedded.

Mobility, warrant the ability to move around some networks in order to carry out their functions.

Cooperation is the ability to cooperate with other agents in order to perform their tasks (associations of agents to make for example group orders to get a better price), for the kind of agents with social ability, i.e. the ability to interact with other agents and possibly humans, a communication language is necessary. This ability can be used to facilitate the agent negotiation on prices, services and transactions.

Information warrant the ability to search information across the "world" by means of "Web Robots", "Spiders" [12], etc, in order to have more information available.

Accuracy and Responsiveness, are characteristics important and which assure that they execute their tasks faithfully.

The agents have the above mentioned characteristics and many functions, but in general they represent owners, and for this they will interact in order to solve their tasks. When they obtain their objectives, they have to notify their owners. At this level there can be two situations: the agent has a previous authorisation to do the transaction and only has to notify the user; or the user has the final decision, and agents have to communicate the existent possibilities. The agent can show his opinion, but the user has the final decision.

To do their functions the agents have the capacity to communicate with others and with the system. In this work we have adopted as communicating language the *standard*, at the moment, KQML [13]. On a semantic point of view the utilisation of shared ontologies warrant the inter-relation between heterogeneous agents.

5   Conclusions

Today there are several Web sites where people can look for a specific good or service, but most of them only serve a small part of the transaction process as it is defined in the CBB model. We believe that by using agents technology, *data mining*, *knowledge discovery* tools and *simulation* techniques we can solve many of the problems presented. We had presented a model for a virtual Market place where users create autonomous agents to buy and to sell goods or services and represent the interests of their owners. The intelligent agents automate the time consuming process of looking for buyers or sellers and can negotiate in order to obtain the best deal.

Our model has many providers for a product or service and many clients that want purchase the product or service. Any transaction has specific parameters and is based in items like price, available stock, delivery policies, terms of guarantee, satisfaction with certain providers, etc. Dynamic pricing according to the actual demand and customers offers is possible too. Four stages of the CBB model are addressed.

Agents are well suited for use in applications that involve distributed computation or communication between components. Agent technology is well suited for use in applications that reason about the messages or objects received over a network. This explains why agent-based approaches are so adequate in applications that use the Internet, like electronic commerce. Multi-agent-systems are also suited for applications that require distributed concurrent processing capabilities.

The analysis that we have made lead to the development of the present model for a Market place. It will be necessary to implement this model and analyse its behaviour to conclude about its effectiveness, efficiency and security. As future work we will implement a prototype Market place based on the presented model, to evaluate the chosen technology and as a means to obtain feedback from possible users. In addition more sophisticated negotiation strategies are envisaged and further development work will include the stage five, "**Purchase and Delivery**", and the stage six, "**Product Service and Evaluation**" from the CBB model.

We also want to explore some implementation details such as the communication language between the agents and the system, and the ontology problem. Even if a universal communication language were to be adopted, the participating agents would still only be using a common syntax. Another important question is about security at the on-line queries and in the system in general.

References

1. Bargain Finder. http://bf.cstar.ac.com/bt
2. OnScale: Live Online Aution House. http://www.onscale.com/
3. United Computer Exchange http://www.uce.com
4. Global Shop http://www.globalshop.pt
5. P. Maes. "Intelligente Software". Scientific American, Vol. 273, N° 3, pag. 84-86. Scientific American, Inc. September, 1995.
6. R. Guttman, A. Moukas, P. Maes. "Agent-mediated Electronic Commerce: A Survey. http://ecomerce.media.mit.edu/papers/ker98.pdf
7. Amazon.com, http://www.amazon.com
8. Kasbah, http://kasbah.media.mit.edu
9. J. Kephart, J. Hanson, J.Sairamesh: Price-War Dynamics in a Free-Market Economy of Software Agents, presented at the Artificial Life VI Conference, University of California at Los Angeles. California, June 29, 1998.
10. http://www.haas.berkeley.edu/citm/auction/toc.html.
11. O. Belo, A. Ribeiro. "A distributed Multi-Agent System Environment, A Web Approach". Proceedings of the IASTED International Conference, 1996.
12. Hyacinth S. Nwana. "Software Agents: An Overview". Knowledge Engineering Review., 1996
13. Y. Labrou, T. Finin. "A Semantics Approach For KQML: A General Purpose Communication Language for Software Agents." Proceedings of CIKM'94, New York, 1994.

On the Formal Specification of Electronic Institutions

Marc Esteva, Juan-Antonio Rodríguez-Aguilar,
Carles Sierra, Pere Garcia, and Josep L. Arcos

Artificial Intelligence Research Institute, IIIA
Spanish Council for Scientific Research, CSIC
08193 Bellaterra, Barcelona, Spain.
{marc,jar,sierra,pere,arcos}@iiia.csic.es
http://www.iiia.csic.es

Abstract. In this article we argue that open agent organisations can be effectively designed and implemented as institutionalized electronic organisations (*electronic institutions*) composed of a vast amount of heterogeneous (human and software) agents playing different roles and interacting by means of speech acts. Here we take the view that the design and development of electronic institutions must be guided by a principled methodology. Along this direction, we advocate for the presence of an underlying formal method that underpins the use of structured design techniques and formal analysis, facilitating development, composition and reuse. For this purpose we propose a specification formalism for electronic institutions that founds their design, analysis and development.

1 Introduction

According to [20], human interactions are guided by institutions, which provide a structure to everyday life. Institutions represent the rules of the game in a society, including any (formal or informal) form of constraint that human beings devise to shape human interaction. Therefore, they are the framework within which human interaction takes place, defining what individuals are forbidden and permitted and under what conditions. Institutions must be created (f.i. the Constitution), and may evolve over time (f.i. the common law). A distinguishing feature of institutions is the clear distinction drawn between the rules and the players. Establishing a stable structure to human interaction appears as the *raison d'être* of institutions.

At this point it is convenient to refer to the crucial distinction between institutions and organisations. Following the rational view of organisations provided by [10] "organisations are social units (or human groupings) deliberately constructed and reconstructed to seek specific goals". Organisations include political, economic, social and educational bodies (f.i. political parties, trade unions, clubs, universities). In [24] *goal specificity* and *formalization* are identified as the two main characteristics of organisations, meaning by formalization the attempt

F. Dignum and C. Sierra (Eds.): Agent Mediated Elec. Commerce, LNAI 1991, pp. 126–147, 2001.
© Springer-Verlag Berlin Heidelberg 2001

to standardize and regulate the behavior of the roles interacting within an organization. Therefore roles are understood as standardized patterns of behavior required of all agents playing a part in a given functional relationship in the context of an organization.

The way organisations are created and how they evolve are fundamentally influenced by the institutional framework, and, in turn they influence how the institutional framework evolves. Organisations must conform to the rules of institutions in order to receive legitimacy and support.

In this paper we adopt as a main goal the design and development of efficient and robust open agent organisations. At the outset we wonder whether we can follow a mimetic strategy that permits us to borrow and adapt well-know social mechanisms and concepts that have proven valuable when employed for articulating human societies. For this purpose, we firstly make explicit the major issues arising in our principal task taking inspiration on the analysis already presented in [8].

- *Heterogeneity.* The society must be capable of coping with and supporting heterogeneous agents, i.e. agents developed in different languages, with different purposes (objectives) and preferences, and endowed with varying degrees of sophistication.
- *Trust and Accountability.* Agents are not always expected to reliably follow the rules of the society due to multiple reasons (bugs, bounded rationality, etc.), and therefore the society must be equipped with the appropriate mechanisms for monitoring and conveniently managing malicious, fraudulent agent behavior.
- *Exception Handling.* We must contemplate the capability of detecting, preventing, and recovering from failures resulting from unintended disfunctional behaviors that may jeopardize the overall functioning of the society.
- *Societal change.* Agent societies are not static; they may evolve over time by altering, eliminating or incorporating rules. Hence the need of demanding flexible agent societies capable of accommodating future changes.

We observe that indeed human societies successfully deal with the issues above by deploying institutions that:

- determine what individuals are prohibited from doing and what are permitted to undertake;
- costlinessly ascertain violations and the severity of the punishment to be enacted; and
- evolve and are altered by human beings.

We uphold that agent organisations can be effectively designed and implemented as *institutionalized agent organisations* —that henceforth we shall term *electronic institutions*, or *e-institutions* for shorter. From this follows that one of our main purposes will be to model the creation, evolution, and consequences of the rules defining institutions and their incorporation into agent organisations.

Notice that the kind of electronic institutions that we will be considering are populated by a vast amount of heterogeneous (human and software) agents playing different roles and interacting by means of speech acts [25]. In other words, we make the assumption that any interacting activity taking place within our electronic institutions is purely dialogic.

Throughout this paper, we focus on the macro-level (societal) aspects referring to the infrastructure of electronic institutions, instead of the micro-level (internal) aspects of agents. Such a task is widely admitted by the multi-agent community as highly delicate [18]. This fact makes us advocate for adopting a principled, engineering approach founded on a formal specification of electronic institutions, continuing the work presented in [22,26], that founds their design, analysis and development of architecturally-neutral electronic institutions. As the most salient result, we obtain a graphical specification language that is intended to be embedded into a development environment that assists e-institutions' designers at all the stages of the development cycle.

The rest of the paper is organized as follows. In Section 2 we argue on the need of a formal method that underpins the specification, analysis and development of electronic institutions. Next, in Section 3 we provide a mathematically sound, unambiguous, abstract definition of electronic institutions. In order to illustrate how to specify in practice electronic institutions, we offer in Section 4 an example corresponding to the fish market an electronic auction house. In Section 5 we summarize and highlight the major benefits arising from our contribution, and discuss the open issues that can be faced taking our proposal as the starting point.

2   A Formal Specification Approach

Formal methods in software building comprise two main activities, namely *formal specification* and *verified design*, that is the precise specification of the behaviour of a piece of software, so that such software can be subsequently produced, and the proof of whether the implementation complies with the specification. Thus, the role of any formal method is to provide a clear and precise description of *what* a system is supposed to do, rather than a formulation of *how* it operates [9]. The presence of an underlying formal model will support the use of structured design techniques and formal analysis, facilitating development, composition and reuse.

In this section we take such formal approach with the purpose of specifying software infrastructures for electronic institutions. Our formal specification will be based on a purposely devised specification language enabled to produce both visual and textual specifications of infrastructures for electronic institutions. In other words, such specification language shall serve to produce sound an unambiguous specifications of the *rules* of the game of an electronic institution. It is apparent that at a further stage the specification language can be extended in order to allow for the specification of the *players* of the game. Such extension is expected to support the specification of micro (internal) aspects of agents, i.e. their architectures and logics. As a result, it would be possible the complete specification (infrastructure and agents) of an electronic institution.

In this work we solely focus on the specification of infrastructures. As a first step, we identify the core notions on which our current conception of electronic institution, and so our specification language, is to be founded:

- *Agents and Roles.* Agents are the players in an electronic institution, interacting by the exchange of speech acts, whereas roles are defined as standardized patterns of behaviour. The identification and regulation of roles is considered as part of the formalization process of any organisation [24]. Any agent within an electronic institution is required to adopt some role(s). A major advantage of using roles is that they can be updated without having to update the actions for every agent on an individual basis. Recently, the concept of role is becoming increasingly studied by software engineering researchers [21, 16], and even more recently by researchers in the agents' community [4,17, 28,6,5].
- *Dialogic framework.* Some aspects of an institution such as the objects of the world and the language employed for communicating are fixed, constituting the context or framework of interaction amongst agents. In a dialogic institution, agents interact trough speech acts. Institutions establish the acceptable speech acts by defining the ontology (vocabulary) —the common language to represent the "world"— and the common language for communication and knowledge representation which are bundled in what we call dialogic framework. By sharing a dialogic framework, we enable heterogeneous agents to exchange knowledge with other agents.
- *Scene.* Interactions between agents are articulated through agent group meetings, which we call *scenes*, with a well-defined communication protocol. We consider the protocol of a scene to be the possible dialogues agents may have.
- *Performative structure.* Scenes can be connected, composing a network of scenes, the so-called performative structure, which captures the existing relationships among scenes. The specification of a peformative structure contains a description of how the different roles can legally move from scene to scene. Agents within a performative structure may be possibly participating in different scenes, with different roles, and at the same time.
- *Normative Rules.* Agent actions in the context of an institution may have consequences that either limit or enlarge its subsequent acting possibilities. Such consequences will impose obligations to the agents and affect its possible paths within the performative structure.

Next, in Section 3 we offer a detailed analysis of the notions introduced above that helps us gradually construct a formal specification of an electronic institution infrastructure.

3 Electronic Institutions' Structure

First of all, and for notational purposes, we introduce some definitions that will apply henceforth. Let $Agents = \{a_1, \ldots, a_n\}$ be a finite set of agent identifiers, and $Roles = \{r_1, \ldots, r_m\}$ a finite set of role identifiers respectively. At the specification level we regard agents and roles simply as symbols and type names. Then by $a_i : r_j$ we mean that agent a_i is of type r_j. Moreover, we define the sets $V_A = \{x_1, \ldots, x_A\}$ and $V_R = \{\rho_1, \ldots, \rho_R\}$ as a finite set of agent variables and a finite set of role variables respectively.

3.1 Roles

We have already identified the notion of role as central in the specification of electronic institutions. Roles allow us to abstract from the individuals, the agents, that get involved in an institution's activities. In order to take part in an electronic institution, an agent is obliged to adopt some role(s). Thereafter an agent playing a given role must conform to the pattern of behaviour attached to that particular role. Therefore, all agents adopting a very same role are guaranteed to have the same rights, duties and opportunities. Notice that we can think of roles as agent types. More precisely, we define a role as a finite set of dialogic actions. Such actions are intended to represent the capabilities of the role. For instance, an agent playing the buyer role is capable of submitting bids and an agent playing the auctioneer role can offer goods at auction.

There are several issues concerning role/role relationships. As an agent may possibly play several roles at the same time, role/role associations standing for conflict of interests must be defined with the purpose of protecting the institution against an agent's malicious behaviour.

Thus, in general, the management of agent/role and role/role relationships becomes a fundamental issue for electronic institutions. *Role-based Access Control Models* (RBAC) [23] developed in the computer security arena offer well-founded mechanisms for handling both types of relationships. Fundamentally, RBAC has been successfully employed for managing the security administration of organisations [3,2]. But more interestingly, RBAC has been accurately formalized [12,14,13]. In order to solve the agent/role and role/role relationships, we borrow and adapt the formalisation of the rules for RBAC offered by the NIST RBAC model [14,13,12], which extends the basic RBAC model by adding role hierarchies, cardinality, and conflict of interests relationships.

Although RBAC manages three types of associations, namely associations between users (agents) and roles, associations between roles, and associations between roles and permissions[12], in this section we solely concentrate on the role/role associations.

When analysing human institutions we observe that the roles played by humans are hierarchically organised. There are many ways of constructing of a role hierarchy to express different types of relationships among roles. Here we consider that roles are organised as a partially ordered set (poset), represented as a pair $\mathcal{R} = \langle Roles, \succeq \rangle$, reflecting a role hierarchy. Then if $r \succeq r'$ holds we say that r subsumes r' or an agent playing role r is also enabled to play role r'.

We also realise that there are conflicting roles within an institution. For instance, in the fish market the *boss* and *buyer* roles are mutually exclusive in the sense that no one can *ever* act as the boss of the market and as a buyer. In a bank, the *teller* and *auditor* roles are also considered as mutually exclusive. We define a policy of static separation of duty (ssd) to mean that roles specified as mutually exclusive cannot be both authorised to an agent.

We represent the static separation of duties as the relation $ssd \subseteq Roles \times Roles$. A pair $(r, r') \in ssd$ denotes that r, r' cannot be authorised to the very same agent. Observe that the static separation of duties will be considered when assigning roles to an agent entering the institution and it restricts the possible assignations of roles to an agent.

Summarising, the adoption of a policy of separation of duties will allow us to express constraints on the role/role associations indicating conflicts of interests. It seems obvious that ssd must satisfy some constraints respect to the relation $\succeq$.

Finally, we explicitly state the requirements identified so far as necessary for managing the role/role relationships:

(i) The static separation of duties relation is symmetric. Formally, for all $r_i, r_j \in Roles$ $(r_i, r_j) \in ssd \Rightarrow (r_j, r_i) \in ssd$.
(ii) If a role subsumes another role, and that role is in static separation of duties with a third role, then the first role is in static separation of duties with the third one. Formally, for all $r, r_i, r_j \in Roles, r \succeq r_i, (r_i, r_j) \in ssd \Rightarrow (r, r_j) \in ssd$.
(iii) If a role subsumes another role, then the two roles cannot be in static separation of duties. Formally, $r_i \succeq r_j \Rightarrow (r_i, r_j) \notin ssd$.

Observe that from the last requirements the following properties can be inferred:

(i) For all $r \in Roles \Rightarrow (r, r) \notin ssd$ since the $\succeq$ relation is reflexive.
(ii) If $(r_i, r_j) \in ssd$ then for all $r \succeq r_i$ and for all $s \succeq r_j \Rightarrow (r, s) \in ssd$.
(iii) If exists r such that $r \succeq r_i$ and $r \succeq r_j \Rightarrow (r_i, r_j) \notin ssd$.

3.2   Dialogic Framework

In the most general case, each agent immersed in a multi-agent environment is endowed with its own inner language and ontology. In order to allow agents to successfully interact with other agents we must address the fundamental issue of putting their languages and ontologies in relation. For this purpose, we propose that agents share when communicating what we call the *dialogic framework* [19], composed of a communication language, a representation language for domain content and an ontology. By sharing a dialogic framework, we enable heterogeneous agents to exchange knowledge with other agents.

Definition 1. *We define a* dialogic framework *as a tuple* $DF = \langle O, L, I, CL, Time \rangle$ *where*

- *O stands for an ontology (vocabulary);*
- *L stands for a representation language for domain content;*

- I is the set of illocutionary particles;
- CL is the (agent) communication language;
- $Time$ is a discrete and partially ordered set of instants.

Within a dialogic framework the representation language (KIF [15], first-order logic, etc.) allows for the encoding of the knowledge to be exchanged among agents using the vocabulary offered by the O ontology. The propositions built with the aid of L, the "inner" language, are embedded into an "outer language", CL, which expresses the intentions of the utterance by means of the illocutionary particles in I. We take this approach in accord to speech act theory [25], which postulates that utterances are not simply propositions that are true or false, but attempts on the part of the speaker that succeed or fail.

We consider that CL *expressions* are constructed as formula of the type $\iota(\alpha_i : \rho_i, \alpha_j : \rho_j, \varphi, \tau)$ where $\iota \in I, \alpha_i$ and α_j are terms which can be either agent variables or agent identifiers, ρ_i and ρ_j are terms which can be either role variables or role identifiers, $\varphi \in L$ and τ is a term which can be either a time variable or a value in $Time$. We say that a CL expression is an *illocution* when α_i, α_j are agent identifiers, ρ_i and ρ_j are role identifiers and τ is a value in $Time$ time-stamping the illocution. We say that a CL expression is an *illocution scheme* when some of the terms corresponds to a variable. This distinction will be valuable when specifying scenes in the following section.

During the execution of a scene, variables in CL expressions will be bound to concrete values. For the purpose of allowing to change the value of a bound variable, we will denote it differently. By $\tilde{t}$ we denote that once bound t it can be assigned new values. In this way, we provide a way of representing that the value of a variable can be overwritten.

Henceforth we shall employ question marks to differentiate variables in CL expressions, including the expression corresponding to the contents, from other terms.

Next we present examples of CL expressions:

- $request(?x_i : pra, ?x_j : pra, appointment(?t), ?t')$ is an illocution scheme.
- $request(KQLAT : pra, marc : pra, appointment(tomorrow), 5)$ is an illocution that instantiates the schema above. We interpret this CL expression as a request sent by agent $KQLAT$ playing the pra (personal representative assistant) role to agent $marc$ playing the same pra role for arranging an appointment to meet *tomorrow*.

Finally, we would like to stress the importance of the dialogic framework as the component containing the ontologic elements on the basis of which any agent interaction can be specified as illustrated next when introducing the notion of scene. Thus, a dialogic framework must be regarded as a necessary ingredient to specify scenes.

3.3   Scene

Before formally defining a scene, we must precisely understand what a scene is. Recall that the whole activity within an electronic institution was described above as a composition of multiple, well-separated, and possibly concurrent, dialogic activities, each one involving different groups of agents playing different roles. For each activity, interactions between agents are articulated through agent group meetings, which we call *scenes*, that follow well-defined communication protocols. In fact, no agent interaction within an institution takes place out of the context of a scene. We consider the protocol of each scene to model the possible dialogic interactions between roles instead of agents. In other words, scene protocols are patterns of multi-role conversation.

A scene protocol is specified by a graph where the nodes of the graph represent the different states of the conversation and the arcs connecting the nodes are labelled with illocution schemes that make scene state change. The graph has a single initial state (non-reachable once left) and a set of final states representing the different endings of the conversation. There is no arc connecting a final state to some other state.

Normally the correct evolution of a conversation protocol requires a certain number of agents for each role involved in it. Then a minimum and maximum number of agents for role is defined and the number of agents playing each role has to be always between them.

Because we aim at modelling multi-agent conversations whose set of participants may dynamically vary, scenes will allow that agents either join in or leave at some particular moments during an ongoing conversation. For this purpose, we differentiate for each role the sets of access and exit states. The incorporation or exit of agents has to satisfy the restriction mentioned above about the number of agents for role. Obviously, the final states have to be an exit state for each role, in order to allow all the agents to leave when the scene is finished. On the other hand, the initial state has to be an access state for the roles whose minimum is greater than zero, in order to start the scene.

Definition 2. *Formally, a scene is a tuple* [1]*:*

$$S = \langle R, DF, W, w_0, W_f, (WA_r)_{r \in R}, (WE_r)_{r \in R}, \Theta, \lambda, min, Max \rangle$$

where

- R *is the set of roles of the scene;*
- DF *is a dialogic framework;*
- W *is a finite, non-empty set of scene states;*
- $w_0 \in W$ *is the initial state;*
- $W_f \subseteq W$ *is the non-empty set of final states;*
- $(WA_r)_{r \in R} \subseteq W$ *is a family of non-empty sets such that WA_r stands for the set of access states for the role $r \in R$;*
- $(WE_r)_{r \in R} \subseteq W$ *is a family of non-empty sets such that WE_r stands for the set of exit states for the role $r \in R$;*
- $\Theta \subseteq W \times W$ *is a set of directed edges;*

---

[1] When we need to differentiate the elements of two scenes s and s' we will use a superindex s or s'.

- $\lambda : \Theta \longrightarrow CL$ is a labelling function;
- $min, Max : R \longrightarrow I\!N$ $min(r)$ and $Max(r)$ return respectively the minimum and maximum number of agents that must and can play the role $r \in R$;

Notice that not every illocution scheme is valid to label an arc. In general, a CL expression $\iota(\alpha_i : \rho_i, \alpha_j : \rho_j, \varphi, \tau)$ can label an arc if it satisfies:

- α_i and α_j are agent variables;
- ρ_i and ρ_j are either role variables or role identifiers in R_s; and
- τ is a time variable;

These variables will be bound to concrete values during the execution of the scene. For example, agent variables in an illocution scheme will be bound respectively to the identifier of the agent that has uttered the illocution and to the identifier of the agent who has received the illocution. Then at each moment the bindings of the variables will be the context of the scene execution.

Next, we describe an example of a scene extracted from the case of study presented in Section 4, that we subsequently employ to illustrate how designers can construct graphical specifications of scenes.

Case Study. We have selected as example, the scene representing the main activity within the marketplace: the auctioning of goods in the auction room. This scene is governed by the auctioneer making use of the downward bidding protocol (DBP) that next we state explicitly:

[**Step 1**] The auctioneer chooses a good out of a lot of goods that is sorted according to the order in which sellers deliver their goods to the sellers' admitter.

[**Step 2**] With a chosen good, the auctioneer opens a *bidding round* by quoting offers downward from the good's starting price, previously fixed by the sellers' admitter, as long as these price quotations are above a *reserve price* set by the seller.

[**Step 3**] For each price called by the auctioneer, several situations might arise during the open round:

Multiple bids. Several buyers submit their bids at the current price. In this case, a collision comes about, the good is not sold to any buyer, and the auctioneer restarts the round at a higher price. Nevertheless, the auctioneer tracks whether a given number of successive collisions is reached, in order to avoid an infinite collision loop. This loop is broken by randomly selecting one buyer out of the set of colliding bidders.

One bid. Only one buyer submits a bid at the current price. The good is sold to this buyer if his credit can support his bid. Whenever there is an unsupported bid the round is restarted by the auctioneer at a higher price, the unsuccessful bidder is punished with a fine, and he is expelled out from the auction room unless such fine is paid off.

No bids. No buyer submits a bid at the current price. If the reserve price has not been reached yet, the auctioneer quotes a new price which is obtained by decreasing the current price according to a price step. If the reserve price is reached, the auctioneer declares the good *withdrawn* and closes the round.

[**Step 4**] The first three steps repeat until there are no more goods left.

Graphical Representation. The purpose of the formal definition above is to give a a mathematically sound definition of scene. However in practice scenes will be graphically specified. For instance, Figure 1 depicts the graphical specifications of the scene presented above.

As to the *auction* scene (see Figure 1), we observe that the specification of the role set requires the participation of exactly one auctioneer(A) and, at least, two buyers(b)(min), although up to ten buyers might be allowed to participate(Max). The graph depicts the states of the scene, along with the edges representing the legal transitions between scene states, and labelled with illocution schemes of the communication language of the dialogic framework. The information contents of such schemes is expressed in first-order logic (*FOL*) making use of the concepts in the *e-auctions* ontology. The type of performative is specified in the set I — which contains the types of performatives identified in [7]— listed in the *Particles* area.

Notice that some states are identified as access and exit states. Apart from the initial and final states, the w_1 state is labelled as an access and exit state for buyers —meaning that after either a collision, sanction or expulsion, new buyers might be admitted into the scene— while ω_3 is uniquely an access state.

3.4   Performative Structure

The notion of performative structure is the most complex and interesting of this formalism, since it models the relationships among scenes. Notice that although conversations (scenes) are currently admitted as the unit of communication between agents, limited work has been done concerning the modelling of the relationships among different scenes. This issue arises when these conversations are embedded in a broader context, such as, for instance, organisations and institutions. If this is the case, it does make sense to capture the relationships among scenes. Thus, while a scene models a particular multi-agent dialogic activity, more complex activities can be specified by establishing relationships among scenes that allow:

- to capture *causal dependencies* among scenes (f.i. a patient cannot undergo an operation without being previously diagnosed by a doctor);
- to define *synchronisation* mechanisms involving scenes (f.i. within an exchange house, we might synchronise traders before allowing them to start off a negotiation scene);

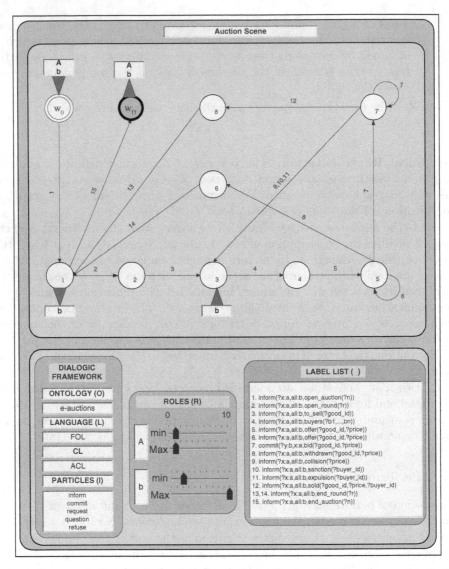

Fig. 1. Graphical Specification of an Auction Scene

- to establish *parallelism* mechanisms involving scenes (f.i. in an auction house, several auctions might be run at the same time);
- to define *choice points* that allow roles leaving a scene to choose their destination (f.i. an agent attending a conference is expected to opt for one of various, simultaneous talks);
- to establish the *role flow policy* among scenes, i.e. which paths can be followed by the roles leaving a scene and which target scenes they can reach. In a conference centre, a speaker, after finishing off his talk, is permitted

to leave the conference room and make it for another conference room to attend an ongoing talk. Notice that, for this particular case, the migration of this speaker also involves the adoption of another role.

In general, the activity represented by a performative structure can be depicted as a collection of multiple, concurrent scenes. Agents navigate from scene to scene constrained by the rules defining the relationships among scenes. Moreover, the very same agent can be possibly participating in multiple scenes at the same time. Hence, it is our purpose to propose a formal specification of performative structures expressive enough to facilitate the specification of such rules.

From a structural point of view, performative structures' specifications must be regarded as networks of scenes. At execution time, a performative structure becomes populated by agents that make it evolve whenever these comply with the rules encoded by the specification. Concretely, an agent participating in the execution of a performative structure devotes his time to jointly start new scene executions, to enter active scenes where the agent interacts with other agents, to leave active scenes to possibly enter other scenes, and finally to abandon the performative structure.

At this point we must notice that the way agents move from scene to scene depends on the type of relationship holding among the source and target scenes. As mentioned above, sometimes we might be interested in forcing agents to synchronise before jumping into either new or existing scene executions, or offer choice points so that an agent can decide which target scene to incorporate into, and so on. Summarising, in order to capture the type of relationships listed above we consider that any performative structure contains a special elements that we call *transition*, devoted to mediate different types of connections among scenes. Each scene may be connected to multiple transitions, and in turn each transition may be connected to multiple scenes. In both cases, the connection between a scene and a transition is made by means of a directed arc. Then we can refer to the source and target of each arc. And given either a scene or a transition, we shall distinguish between its incoming and outgoing arcs. Notice that there is no direct connection between two scenes, or, in other words, all connections between scenes are mediated by transitions. We do not allow also the connection of transitions.

Agents will be moving from a scene instance (execution) to another by traversing the transition connecting the scenes and following the arcs that connect transitions and scenes. Transitions must be regarded as a kind of routers that contain local information about the scene instances that they connect. Therefore, instead of modelling some activity, they are intended to route agents towards their destinations in different ways, depending on the type of transition.

The arcs connecting transitions to scenes play also a fundamental role. Notice that as there might be multiple (or perhaps none) scene executions of a target scene, it should be specified whether the agents following the arcs are allowed to start a new scene execution, whether they can choose a single or a subset of scenes to incorporate into, or whether they must enter all the available scene executions.

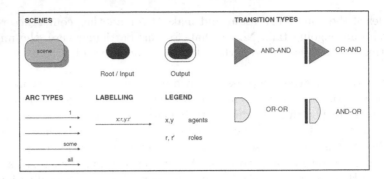

Fig. 2. Graphical Elements of a Performative Structure

We define a set of different types of transitions and arcs whose semantics will highly constrain the mobility of agents among the scene instances (the ongoing activities) of a performative structure. The differences between the diverse types of transitions that we consider are based on how they allow to progress the agents that they receive towards other scenes. Let us divide each transition into two parts: the *input*, through which it receives agents from the incoming arcs, and the *output*, through which agents leave following the outgoing arcs towards other scenes. Then, the following classification of transitions is based on the behaviour that they exhibit on their input and output sides:

- **And/And**: They establish synchronisation and parallelism points since agents are forced to synchronise at their input to subsequently follow the outgoing arcs in parallel.
- **Or/Or**: They behave in an asynchronous way at the input (agents are not required to wait for others in order to progress through), and as choice points at the output (agents are permitted to select which outgoing arc, which path, to follow when leaving).
- **And/Or**: They are a hybrid of the two types of transitions above: on the one hand, likewise *and/and* transitions, they force agents to synchronise on the input side, while on the other hand, likewise *or/or* transitions, they permit agents to individually make the choice of which path to follow when leaving.
- **Or/And**: They are also a hybrid of *and/and* and *or/or* transitions. Agents are not required to wait for others on the input side, but they are forced to follow all the possible outgoing arcs.

According to this classification, we define $\mathcal{T} = \{and/and,\ or/or,\ and/or,\ or/and\}$ as a set of transition types.

Depending on the path followed by the agents when traversing a transition, they may either start scenes or incorporate to one or more ongoing scenes. Thus there are also different types of paths, arcs, for reaching scenes after traversing transitions. We define $\mathcal{E} = \{1, some, all, *\}$ as the set of arc types. Following a *1-arc* constrains agents to enter a single scene instance of the target scene, whereas a *some-arc* is less restrictive and allows the agents to choose a subset of scene instances to enter, and an *all arc* forces the agents to enter all the scene instances to which the paths lead. Finally, a **- arc* fires the creation of a new scene instance of the target scene. Furthermore, each arc will be labelled with the collection of roles that are allowed to follow the arc.

Within the transitions agents are informed about current active scenes and request for their destination. Thus they constitute an intermediate state for agents that move from scene to scene. Transitions are employed by the institution for brokering purposes between agents and the active scenes connected to the transition. Thus within transitions agents will be informed about the active scenes that they can reach so that they choose their destination, i.e. either some active scene to join or some scene to be started. Each transition has an institutional agent that interact with arriving agents. The dialogue in transition can be specified as the dialogue in the scenes with the vision of the institutional agent and one arriving agent i.e. as a conversation with the institutional agent and another agent. When an agent arrives it is informed about its possibilities that depend on the type of the transition and the type of the arcs connecting the transition to the target scene(s). The difference between a transition and the rest of the scenes is that there is not a global state of the transition and any agent can be in a different state[2]. For example, new agents after arrive are in the initial state while other agents are in a middle state after been informed of their destination or waiting to synchronize with other agents or some agents can be in a final state waiting to move to their destinations. Agents requesting to move to a transition are always accepted and they are incorporated to the initial state. After they have selected their target scenes they wait in a final state until the target scene(s) arrives to an access state when.

Figure 2 depicts the graphical representations that we will employ to represent the performative structure's components introduced so far. From the point of view of the modeller, such graphical components are the pieces that serve to construct graphical specifications of performative structures.

Before stating a concrete definition of performative structure, there is a last element to be considered. Notice that although two scenes may be connected by a transition, the eventual migration of agents from a source scene instance to a target scene instance not only depends on the role of the agents but also on the results achieved by agents in the source scene. Thus, for instance, in the fish market, although a registration scene is connected to an auction scene, the access of a buying agent to the execution of the auction scene is forbidden if it has not successfully completed the registration process when going through a registration scene. In a conference centre environment, two agents are not allowed to meet to talk at a meeting room unless they have previously arranged and committed to some appointment. This fact motivates the introduction of constraints over the arcs connecting scenes and transitions. We will require that agents satisfy the constraints, conditions, over the arc solicited to be followed

---

[2] Transitions can be seen as scenes where the state of the scene is the Cartesian product of the state of each agent

when attempting to reach a destination scene. Therefore, conditions must also appear in our formal definition of performative structure.

Finally, we bundle all the elements introduced above to provide a formal definition of a performative structure specification:

Definition 3. *Formally, given a meta-language ML, a performative structure is a tuple*

$$PS = \langle S, T, s_0, s_\Omega, E, f_L, f_T, f_S, f_E, C, \mu \rangle$$

where

- *S is a finite, non-empty set of scenes;*
- *T is a finite and non-empty set of transitions;*
- *$s_0 \in S$ is the root scene;*
- *$s_\Omega \in S$ is the output scene;*
- *$E = E^I \bigcup E^O$ is a set of arc identifiers where $E^I \subseteq (WE_S) \times T$ is a set of edges from exit states of scenes to transitions where $WE_S = \bigcup_{s \in S} \bigcup_{r \in R} WE_r^s$, and $E^O \subseteq T \times S$ is a set of edges from transitions to scenes;*
- *$f_L : E \longrightarrow 2^{V_A \times R}$ is the labelling function;*
- *$f_T : T \longrightarrow \mathcal{T}$ maps each transition to its type;*
- *$f_E : E \longrightarrow \mathcal{E}$ maps each arc to its type;*
- *$C : E \longrightarrow ML$ maps each arc to a meta-language expression of type boolean, i.e. a predicate, representing the arc's constraints;*
- *$\mu : S \longrightarrow I\!N$ sets the upper bound on the number of allowed simultaneous scenes for the scene scheme represented by each scene node.*

In order to present the requirements to be satisfied by the elements above, some previous definitions are needed. Let $s \in S$ be a scene such that $s = \langle R, DF, W, w_0, W_f, (WA_r)_{r \in R}, (WE_r)_{r \in R}, \Theta, L, min, Max \rangle$. Let var and roles be two functions over arcs, defined respectively as $var : E \longrightarrow 2^{V_A}$ and $roles : E \longrightarrow 2^{Roles}$, which return for each arc the set of variables and the set of roles contained in the arc label. Then the following requirements must be satisfied by every performative structure:

(i) *All the agent variables labelling the incoming arcs of a given transition must also appear on the outgoing arcs of the transition: for any $t \in T$*
   $$\bigcup_{(s,t) \in E^I} var((s,t)) = \bigcup_{(t,s') \in E^O} var((t,s'))$$

(ii) *For every scene there is a path from the root transition to the output scene passing through the scene. For all $s \in S$ there is a path $s_0, t_1, \ldots, s_m, t_m, s_\Omega$ such that $(s_i, t_i) \in E^I, (t_i, s_{i+1}) \in E^O \quad \forall i = 0, \ldots, m-1$ and $s_i = s$ for some i.*

(iii) *For every scene, the roles labelling its outgoing arcs must belong to its role set and for every role in its role set there is at least one outgoing arc labelled with it, i.e. for all $s \in S \quad \bigcup_{(s,t) \in E^I} roles((s,t)) = R^s$.*

(iv) *For every scene, the roles labelling its incoming arcs must belong to its role set and for every role of its role set there is at least one incoming arc labelled with it, i.e. for every scene $s \in S \quad \bigcup_{(t,s) \in E^O} roles((t,s)) = R^s$.*

(v)   For every scene, there must be at least one access state for every role labelling an incoming arc, i.e. for every arc $(t, s) \in E^O$, and for every role $r \in roles((t, s))$ there is an access state $w \in WA_r^s$ where WA_r^s is the set of access states for the role r in the scene s.

(vi)   For every and/and transition, every outgoing arc has to be connected to a scene containing at least one access state for all the roles labelling the arc. More formally, for every (t, s) such that $f_T(t) = $ and/and then

$$\bigcap_{r \in roles((t,s))} WA_r \neq \emptyset.$$

(vii) For every arc of type $*$ the initial state of the scene must belong to the set of access states for each role labelling the arc. Formally, for each arc $(t, s) \in E^O$ such that $f_E((t, s)) = *$ we require that $w_0 \in \bigcap_{r \in roles((t,s))} WA_r$.

(viii) Agents will not be allowed to progress through an arc of type $*$ if the number of instances of this scene has reached its maximum.

From the definition above, we can simply view a performative structure as a network of scenes interconnected by different types of transitions. The specification of a performative structure amounts to select a collection of scenes, and next create sound connections among them. Complementarity, the limits on the number of scenes, μ, need to be defined. Figure 3 shows how the graphical elements in Figure 2 are combined in order to produce the graphical specification of the performative structure corresponding to the fish market. Observe that the scene that Figure 1 represents, appears in the resulting specification as a particular node.

Notice that we demand any performative structure to contain a root and an output scene. The output scene does not model any activity, and so it must be regarded as the exit point of the performative structure. As to the root scene, it must be regarded as the starting point of any agent accessing the performative structure. Departing from the root scene, agents will make for other scenes within the performative structure.

3.5   Normative Rules

Such as depicted, a peformative structure constrains the behaviour of any participating agents at two levels:

(i) *intra-scene:* Scene protocols dictate for each agent role within a scene what can be said, by whom, to whom, and when.

(ii) *inter-scene:* The connections among the scenes of a performative structure define the possible paths that agents may follow depending on their roles. Furthermore, the constraints over output arcs impose additional limitations to the agents when attempting to reach a target scene.

And yet, we understand that an agent's actions within a scene may have consequences that either limit or enlarge its subsequent acting possibilities out of the scope of the scene.

Such consequences have effect along two different directions. On the one hand some actions will introduce subsequent acting commitments that have to be interpreted as acting obligations. On the other hand, other consequences occurring locally within a scene may vary the paths that an agent can follow in the performative structure because they affect the satisfaction and dissatisfaction of the constraints labelling paths. Both types of consequences will be required to be kept by an institution for each agent on an individual basis. In general, for a given agent we shall refer to such consequences as the agent *context* within the institution.

For instance, a trading agent winning a bidding round within an auction house is obliged to subsequently pay for the acquired good. Considering the performative structure in Figure 3 that implies that the trading agent has to move at some time to the buyers' settlements scene to pay for the acquired good. Notice that although the auction scene is connected to the output scene, the path is disallowed to agents unless they fulfil their pending payments.

In order to represent the deontic notion of obligation, we set out the predicate *obliged* as follows:

– $obliged(x, \psi, s)$ = agent x is obliged to do ψ in scene s.

where ϕ is taken to be, in both cases, an illocution scheme.

Next we introduce a special type of rules, the so-called *normative rules* in order to capture which agent actions (illocutions) have consequences that need to be kept in its context. Given a performative structure and a metalanguage, the normative rules will have the following schema:

$$(s_1, \gamma_1) \wedge \ldots \wedge (s_m \gamma_m) \wedge \phi_1 \ldots \phi_n \Rightarrow \phi_{n+1} \wedge \ldots \wedge \phi_r$$

where $(s_1, \gamma_1), \ldots, (s_m, \gamma_m)$ are pairs of illocution schemes and scenes, and $\phi_1 \wedge \ldots \wedge \phi_r$ are meta-language predicates. Notice that some of these rules will be devoted to the triggering of obligations, while others will be used for inferring facts that will be subsequently employed to determine the access of an agent to other scenes.

Let us consider the following example that will help us illustrate how normative rules are specified[3]:

$$(auction\_room, commit(?x : a, ?y : b, sell(?good, ?y, ?price, ?round))) \Rightarrow$$

$$obliged(?y, commit(?y : b, ?z : c, pay(?good, ?price, ?card), buyers\_settlements) \tag{1}$$

If an auctioneer commits to sell the good at auction at a given buyer, this is obliged to commit to a buyers' accountant in a *settlements* scene to pay for the good.

Summarising the deployment of normative rules is motivated by the need of an institution to infer agents' obligations as well as the consequences of agents' local actions (within scenes) that have effect out of the scope of a scene.

---

[3] a, b, c stand respectively for the auctioneer, buyer and accountant roles.

3.6   Electronic Institution

Finally, we can define an electronic institution choosing a performative structure and defining the rest of its components. These are the institutional roles, the hierarchy between roles, the policy of duties and the normative rules. The institutional roles define a set of roles that can not be played by the external agents. They are like the workers in a human institution. In the case of the hierarchy of roles and the ssd we can to take into account that both are applied to the set of roles of the institution which are all the roles appearing in the different scenes of the performative structure.

Definition 4. *An electronic institution is defined as a tuple*

$$\langle \mathcal{PS}, IR, \succeq, ssd, N_{PS} \rangle$$

where

- *PS stands for a performative structure;*
- *IR is a subset of roles representing the institutional roles;*
- $\succeq$ *stands for the hierarchy partial order over the roles;*
- *ssd is the set of static separation of duties between roles; and*
- N_{PS} *stands for a set of normative rules.*

Notice that the specification of an electronic institution must be regarded as a compositional activity to be undertaken by the institution designer. We can consider that specifications of dialogic frameworks, scenes and peformative structures are to be naturally organised into specification libraries.

Once completed a specification, it must go through a validation process that checks its well-formedness. Ultimately, if such a specification proves to be correct, its equivalent textual representation must be generated in order to be manipulated by the agents intending to participate in the institution. Moreover, the generated textual representations can be also employed for brokering purposes.

In the light of the complexity of the whole process, it is apparent the need of tools that assist the institution designer through the specification, validation, and translation of an electronic institution into a machine-readable format so that it can be easily parsed by agents.

4   Practical Specifications

The purpose of this section is to practically illustrate how to specify electronic institutions. For this purpose we concentrate on the modelling of the fish market an electronic auction house, whose complete graphical specification is shown in Figure 3.

If we look at the example in figure 3 we can see that there are five scenes apart from the root and the output scene. We can observe the different paths that agents can follow depending on their role. Each scene is created by an institutional agent: buyer admitter, seller admitter, auctioneer, buyer accountant

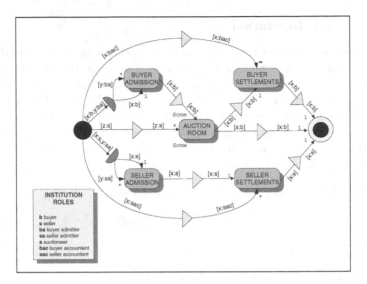

Fig. 3. Graphical Specification of the Fishmarket Performative Structure.

and seller accountant. This agents start one of the scenes and are in charge of it. They will dialogue with the external agents coming to the institutions.

We have two roles that external agents can play, the buyer and the seller roles. Both of them and also the institutional agents go for the root scene when entering the institutions. From the root scene we can see that buyers and sellers have different paths. On the one hand, buyers after entering in the root scene they can only go to the buyer admission scene. There they have to pass the admission process that is mediated by the buyer admitter who will ask the buyer for his login and password. If he is admitted, then he can go to the auction scene. As it can be some auction rooms at the same time, maybe each one auctioning a different kind of goods, he can choose a subset of them to go. For that reason the arc connecting the transition and the auction room is labelled of type *some*. When a buyer wants to leave the auction room it have two possibilities, to go to the output scene and leave the institution or to go to the buyer settlements. If he has won a round he must go to the buyer settlements to pay for the goods and the path going to the output scene is disabled for him. At the buyers settlements he has to pay for the goods corresponding to the round(s) that he has won and then he can leave the institution going to the output scene.

On the other hand, from the root scene sellers can only go to the seller admission scene. There they identify themselves with the sellers admitter and deliver their goods for being auctioned. From there they can go to the seller settlements scene where they receive the money for their goods after they have been auctioned at the auction scene. After receiving the money they can leave the institution moving from the seller settlements scene to the output scene.

5   Summary

In agree with [11], although organisational design is widely admitted as a fundamental issue in multi-agent systems, social concepts have been introduced in a rather informal way. Hence the need for formally incorporating organisational terms and concepts into multi-agent systems.

In this paper we have argued that agent societies can be effectively designed and constructed as electronic institutions. Then we have adopted a formal approach to specify electronic institutions. But why a formal technique? We believe that the following tip [1](page 215) answers the question:

> Use a formal technique when we cannot afford to have the requirements misunderstood.

An this is our case if we consider the high complexity of what we have identified as our main goal: the design and development of architecturally- neutral electronic institutions inhabited by heterogeneous (human and software) agents. In general, the presence of an underlying formal method underpins the use of structured design techniques and formal analysis, facilitating development, composition and reuse. Thus, we defend that successful methodologies must rely on unambiguous formal semantics, though developers are not aware of the existence of such a semantics as pointed out in [27].

Thus, we consider that the development of an electronic institution must be preceded by a precise specification that fully characterise the institution's rules. Some important advantages derive from the creation of specifications (models) of electronic institutions:

- An electronic institution model is a description of the modelled institution that can be used either as a specification or as a presentation. Such a model allows to investigate a new institution before being constructed. This possibility is particularly useful for institutions where design errors may jeopardise security or be expensive to correct.
- Graphical specifications are extremely easy to understand. They are similar to the informal diagrams employed by engineers and designers while designing, constructing and analysing a system.
- An electronic institution's specification offers an explicit description of both states and actions, in contrast to most description languages which describe either the states or the actions.
- The behaviour of an electronic institution model can be analysed, either by means of simulation or by means of more formal analysis methods.
- The process of creating the description and performing the analysis allows the modeller to gain a dramatically improved understanding of the modelled institution.

Acknowledgements. Marc Esteva enjoys the CIRIT doctoral scholarship 1999FI-00012. The research reported in this paper is supported by the ESPRIT LTR 25500-COMRIS *Co-Habited Mixed-Reality Information Spaces* project, the SLIE project IST-1999-10948 and the Spanish CICYT project SMASH, TIC96-1038-C04001.

References

1. *Software Requirements. Objects, Functions and States.* Prentice Hall International, Inc, 1993.
2. J. Barkley. Comparing simple role based access control models and access control lists. In *Proceedings of the Second ACM Workshop on Role-based Access Control,* 1997.
3. J. Barkley, A. V. Cincotta, D. F. Ferraiolo, S. Gavrilla, and D. R. Kuhn. Role based access control for the world wide web. In *20th National Information System Security Conference,* 1997.
4. M. Becht, T. Gurzki, J. Klarmann, and M. Muscholl. Rope: Role oriented programming environment for multiagent systems. In *Proceedings of the Fourth IFCIS Conference on Cooperative Information Systems (CoopIs'99),* 1999.
5. O. Belakhdar and J. Ayel. Modelling approach and tool for designing protocols for automated negotiation in multi-agent systems. In W. van de Velde and J. W. Perram, editors, *Agents Breaking Away,* number 1038 in Lecture Notes in Artificial Intelligence, pages 100–115. Springer-Verlag, 1996.
6. R. J. A. Buhr, M. Elammari, T. Gray, and S. Mankowski. A high level visual notation for understanding and designing collaborative, adaptive behaviour in multiagent system. In *Proceedings of the 31st Annual Hawaii International Conference on System Sciences (HICSS'98),* 1998.
7. P. R. Cohen and H. J. Levesque. Communicative actions for artificial agents. In *Proceedings of the First International Conference on Multi-Agent Systems (ICMAS-95),* pages 65–72, Menlo Park, CA., jun 1995. AAAI Press.
8. C. Dellarocas and M. Klein. Civil agent societies: Tools for inventing open agent-mediated electronic marketplaces. In *Proceedings ACM Conference on Electronic Commerce (EC-99),* 1999.
9. A. Diller. *Z An Introduction to Formal Methods.* John Wiley & Sons, Inc, 1990.
10. A. Etzioni. *Modern Organizations.* Englewood Cliffs, NJ, Prentice-Hall, 1964.
11. J. Ferber and O. Gutknecht. A meta-model for the analysis of organizations in multi-agent systems. In *Proceedings of the Third International Conference on Multi-Agent Systems (ICMAS-98),* pages 128–135, 1998.
12. D. F. Ferraiolo, J. F. Barkley, and D. R. Kuhn. A role based access control model and reference implementation within a corporate intranet. *ACM Transactions on Information Systems Security,* 1(2), 1999.
13. D. F. Ferraiolo, J. A. Cugini, and D. R. Kuhn. Role-based access control (rbac): Features and motivations. In *Annual Computer Security Applications Conference.* IEEE Computer Society Press, 1995.
14. S. I. Gavrila and J. F. Barkley. Formal specification for role based access control user/role and role/role relationship management. In *Proceedings of the Third ACM Workshop on Role-based Access Control,* 1998.
15. M. R. Genesereth and R. E. Fikes. Knowldege interchange format version 3.0 reference manual. Technical Report Report Logic–92–1, Logic Group, Computer Science Department, Standford University, June 1992.
16. I. Jacobson, M. Christerrson, P. Jonsson, and G. Overgaard. *Object-Oriented Software Engineering - A Use Case Driven Approach.* Addison-Wesley, 1996.
17. E. A. Kendall. Agent roles and role models: New abstractions for intelligent agent system analysis and design. In *Proceedings of Intelligent Agents for Information and Process Management (AIP'98),* 1998.

18. V. R. Lesser. Reflections on the nature of multi-agent coordination and its impli-
    cations for an agent architecture. *Autonomous Agents and Multi-Agent Systems*,
    1:89–111, 1998.
19. P. Noriega and C. Sierra. Towards layered dialogical agents. In *Third International
    Workshop on Agent Theories, Architectures, and Languages, ATAL-96*, 1996.
20. D. North. *Institutions, Institutional Change and Economics Perfomance*. Cam-
    bridge U. P., 1990.
21. D. Riehle and T. Gross. Role model based framework design and integration.
    In *Proceedings of the 1998 Conference on Object-Oriented Programming Systems,
    Languages, and Applications (OOPSLA'98)*, pages 117–133. ACM Press, 1998.
22. J. A. Rodríguez-Aguilar, F. J. Martín, P. Noriega, P. Garcia, and C. Sierra. To-
    wards a formal specification of complex social structures in multi-agent systems. In
    J. A. Padget, editor, *Collaboration between Human and Artificial Societies*, volume
    1624 of *Lecture Notes in Artificial Intelligence*, pages 284–300. Springer-Verlag,
    2000.
23. R. Sandhu, E. J. Coyne, H. L. Feinstein, and C. E. Youman. Role based access
    control models. *IEEE Computer*, 29(2), 1996.
24. W. R. Scott. *Organizations: Rational, Natural, and Open Systems*. Englewood
    Cliffs, NJ, Prentice Hall, 1992.
25. J. R. Searle. *Speech acts*. Cambridge U.P., 1969.
26. C. Sierra and P. Noriega. Institucions electròniques. In *Proceedings of the Primer
    Congrès Català d'Intel.ligència Artificial*, 1998.
27. M. Wooldridge and N. R. Jennings. Intelligent agents: Theory and practice. *The
    Knowledge Engineering Review*, 10(2):115–152, 1995.
28. M. Wooldridge, N. R. Jennings, and D. Kinny. A methodology for agent-oriented
    analysis and design. In *Proceedings of the Third International Conference on Au-
    tonomous Agents (AGENTS'99)*, May 1999.

Towards a Flexible Trading Process
over the Internet

Michael Vetter[1] and Stefan Pitsch[2]

[1] Institut für Arbeitswissenschaft und Technologiemanagement der Universität Stuttgart,
Nobelstrasse 12, 70569 Stuttgart, Germany
Michael.Vetter@iao.fhg.de
[2] Fraunhofer-Institut für Arbeitswirtschaft und Organisation,
Nobelstrasse 12, 70569 Stuttgart, Germany
Stefan.Pitsch@iao.fhg.de

Abstract. *The CASBA [1] project is developing an electronic marketplace to improve the quality of existing electronic commerce services, by introducing a higher flexibility and automating trading processes. This is achieved through the use of intelligent agent technology, enabling the market framework to offer timesaving automation of auctions and flexibility through negotiations among the agents. The main objective is to expand the range of business models and transaction scenarios which may be handled online beyond those which are commonplace today and thus enabling a more flexible trading process on the whole. All six stages of the Consumer Buying Behaviour model (CBB) including merchant brokering and payment are addressed.*

1 Introduction

With today's wide availability of adequate security mechanisms there is a growing number of electronic commerce applications on the Internet. Most of these applications are **shops with electronic product catalogues** or **electronic malls** which allow online orders and secure electronic payment transactions. However, these applications have several shortcomings. One of these shortcomings is the lack of flexibility of the trading process.

The main objective of the CASBA system is to expand the range of business models and transactions beyond those that are commonly found on the Internet today. Instead of only supporting transactions that are limited to fixed price, single seller/buyer relationships or simple non-automated auctions, the CASBA system will offer automated negotiations with a wide range of transaction types including brokerage and a variety of agent driven automated auction types [5].

In the following chapters we will first describe our view on the flexible trading process, then how CASBA supports the different CBB stages and the architecture of the system including database access, commerce model and the trading models them selves. A short view on the developed prototype and the currently developed pilot applications concludes the work.

F. Dignum and C. Sierra (Eds.): Agent Mediated Elec. Commerce, LNAI 1991, pp. 148-162, 2001.
© Springer-Verlag Berlin Heidelberg 2001

2 A Flexible Trading Process

In the online markets of today it is not possible to dynamically price a good according to the actual demand or to customise offers to a certain customer (apart from the simple price negotiation in live auctions that are recently spreading on the Internet). The details of the deal cannot be negotiated by the customer and the vendor and the comparison with competitors is usually not supported by these systems.

One goal of our work is to improve the quality of existing electronic commerce services by providing a flexible electronic market place. More complex ways of buying and selling goods like automated auctions and parallel negotiations are supported. Intelligent agent technology is used to automate the time consuming process of looking for business partners and negotiating the details of a deal. The agents can execute routine tasks more efficiently. These autonomous agents differ from common retrieval and filtering agents (shopping bots) in their ability to negotiate with other agents. This will improve online business performance by better addressing the customers needs and by fast adaptation of prices to the market situation. However, we believe that this will not lead to price-wars as sketched in [12], since the CASBA agents have a memory of offers and the price is not the only attribute that is being negotiated.

In addition, most of the current commerce agent systems only support the product and/or merchant brokering stages of the six stages of the Consumer Buying Behaviour (CBB) model [4] that is used to explain the different stages in a deal. Few are going into the negotiation part. But a flexible marketplace tool has to take as many stages into account as it can to be successful. The CASBA system addresses all 6 stages of the CBB model (more or less thoroughly) including the need identification, payment/delivery and service evaluation stages for a better handling of the users needs in e-commerce.

3 Complete CBB Support

The goal of CASBA is to support all stages of the CBB model (at least to some extend for each stage), with the main parts being the stages 3 and 4, while also including parts of the stages 1, 2, 5 and 6.

The **need identification** stage is supported with notification and advertisement features, keeping the consumer up to date with new products and goods available on the market and in current or future auctions, corresponding with the consumers interest profile.

Product brokering is achieved by matching user-set attribute priorities with available products. Related and alternative products can be offered by the sell agents, according to the users preferences.

The **merchant brokering** stage, as one of the main functions of the system, is using the central database in which all agents are registered. Each buy order request is matched with sell agents claiming to supply the desired product. The buyer can then pre-select the sellers he wants to negotiate with, using user-set filtering rules. The buy agent also selects auctions to bid on, if they offer the desired product.

In the **negotiation** stage the agents negotiate with each other, using pre-defined strategies selected by the individual user. The agents can also use strategies when bidding in auctions, depending on the auction type. Auctions in CASBA can be used for fast and efficient prize allocation in certain market types.

The **payment and delivery** stage is supported by using online payment systems. Actual online delivery of the good is possible if the product is in electronic form. Physical goods are shipped the traditional way by the sellers themselves.

Finally, the **service and evaluation** stage is addressed by adding a feedback functionality through which the users can give feedback to the market (evaluating the quality of a deal, including partner reliability and related matters) and the seller directly (providing feedback about the quality of the good and the service). This feedback is voluntarily but in the user's interest in order to be better protected from fraud.

From stage 6 there is a feedback loop towards stage 1 since the seller is able to inform the buyer about new products and goods once a contact between them is established.

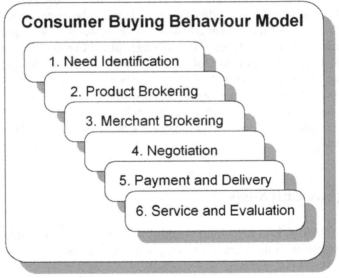

Fig.1: Consumer Buying Behaviour Model

4 CASBA Architecture

CASBA has a distributed open architecture, utilising technology like CORBA, Java and JavaScript. Interfaces to e-commerce components such as payment servers allow the CASBA server to be integrated into existing e-commerce solutions. The email server is used to inform subscribed users about new products or auctions on the market. Furthermore notifications about important actions of the agents can be send via email if the user is not using the CASBA client often.

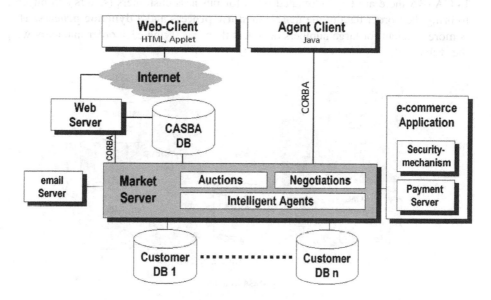

Fig.2: CASBA Architecture

The users of the system have two ways of accessing the CASBA server itself. The first way is via a web-client, using Java-applets and HTML/JavaScript-Interfaces. In contrast to this somewhat limited web-client (where the private user cannot customise everything, since the real agent code is running on the server) there is the agent-client that can be programmed by the professional user himself, using the CORBA methods provided by the CASBA server. This allows companies to compete on the market using their own negotiation strategies and to connect their agents to their ERP system. Furthermore 3rd party service providers could offer advanced agent functionality with access to the market to other users. CORBA was chosen to enable client implementations in different programming languages.

The formerly pursued idea of having the web-client access the server via a CORBA interface has been revoked. Sending CORBA messages through a firewall that most companies use today would require a tunneling process via a CORBA gatekeeper. From a users standpoint it is not acceptable to be forced to install such a gatekeeper (that even would cost extra money). Instead the web-client now uses a Java-Script or Java interface that communicates via the usual HTTP connection, using technologies like servlets, CGI, etc. on the web server.

We evaluated the Grasshopper agent framework which was one of the few commercial tools but decided not to use it because mobile agents still have unsolved security problems. Furthermore we did not want to impose a special tool for the implementation of the agent client.

4.1 Database Access

In CASBA there are two automated ways for business customers (sellers and buyers) to bring their order data to the market, a **static process** and a **dynamic process**. This is more efficient for large numbers of orders than specifying each order manually with the web client.

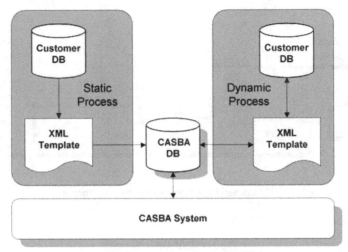

Fig.3: DB connection in CASBA

In the **static process** the customer exports the relevant data from his database using an XML-template converting the data into the XML structured ontology used on the CASBA market. The data is then stored in the CASBA database. The benefit of this method is that the customers do not need to have an online database available all the time. The trade-off however is that the product data is not up-to-date all the time.

In the **dynamic process** the customer has an online database available 24 hours a day. The CASBA agent connects via a special database agent with the external database of the customer using the XML-template to match the structured ontology of the CASBA market to the customers own structure in his database. This enables up-to-date information like product availability, instant product updates and a better tie-in with the whole logistics process. However the product categories and agents of this customer still need to be registered in the CASBA database to enable the matching by the administrator agent.

4.2 CASBA Commerce Model

To fulfil a deal in the CASBA commerce model we need two separate agreement notifications, one from the buyer and one from the seller.

In **negotiations** agents notify each other if they agree to the last offer made by the other agent. Both agents then proceed to submit their agreement information to the AdministratorAgent, who checks the agreement information. If they match the deal is given to the payment server for completion. The payment server then sends the payment result back to the AdministratorAgent (paid or non-paid) and the Administrator-Agent sends the information of the completed (or not completed) deal to the participating agents. There is only one AdministratorAgent per market server but it is multi-threaded and therefore can handle many requests in parallel.

In case of **auctions** one of the agreements is automatically given by the agent that places the auction order on the market. The second agreement is automatically given in each bid a participant in an auction makes. This way we don't need to get the separate agreements after the auction is over and the bids are legally binding as is the initial auction offer.

If the user instructed the agent to not act fully autonomously (i.e. the users confirmation is needed to really make a deal) the agent can only submit a **pending agreement**, this can be either accept by the other agent or not. The pending time is subject to negotiation, but will most likely be the lowest accepted time among the two agents.

The negotiated payment method may involve late payments (not instantaneously, i.e. credit card charge occurs when the product is actually shipped off by the seller). This is also handled by the payment server. The administrator is only notified that the payment agreement has been confirmed via the payment server.

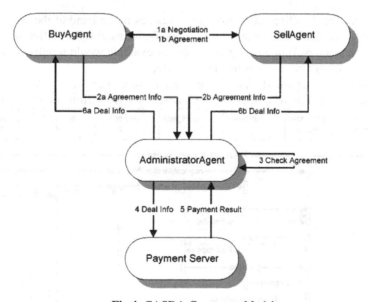

Fig.4: CASBA Commerce Model

4.3 Auctions within CASBA

The CASBA system support four types of auctions, which are the most commonly used auction types on today's markets [2]. Additional auction types can be implemented on the server side by extending the framework using inheritance.

In the **English auction**, the auctioneer begins with the low starting price and proceeds to solicit successively higher bids from the buyers until no one increases the bid any more. The item is sold to the highest bidder at the price of the last bid.

In the **Dutch auction**, bidding starts at an extremely high price and is progressively lowered until a buyer claims an item by calling the price. When multiple units are auctioned, normally more takers are present. The first winner takes his prize and pays his price and later winners pay less. When the goods are exhausted, the bidding is over.

In the **first-price sealed bid auction** (one unit up for sale) each bidder submits one bid in ignorance of all other submitted bids. The highest bidder wins and pays the amount he bid. In the *discriminatory* subtype multiple units of the good are available. The bids are sorted from high to low and the units are sold to the bidders (starting with the highest) until the supply is exhausted. Each bidder has to pay the amount he bid, resulting in different prices for the winners.

Like the first-price sealed bid auction, the **Vickrey auction** (also knows **as uniform second-price**) is working with sealed bids. The difference is that in the Vickrey auction the bidder who made the highest bid gets the good at the price of the highest non-winning bid. If multiple units are being auctioned, all winners pay the price of the highest non-winning bid.

The choice for the different auction styles resides in the hand of the seller. He can chose the type of auction depending on the good he wants to sell as different goods ask for different methods. Unique and rare goods for example would usually be sold in an English auction but almost never in a Dutch style.

The following diagram shows a sample interaction chart for the Vickrey-auction type as implemented in the CASBA system, describing the information flow [6].

Fig.5: CASBA Interaction Chart; Vickrey

4.4 Negotiations within CASBA

Negotiation as the traditional way of allocation can be a tedious and long lasting process if the participating parties are human, since human negotiators tend to include non-subject related preferences in their negotiation processes, like pride, ego and culture [3]. However, agents following rule based strategies can be used to maximise the users gain from a negotiation without incorporating such tendencies.

CASBA supports full parallel negotiations, where all the negotiable details are evaluated at once rather then being negotiated sequentially, which would be time-consuming and, most importantly, impractical due to the relations between the attributes. It is possible in sequential negotiations that a potential deal is not reached because some attributes are already fixed to the wrong values and cannot be changed any more when negotiating about other attributes.

Negotiable attributes can be classified into two sets. General attributes such as price, payment date, delivery date, quantity, etc. are applicable to almost all sorts of goods because they refer to the contract conditions. Specific attributes in contrast describe the properties of the product itself. They can be used to enable product brokering or to negotiate about variants of a good.

The negotiations follow rule-based strategies, which can be adapted by the user and will evolve through learning methods. The strategies are usually computed on the server but can also be implemented in special agent clients. The use of rules allows a simpler coordination of 1:n or m:n negotiation scenarios than a strictly procedural approach. Combined with calculation functions the rules determine when to accept or reject an offer from an other agent and when to create a new counter offer. One example rule is waiting for a certain number of competing offers from other agents (unless a timeout is reached) before it creates a new offer. Learning will adapt the parameters and weights that are used in the strategy functions to changing market situations and to better cope with other agents behaviour.

The basis for a strategy is the utility function that evaluates each offer and counter offer. Based on the user's order input the utilities for each attribute value are calculated separately and combined with a weighted arithmetic mean function. For the use in a domain where only certain combinations of attribute values are useful special utility functions need to be defined. In addition special attribute types that do not have monotonous utility functions (e.g. strings) also require the implementation of new classes. The framework is designed to be easily extensible cope with these problems.

Special rules determine the conditions for these ongoing negotiations, taking into account risk factors, domain knowledge, dependencies between attributes as well as positive (agreement) and negative (termination of negotiation) end conditions. Someone who is willing to take a high risk of not getting a desired product for the specified conditions can use a tougher negotiation strategy to get a better deal.

Each agent has exactly one order to fulfil (either to sell or buy) but can be involved in negotiations with many other agents at the same time. However, it can only give its (pending or final) agreement to exactly one offer regarding the object of its order. Special cases erupt when an agent is making various deals to fulfil one order, i.e. in order to buy 50 pieces of a good it has to buy them in smaller chunks if no seller is able to deliver the asked amount. Here a co-ordination routine prevents the agent from overbuying his amount.

The agent can be either thoroughly instructed on how to complete its order in regard to the used trade technique (auction or negotiation, what type of auction, etc.) and strategy or the user can leave that decision to the agent itself, which will then use the default values and react to the current market situation using the best strategy applicable.

The following diagram shows the interaction chart for a negotiation cycle as implemented in the CASBA system, describing the information flow. The method names are inspired by the FIPA agent communication language but do not conform strictly to their specification. This scenario is buyer centric where a single buyer has the choice between several sellers. The number of negotiation steps (propose) is usually much larger than shown here.

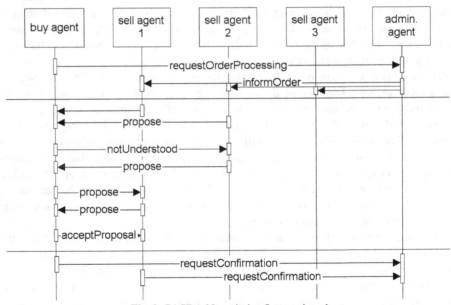

Fig.6: CASBA Negotiation Interaction chart

4.4.1 A Sample Strategy

The negotiation strategies in CASBA are similar to the ones described in [13]. We also use a combination of several tactics that take available resources and time into account. However we do not apply the tactic functions on each attribute but on the utility of the complete offer. This way an agreement is more likely when imitating tactics are used. The difficulty with this approach is to calculate an optimal set of attribute values that has the desired utility. The details of the strategy will most likely be non-public to avoid exploitation by other parties and negotiation partners. Third party developers can implement their own strategies and compete with the standard CASBA agents.

To illustrate the use of a negotiation strategy in CASBA we present the following simple imitating strategy which imitates the opponents behaviour in a 1:1 scenario. Note that this is just an example and is in no form intended to be comprehensive. More sophisticated strategies would include relations between attributes and their respective values among other things.

Each good has a number of negotiable attributes (AT_1 to AT_n) that have assigned a priority number in form of percentages of their contribution to the total utility function output value (UFOV). To clarify which attribute value belongs to whose offer, we use the indices A (our agent's offer) and B (counter offer). So the value of AT_{A1} is the first attribute in our agent's offer.

The new offer is calculated on the basis of the last two counteroffers our agent received, while incorporating a risk value factor (RVF) for different strategic approaches (high, medium and low risk). Since this strategy really starts developing at t=2 we need a starting constant (StartConst) for the initial negotiation step.

```
// for t=0 the initial order values are used
// Offer is our agent's offer
// COffer is the received counter offer
t=1
FOR n=1 to NrNegoAttrib
{
    ATAn(t) = ATAn(t-1) + StartConst * RVF
}
REPEAT
{
    t=t+1
    FOR n=1 to NrNegoAttrib
    {
        ATAn(t) = ATAn(t-1) + (ATBn(t-2) - ATBn(t-1)) * RVF
    }
}
UNTIL ( (UFOV(COffer(t)) > UpperThreshld)
    or ((UFOV(Offer(t)) - UFOV(COffer(t)))    DiffThreshld)
    or (UFOV(COffer(t))    UFOV(Offer(t)))
    or (t == MaxSteps) )
```

There are three positive (agreeing) end conditions in this strategy upon which an agreement is reached. UpperThreshld sets an upper UFOV limit, DiffThreshld defines an UFOV window and if the counteroffer's UFOV is higher then the last own UFOV the third condition is met. The single negative (termination) end condition is triggered when a predefined number of negotiation steps has been reached without an agreement.

5 CASBA Prototype and Pilots

A prototype has been developed by the CASBA consortium to evaluate the chosen technology and as a means to obtain feedback from possible users. The prototype consists of a server application and three Applets. These components were written in Java, using CORBA for the client-server communication, and an expert system shell for implementing the rules of a negotiation strategy.

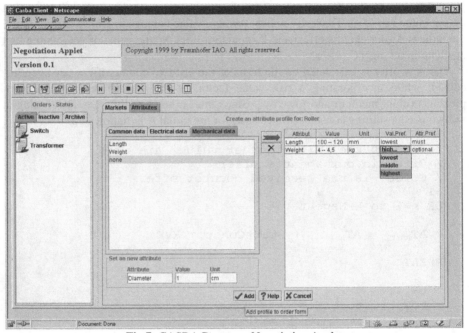

Fig.7: CASBA Prototype Negotiation Applet

The prototype consists of the following three applets that can access the agent server:

- The auction applet was specially designed to handle (last minute) airline tickets, a good that has a clear ontology and therefore is well suited for automated auctions.
- The negotiation applet (fig. 7) in contrast can be used with any kind of good. It is used to demonstrate the specification of orders for negotiations between agents, using complex ontologies that need to be defined for each marketplace (e.g. electronic parts). New ontologies for different goods are dynamically loaded from the server.
- The administration applet can display the administrative issues on a CASBA market server, like information about registered users, available markets, running agents and completed deals.

The experiences made with the prototype helped designing the pilot applications that are currently under development by the consortium partners and showcase a variety of possibilities of the CASBA system. The first pilot (see fig. 8) is focussing on negotiating deals on online advertising space for an Internet provider in Greece, the second is an extension to the airline ticket prototype used in Germany and the third will be a full grown online auction house with sequential English auctions added to an Internet market system in England.

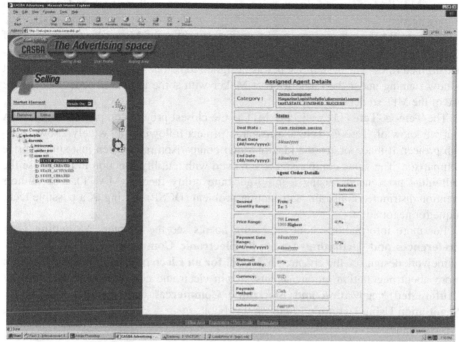

Fig.8: CASBA "The Advertising space" pilot application

6   Related Work

There are several research projects addressing the problems of online electronic commerce, often using agent technology as well. The following paragraphs describe the projects that are closely related to CASBA. However most of them only negotiate about price.

The **Michigan Internet AuctionBot** [7] is a project at the University of Michigan, Artificial Intelligence Laboratory. It sees itself as an information service, that collects the bids, determines the resulting price (using the auction-specific rules) and notifies the participating parties about the outcome. It does not support transactions of any kind or the exchange of the goods. However, the AuctionBot has an API that can be accessed from interested parties to 'include' AuctionBot into their own market solutions.

The **Fishmarket** [8] project is another approach at recreating real-life auctions on the internet via agents. Originally using the Dutch auction method, the Fishmarket now supports various kinds like English, Vickrey and others. Currently the system is used for evaluating competing strategies in a form of contest.

The **MAGMA** [9] (now with a slightly different focus known as MAGNET) project at the University of Minnesota uses agents that can negotiate among themselves. The system consists of trader agents, communicating with each other via a relay server. MAGMA supports direct price negotiation as well as brokered negotiation among agents.

The **KASBAH** project of the AmEC Initiative [10] at the Massachusetts Institute of Technology introduced agents that were negotiating about price following three time-constrained rules. The system itself was designed to be one huge double auction and it is now running under the name Market Maker with some improved functions for the use of the MIT students.

The **Tete-@-Tete** [11] project at MIT is the closest project comparable to CASBA that we know of. Tete-@-Tete is a research project following the widely known Kasbah project. It incorporates the idea of value comparison rather then just simple prize comparison. The value comparison is achieved with a utility function to maximise the individual users needs, using a multi-attribute utility theory (MAUT). The authors mention distributed constraint satisfaction problem (DCSP) solving as a possible technique for negotiation.

For more information about mediating agents see the chapter "**Modelling User Preferences and Mediating Agents in Electronic Commerce**", for an alternative framework design see the chapter "**A Model for an Electronic MarketPlace**" and for more about negotiation among agents and in electronic commerce see the chapters "**Automated Negotiation and Electronic Commerce**" and "**Formal Models for Negotiation Using Dynamic Logic**" in this book.

7 Conclusion

The CASBA market system incorporates the benefits of multiple intelligent agents in an electronic marketplace. The agents automate routine tasks and allow flexible market mechanisms such as auctions and integrative negotiations following evolving strategies. By spanning all stages of the CBB model this automated marketplace offers a comprehensive and flexible way of trading over the internet.

During the project it became obvious that a lot of work still needs to be done on a product specifications standard. While the tools to develop and implement such a standard are available today, no single standard has yet emerged.

Further development work will enable more sophisticated negotiation strategies using probabilities and AI learning technology to improve the agents performance. Simulation results will be used to find the best choices for the many parameters and weights of the strategy functions. We are also investigating how the strategy of the negotiation partner could be recognized and how this knowledge could be used.

Acknowledgements

This work is funded by the ESPRIT Project 27064 CASBA (Competitive Agents for Secure Business Applications) [1]. We would like to thank our project partners from Exodus, Tradezone, Pixelpark, HexMac and Compulink for their co-operation.

References

It is not possible to ensure that the World Wide Web URLs listed below will be still available after this paper is published. The date in brackets indicates the date when the URL was accessed the last time.

1. The CASBA project, homepage, http://www.casba-market.org/ (11/23/2000)
2. Agorics, Inc.; Going, Going, Gone! A Survey of Auction types, http://www.webcom.com/~agorics/new.html (11/23/2000)
3. Beam, C.; Segev, A.; Shanthikumar, J.G.; Electronic Negotiation through Internet-based Auctions, CITM Working Paper 96-WP-1019, December 1996, http://haas.berkeley.edu/~citm/WP-1019.PDF (11/23/2000)
4. Guttman, R. H.; Moukas, A. G.; Maes, P.: Agent-mediated Electronic Commerce: A Survey, Knowledge Engineering Review, Cambridge University Press, June 1998, http://ecommerce.media.mit.edu/papers/ker98.pdf (11/23/2000)
5. Vetter, M.; Pitsch, S.; Using autonomous agents to expand business models in electronic commerce, in: Roger, Y.; Stanford-Smith, B.; Kidd, P. T.; Business and Work in The Information Society, EMMSEC'99, IOS Press, Amsterdam, 1999
6. Vetter, M.; Pitsch, S.; An Agent-based Market Supporting Multiple Auction Protocols, Agents 99, WS 4: Agent-Based Decision-Support for Managing the Internet-Enabled Supply-Chain, http://www.research.ibm.com/CoopDS/Agents99/vetter.pdf (11/23/2000)
7. Wurman, P. R.; Wellman, M. P.; Walsh, W. E.: The Michigan Internet AuctionBot: A Configurable Auction Server for Human and Software Agents, Proceedings of the 2nd International Conference on Autonomous Agents (Agents'98), Minneapolis, May 1998, ftp://ftp.eecs.umich.edu/people/wellman/agents98wurman.ps.Z (11/23/2000)
8. Rodríguez-Aguilar, J. A.; Martín, F. J.; Noriega, P.; Garcia, P.; Sierra, C.: Towards a Testbed for Trading Agents in Electronic Auction Markets, AI Communications, ISSN 0921-7126, IOS Press, 1998, http://wwwiiia.csic.es/Projects/fishmarket/aicom.ps.gz (11/23/2000)
9. Collins, J.; Youngdahl, B.; Jamison, S.; Mobasher, B.; Gini, M.: A Market Architecture for Multi-Agent Contracting, Proceedings of the 2nd International Conference on Autonomous Agents (Agents'98), Minneapolis, May 1998, pp. 285-292, http://www.cs.umn.edu/Research/airvl/magnet/papers/agents98.pdf (11/23/2000)
10. Chavez, A.; Maes, P. : Kasbah: An Agent Marketplace for Buying and Selling Goods, Proceedings of the First International Conference on the Practical Application of Intelligent Agents and Multi-Agent Technology (PAAM'96), London, UK, April 1996, http://lcs.www.media.mit.edu/groups/agents/Publications/kasbah-paam96.ps (11/23/2000)

11. R. Guttman and P. Maes. "Agent-mediated Integrative Negotiation for Retail Electronic Commerce." Proceedings of the Workshop on Agent Mediated Electronic Trading (AMET'98). Minneapolis, Minnesota, May 1998.
   http://ecommerce.media.mit.edu/papers/amet98.pdf (11/23/2000)
12. Kephart, J.O.; Hanson, J.E.; Sairamesh, J.: Price-War Dynamics in a Free-Market Economy of Software Agents, Artificial Life journal, volume 4 issue 1, MIT Press, 1998
   http://www.ibm.com/iac/reports-technical/pricewar-dyn/index.html (11/23/2000)
13. C. Sierra, P. Faratin, and N. R. Jennings. A service-oriented negotiation model between autonomous agents. In M. Boman and W. Van de Velde, editors, Multi-Agent Rationality: Proceedings of the 8th European Workshop on Modelling Autonomous Agents in Multi-Agent World, MAAMAW'97, number 1237 in Lecture Notes in Articial Intelligence, pages 17-35. Springer-Verlag, 1997.

Modeling User Preferences and Mediating Agents in Electronic Commerce

Mehdi Dastani[1], Nico Jacobs[2], Catholijn M. Jonker[1], and Jan Treur[2]

[1]Department of Artificial Intelligence, Vrije Universiteit Amsterdam,
De Boelelaan 1081a, 1081 HV Amsterdam, The Netherlands
{mehdi,jonker,treur}@cs.vu.nl
http://www.cs.vu.nl/~{mehdi,jonker,treur}

[+] Dept. of Computer Science, Katholieke Universiteit Leuven,
Celestijnenlaan 200A, B-3001 Heverlee, Belgium
Nico.Jacobs@cs.kuleuven.ac.be
http://www.cs.kuleuven.ac.be/~nico

Abstract. *An important ingredient in agent-mediated Electronic Commerce is the presence of intelligent mediating agents that assist Electronic Commerce participants (e.g., individual users, other agents, organisations). These mediating agents are in principle autonomous agents that will interact with their environments (e.g. other agents and web-servers) on behalf of participants who have delegated tasks to them. For mediating agents a (preference) model of participants is indispensable. In this paper, a generic mediating agent architecture is introduced. Furthermore, we discuss our view of user preference modeling and its need in agent-mediated electronic commerce. We survey the state of the art in the field of preference modeling and suggest that the preferences of electronic commerce participants can be modelled by learning from their behaviour. In particular, we employ an existing machine learning method called inductive logic programming (ILP). We argue that this method can be used by mediating agents to detect regularities in the behaviour of the involved participants and induce hypotheses about their preferences automatically. Finally, we discuss some advantages and disadvantages of using inductive logic programming as a method for learning user preferences and compare this method with other approaches.*

1 Introduction

The explosive growth of electronic markets and retail Electronic Commerce has resulted in an overload of online information and products. The effectivity and success of this market depends on the amount of automated Electronic Commerce processes and services that are available online. Finding, comparing, buying, selling and customising items via the World Wide Web, automatic negotiation and personalised recommendation services are examples of such processes and services. Some of these processes and services are already available on the World Wide Web though in limited forms. For example, search engines like Altavista and Yahoo help people to locate items on the web and online shop sites such as Jango [44], Amazon [39] and Moviefinder [46] offer personal recommendation services to advise their customers about products that may be interesting to them. Also, online auction sites such as eBay

F. Dignum and C. Sierra (Eds.): Agent Mediated Elec. Commerce, LNAI 1991, pp. 163-193, 2001.
© Springer-Verlag Berlin Heidelberg 2001

[42] and AuctionBot [40] provide automatic bid proposal services such that a customer needs not to be online during a chosen auction. Finally, in the forthcoming marketplaces such as MarketMaker [45] users can create agents and delegate various tasks such as buying, selling, and searching items to them. These agents are able to negotiate with each other in order to perform delegated tasks. These services help customers to avoid the large search space of available items or the need to be involved in all required activities.

In general, to support users on the World Wide Web, various types of agents can be developed. For example, to support brokering processes in electronic commerce, agents can be developed that support a user offering products (or services) at the World Wide Web. Also, agents can be developed that support a user searching for information or products within the scope of user's interest. Of course, agents can be developed to combine both functionalities as well. Moreover, mediating agents can be developed that communicate with both agents, i.e. with agents that provide information or products and with agents that ask for information or products. Recently a few applications of mediating agents have been addressed for this area; for example, see [9], [10], [22], [27], [33], [35]. In general, applications like these are implemented in an ad hoc fashion without an explicit design at a conceptual level.

The aim of this paper is twofold. On the one hand, a generic agent architecture for mediating agents acting in brokering processes is introduced which has been designed in a principled manner, using the compositional development method for multi-agent systems DESIRE. The agent architecture can be instantiated by adding specific types of knowledge to support functionalities and behaviour required. Depending on the choice of these requirements, an agent is created for a specific application by including the appropriate types of knowledge. For example, a search agent with functionality restricted to (incidental) search for information upon a user's request can be built by adding only knowledge needed for this task. Such an agent, for example, is not able to store and maintain the user's query or information that has been found, nor is it able to provide information to other agents. If these functionalities are required as well, the necessary types of knowledge have to be added. On the other hand, we present an overview of some existing approaches in preference *modeling* and briefly discuss them. It is discussed that each approach is appropriate for certain classes of applications. Finally, we explore in more detail the use of Inductive Logic Programming (ILP) as a possible method for automatic preference *modeling*. We explain how this method can be employed in order to induce preference models. The (dis)advantages of this method are discussed and some experimental results are presented.

In Section 2 an example problem domain for brokering processes is sketched. Section 3 introduces the design of the generic architecture for mediating agents. The different types of knowledge are presented in Section 4. In Section 5 the behaviour of the system is analysed by giving an overview of which types of knowledge are needed for which types of basic functionalities. In Section 6 an overview is given of recent literature on preference *modeling*, showing the need for an automatic approach to user preference *modeling*. Finally, Section 7 shows that Inductive Logic Programming is a possible technique for constructing preference models and may be useful as an algorithm for the production of a classification tree that can be used to match products against preferences.

2 Electronic Commerce and Brokering

The process of brokering as often occurs in Electronic Commerce involves a number of agents. A provider agent that provides information about products to other (human or computer) agents may support a user offering products. A user looking for products may be supported by a personal assistant agent that takes its user's queries and contacts other agents or looks at the Web directly to find information on products within the user's scope of interest. Such a personal assistant agent may contact either provider agents immediately, or mediating agents, which in turn have contact with provider agents, or other mediating agents. Depending on the application, the chain of agents involved may include zero or more mediating agents.

The domain analysed for the agent architecture presented here is the domain of brokering (scientific) papers. Although this domain might not be considered as a real electronic commerce application (for instance because electronic commerce applications usually involve money as an important attribute of domain items), we have chosen it because of the easy access to data needed to do experiments. Moreover, we believe that our approach is general and thus can be applied to any domain consisting of any set of attributes. In particular, we will show that both proposed learning method and the agent architecture are flexible enough to be applied to real electronic commerce applications.

The domain of scientific papers has a number of aspects in common with other domains within the area of electronic commerce. The task of a provider agent is to inform other researchers on papers available on Internet (a marketing aspect). For example, an agent related to a Web site of a research group announces new papers included in their Web site. If a researcher is looking for a paper with certain characteristics (scope), a personal assistant agent can ask other agents for information on papers with these characteristics. To be able to tune the information provided to users, a number of scopes of interest can be maintained for each of the users. For example, one of the users may be interested in papers on certain topics, such as work flow management systems, but also in papers on agents and the World Wide Web.

Topics can be basic (e.g., 'work flow management systems', or 'agents', or 'World Wide Web'), or a combination of a number of topics (e.g., 'agents and World Wide Web'). In the latter case the user interest is limited to papers which address both topics. Moreover, if it is added that the user is only interested in papers from the years 1995 to 1997, then either year in the range 1995-1997 is meant. Topics can be matched with, for instance, the set of keywords of a paper, or with the abstract, or the paper as a whole. In some disciplines, such as Medicine, an ontology of topics has been developed that serves more or less as a standard. Besides topics also other attributes of papers can be used to define a scope of interest, for example an author, a year, a research group, et cetera. These attributes can also be used in combination with each other. For this example, a shared ontology of topics is assumed. All agents in the brokering process express their information and interests using this shared ontology. It is assumed that the following attributes of a paper are available and can be used: title, authors, affiliation(s) of the authors, location on the World Wide Web where it can be found, topics covered by the paper, abstract, year, and reference. This information can be used to identify papers that are of interest to a user, but also forms the source for the information that can be provided to a user when a paper is proposed to him or her.

3 Design of the Generic Mediating Agent

The generic mediating agent presented in this paper offers a reusable agent that can be applied (reused) in the context of a multi-agent system which can take different forms. One simple possibility is that the mediating agent serves as a personal assistant representing a buyer and communicates with this user and with other software agents that represent sellers. The generic mediating agent supports the user profiling involved, but also maintenance of information on sellers. More complex possibilities can involve, in addition, communication between buyer personal assistant agents, for example, to combine requests and form coalitions. The generic mediating agent does not exclude this possibility, but no explicit structures have been added yet to support this. Another possibility is to use the generic mediating agent as the basis for a broker agent which communicates both with buyer representative agents and seller representative agents.

For the design of the generic mediating agent the following main aspects are considered: process composition, knowledge composition, and relations between knowledge and process composition, as discussed in [6]. A compositional generic agent model (introduced in [8]), supporting the weak agency notion (cf. [37]) is used. At the highest abstraction level within an agent, a number of processes can be distinguished that support interaction with the other agents. First, a process that manages communication with other agents, modelled by the component agent interaction management in *Figure* 1. This component analyses incoming information and determines which other processes within the agent need the communicated information. Moreover, outgoing communication is prepared. Next, the agent needs to maintain information (including indications of specific interests and preference models built over time) on the other agents with whom it co-operates: maintenance of agent information. The component maintenance of world information is included to store world information (e.g., information on attributes of products). The process own process control defines different characteristics of the agent and determines foci for behaviour. The component world interaction management is included to model interaction with the world (with the World Wide Web world, in the example application domain): initiating observations and receiving observation results.

The agent processes discussed above are generic agent processes. Many agents perform these processes. In addition, often agent-specific processes are needed: to perform tasks specific to one agent, for example directly related to a specific domain of application. In the current example the agent has to determine proposals for other agents. In this process information on available products (communicated by information providing agents and kept in the component maintenance of world information), and about the interests of agents and their preference models (kept in the component maintenance of agent information), is combined to determine which agents might be interested in which products. For the mediating agent this agent-specific task is called determine proposals. *Figure* 1 depicts how the mediating agent is composed of its components.

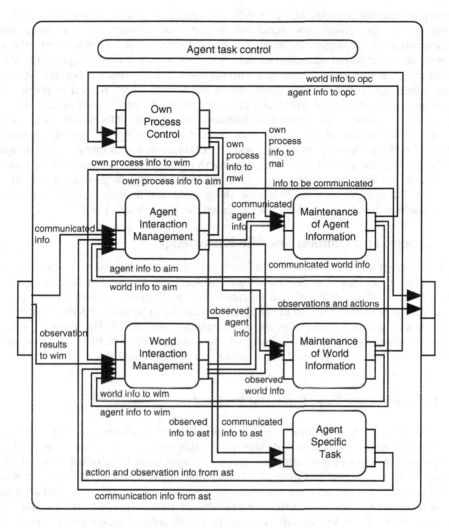

Fig. 1. Composition at the highest level within the mediating agent

Part of the exchange of information within the generic agent model can be described as follows. The mediating agent needs input about interests, put forward by agents, and information about attributes and evaluations of available products that are communicated by information providing agents. It produces output for information agents about proposed products and the attributes of these products. Moreover, it produces output for information provider agents about interests. In the information structures (called information types) that express communication information, the subject of the communication and the agent from or to whom the communication is directed are expressed. This means that communication information consists of statements about the subjects that are communicated.

Within the mediating agent, the component own process control uses belief input information and generates focus information: to focus on a scope of interest to be given a preferential treatment, i.e., pro-active behaviour will be shown with respect to this focus. The component agent interaction management has the same input information as the agent (incoming communication), extended with belief info and focus info. The output generated includes part of the output for the agent as a whole (outgoing communication), extended with maintenance info (information on the world and other agents that is to be stored within the agent), which is used to prepare the storage of communicated world and agent information. Information on attributes of products is stored in the component maintenance of world information. In the same manner, the beliefs of the agent with respect to other agents' profiles (provider attribute info, preference model info, and interests) are stored in maintenance of agent information. The agent specific task determine proposal uses information on product attributes, preference models, and agent interests as input to generate proposals as output. For reasons of space limitation the generic and domain-specific information types within the agent model are not presented; for more details [19].

4 Generic and Domain Specific Knowledge

The different knowledge abstraction levels introduced for information types can also be exploited to structure the knowledge. Abstract knowledge can be formulated in terms of scopes, abstracting from attributes and values. Other more specific knowledge is used to perform the abstraction step: it can be used to derive conclusions in terms of scopes from input in terms of attributes and values. The knowledge bases are discussed below in the context of the component in which they are used. Knowledge bases not specified in this paper can be found in [19].

4.1 Agent Specific Task: Determine Proposals

To determine proposals fitting a given scope of interest, information on products has to be compared to this scope of interest. To this end, the information on products, expressed in terms of their attributes has to be aggregated to information in terms of scopes. This can be derived using two knowledge bases, attribute and scope kb, which defines the relations between attributes and scopes in general, and product scope abstraction kb, which identifies for which scope(s) a product is relevant. The composition of the knowledge in these two knowledge bases supports reuse. For example, if in one of the two knowledge bases, modifications are made, the other knowledge base still can be used. Moreover, the first knowledge base is specified independent of knowledge about products. It can be (re)used within the component maintenance of agent information as well, as will be shown below. Given information on the scopes of products, by the knowledge base strict match kb it is defined how proposals to agents can be generated by matching the scopes of products and the scopes in which an agent is interested. For strict matching it consists of only one element.

Knowledge base strict match kb

if   interested_in(A:AGENT, S:SCOPE)

   and in_scope(P:PRODUCT, S:SCOPE)

then is_possibly_interesting_for(P:PRODUCT, A:AGENT, S:SCOPE)

This knowledge simply states that if a product is in a scope an agent is interested in, then this product is possibly interesting for this agent. Alternative knowledge bases can be used for non-strict matching. Using a method to determine a predicted rating (e.g., the classification tree that is constructed by the learning algorithm described in Section 7), the products that are possibly interesting for a user are classified with a predicted rating. In a selection phase only those products that have a sufficiently high predicted rating are presented to the user.

Knowledge base proposal_selection kb
if   is_possibly_interesting_for(P:PRODUCT, A:AGENT, S:SCOPE)
   and has_acceptable_predicted_rating(P:PRODUCT, A:AGENT)
then is_interesting_for(P:PRODUCT, A:AGENT, S:SCOPE)

By adapting the predicted rating to his or her own preferences the user influences the learning method contained within the component maintenance of agent information and thereby indirectly influences the predicted rating knowledge (e.g., the form of the classification tree discussed in Section 7) used within the current component (determine proposals).

4.2 Agent Interaction Management

The component agent interaction management makes use of five knowledge bases: (1) for incoming communication from agents asking for information on products, (2) incoming communication from agents giving their evaluation of products (necessary for constructing preference models), (3) incoming communication from agents providing information, (4) outgoing communication to agents interested in information on products, and (5) outgoing communication to agents providing information.

4.2.1 Incoming Communication
If an agent communicates her or his interests to a mediating agent, then this information is identified as new agent interest information that is currently believed (which can be forgotten after the agent has reacted on it: knowledge base agent interest identification kb) or that has to be stored (in which case it can be remembered later: knowledge base agent interest maintenance identification kb). A condition for storage of interests information is that the type of contract is persistent. For agents with a weaker type of contract no requests are stored, and instead of building a user specific preference model a default preference model can be used.

Knowledge base agent interest maintenance identification kb

if   communicated_by(interest(S:SCOPE), V:SIGN, A:AGENT)
   and belief(has_contract(A:AGENT, contract_type(persistent, Y)), pos)
then new_agent_info(interested_in(A:AGENT, S:SCOPE), V:SIGN)

If an agent communicates that he or she wants to subscribe for a contract of a certain type, then this information is identified as new contract information that has to be stored. This identification makes use of the following knowledge base.

Knowledge base subscription identification kb
if   communicated_by(subscription_for(C:CONTRACT_TYPE),
                                                    V:SIGN, A:AGENT)
then new_agent_info(has_contract(A:AGENT, C:CONTRACT_TYPE), V:SIGN)

If an agent has a persistent type of contract with the mediating agent, then evaluations of products given by that agent have to be identified, so that they can be used in the maintenance of his/her preference model.

Knowledge base agent preference information identification kb

if   communicated_by(is_rated_as(P: PRODUCT, R: RATING),

V:SIGN, A:AGENT)

and belief(has_contract(A:AGENT, contract_type(persistent, Y)), pos)

then new_agent_info(is_rated_as_by(P: PRODUCT, R: RATING, A:AGENT),

V:SIGN)

If an agent communicates information about products it provides, this incoming information is analysed, new world information is identified as new information that can be used immediately and forgotten afterwards (knowledge base provider info identification kb), or has to be stored (knowledge base provider info maintenance identification kb). If an agent communicates information about products it provides, this incoming information can also be analysed, in order to obtain new agent information on the scopes of the information the agent (apparently) can provide. This is expressed by:

Knowledge base provider scope maintenance identification kb:

if   communicated_by(attribute_has_value(P:PRODUCT,

A:ATTRIBUTE, V:VALUE), pos, A:INFO_PROVIDER)

then new_agent_info(can_provide(A:INFO_PROVIDER, A:ATTRIBUTE,

V:VALUE), pos)

4.2.2 Outgoing Communication

New information (product identification, scope, predicted rating, or attribute information) on a product that may be interesting for an agent is communicated to this agent. This is expressed in the following knowledge base:

Knowledge base proposal communication kb:

if   belief (is_interesting_for(P:PRODUCT, A:AGENT, S:SCOPE), pos)

and belief(attribute_has_value(P:PRODUCT, A:ATTRIBUTE, V:VALUE), pos)

and belief(product_has_predicted_rating_for(P:PRODUCT, R: RATING,

A: AGENT), pos)

then to_be_communicated _to(is_interesting(P:PRODUCT, S:SCOPE), pos,

A:AGENT)

and to_be_communicated_to(attribute_has_value(P:PRODUCT,

A:ATTRIBUTE, V:VALUE), pos, A:AGENT)

and to_be_communicated_to(product_has_predicted_rating(P:PRODUCT,

R: RATING), pos, A: AGENT)

The agent only communicates to an information provider if a scope has been taken as a focus, and if the information provider can provide products on this scope. This is expressed by:

Knowledge base info provider request kb

if   in_search_focus(S:SCOPE)

and belief(can_provide_scope(A:AGENT, S:SCOPE), pos)

then to_be_communicated _to(interest(S:SCOPE), pos, A:AGENT)

4.3 Own Process Control

The types of proposals to be determined and the scopes on which to focus search are determined by means of the knowledge base focus kb, as indicated by the following knowledge base. The knowledge base focus kb is used within own process control component. For example, in the first knowledge element it is expressed that for an agent with a contract of any type, proposals will be determined that fit the agent's interests. This is in contrast with, for example, the second knowledge element which expresses that only for agents with a persistent contract type, their scopes of interests will be chosen as persisting search foci (otherwise these scopes of interest will be forgotten after being handled).

Knowledge base focus kb
if   belief(has_contract(A:AGENT, C:CONTRACT:TYPE))
    and belief(interested_in (A:AGENT, S:SCOPE), pos)
then   product_to_be determined(in_scope (P:PRODUCT, S:SCOPE))
    and proposal_to_be determined(is_interesting_for(P:PRODUCT, A:AGENT,
                                                                    S:SCOPE))

if   belief(has_contract(A:AGENT, contract_type(persisting, search_for_info)))
    and belief(interested_in (A:AGENT, S:SCOPE), pos)
then   in_persisting_search_focus(S:SCOPE)

if   belief(has_contract(A:AGENT, contract_type(incidental, search_for_info)))
    and belief(interested_in (A:AGENT, S:SCOPE), pos)
    and not search_focus_processed_for(S:SCOPE, A:AGENT)
then   in_incidental_search_focus(S:SCOPE)
    and search_focus_chosen_for(S:SCOPE, A:AGENT)

if   in_persistent_search_focus(S:SCOPE)
then   in_ search_focus(S:SCOPE)

if   in_incidental_search_focus(S:SCOPE)
then   in_ search_focus(S:SCOPE)

if   in_ search_focus(S:SCOPE)
then   provider_to_be_determined_for(S:SCOPE)

4.4 World Interaction Management

The component world interaction management allows the agent to look for information by observation. This entails generation of observations to be performed and obtaining the observation results. The obtained observation results can be used incidentally after which the information is forgotten (using knowledge base observation info identification kb) or maintained to be used later as well (using knowledge base observation maintenance identification kb), similar to agent interaction management. The agent only observes if a scope has been taken as a focus. This is expressed using knowledge base observation initiative kb.

Knowledge base observation initiative kb
if   in_search_focus(S:SCOPE)
then   to_be_observed(S:SCOPE)

The actual execution of the observation does not take place within the agent, but in the external world. As part of the external world an engine can be used to search for products matching the pattern defined by the specified scope. The result of such an observation will be all information of any product that matches the scope. The knowledge base specified above is kept rather simple. To avoid too frequent repetition of observation, more sophisticated knowledge can be specified.

4.5 Maintenance of World and Maintenance of Agent Information

In principle, the components maintenance of world information and maintenance of agent information store information. The knowledge base attribute and scope kb defined above is also used in the component maintenance of agent information. In addition, the knowledge base provider scope abstraction kb is defined; it is similar to the knowledge base product scope abstraction kb mentioned above. But most importantly with respect to user preference *modeling*, the product evaluations (as given by the user in response to products presented to him/her) are used to adapt the user preference model within the component maintenance of agent information. An example of a technique to be used is described in Section 7.

5 The Behaviour

The behaviour of the mediating agent can be analysed in different ways. One way is to consider its basic functionalities with respect to its brokering task, and use these as building blocks to obtain behaviour. For example, its behaviour in terms of the weak notions of agency (autonomy, social ability, reactivity, and pro-activity) can be determined in terms of basic functionalities. Moreover, basic functionalities can be related to knowledge bases that are available within the agent. Using these two relationships, a relation can be identified between behaviour and available knowledge within the agent.

5.1 Basic Functionalities Depending on the Agent's Knowledge

The mediating agent shows behaviour depending on certain basic functionalities. For the agent model presented, these basic functionalities have been specified in a declarative manner by the agent's knowledge. For each of the basic properties of the agent it has been established which knowledge bases are required. By varying the choice of knowledge for the agent, different types of agents can be designed.

1. *Observation of information available within a certain part of the world*
Observation requires the ability to initiate observations, specified in the knowledge base observation initiative kb, and the ability to identify the information resulting from an observation, specified in the knowledge base observation info identification kb. Both knowledge bases can be used within the component world interaction management.

2. Communication with agents asking for information on products

The basic functionality to communicate with agents asking for information on products requires the processing of incoming communication of asking agents and preparation of outgoing information. The incoming information may refer to scopes of interests of the asking agent, evaluations of products, or to subscription. The communicated scopes of interest are identified using the knowledge base agent interest identification kb. That an agent is providing feedback information regarding products is identified using knowledge base agent preference information identification kb. Incoming communication on subscription is identified using knowledge base subscription identification kb. Outgoing communication containing product information to agents that ask for information is prepared using knowledge base proposal communication info. All these knowledge bases are used within the component agent interaction management.

3. Communication with agents providing information on products

Communicated information on products can be processed in two different ways. First, the product information can be identified, using knowledge base provider info identification kb. Second, from the fact that information is provided on a product with certain characteristics, it can be abstracted (from the given product) that this provider is able to offer (at least some) products with these characteristics in general. This is done using knowledge base provider scope identification kb. Communication to an agent that may be able to provide information is prepared using knowledge base provider request kb. All these knowledge bases are used within component agent interaction management.

4. Maintenance of acquired information on products

The agent can identify that all communicated information on products has to be stored, using knowledge base provider info maintenance identification kb within component agent interaction management. Moreover, by knowledge base observation info maintenance identification kb, within component world interaction management, new observation results on products to be stored can be identified.

5. Maintenance of scopes of interest of agents and the preference models

The agent can identify that the incoming requests of agents are to be maintained. This functionality is specified by the knowledge base agent interest maintenance identification, used within component agent interaction management. Feedback information regarding products is identified using knowledge base agent preference information identification kb, this knowledge base is also used within component agent interaction management. The feedback information itself is used for the maintenance of user preference models; for an example see Section 7.

6. Maintenance of scopes of products agents can provide

Scopes of information agents can provide are stored, if the incoming communication is handled in an appropriate way using knowledge base provider scope maintenance identification kb, used within component agent interaction management.

7. Own control

Control of the agent's own processes is defined by the knowledge base focus kb, used within component own process control.

8. *Determining matches between products and scopes of interests*

To determine matches between products and scopes of interest the agent can use the knowledge bases attribute and scope kb, product scope abstraction kb, proposal selection kb, and strict match kb within component determine proposals.

basic functionality	*knowledge specifying functionality*	*in component*
1. observation	observation initiative kb observation info identification kb	WIM WIM
2. communication with agents asking for information	agent interest identification kb subscription identification kb proposal communication kb agent preference information identification kb	AIM AIM AIM AIM
3. communication with agents providing information	provider info identification kb provider scope identification kb provider request kb	AIM AIM AIM
4. maintenance of product information	observation info maintenance identification kb provider info maintenance identification kb	WIM AIM AIM
5. maintenance of scopes of interest and preference models	agent interest maintenance identification kb agent preference information identification kb	AIM AIM
6. maintenance of scopes of products agents can provide	provider scope maintenance identification kb provider scope abstraction kb attribute and scope kb	AIM MAI MAI
7. own control	Focus kb	OPC
8. match between products and scopes of interests	attribute and scope kb product scope abstraction kb strict match kb proposal selection kb	DP DP DP DP

Fig. 2. Relation between basic functionalities and knowledge required

Combinations of these functionalities define specific types of agents. For example, if a provider agent is designed, functionalities 2, 4, 5, 8 may be desired, whereas functionalities 1, 3, 6, 7 could be left out of consideration. If an agent is designed to support a user in finding information on products within a certain scope, functionalities 1, 3, 6, 8 (and perhaps 4) may be desired, whereas 2 and 5 may be less relevant. For a mediating agent, or for an agent that has to play different roles, almost all functionalities (i.e., 1 to 8) may be desired. The generic agent architecture introduced in Sections 3 and 4 can be instantiated in different manners to obtain, among others, the types of agents mentioned. The relation between the agent's basic functionalities, its knowledge, and where the knowledge is used is summarised in the table in *Figure* 2.

5.2 Reactive, Pro-active, and Other Forms of Behaviour

Depending on the choices made, the mediating agent can show reactive behaviour towards agents asking for information on products and provider agents.

In reaction to an agent that asks for products within a certain scope, the mediating agent determines which of the products it knows, fit to this scope, using either an already known preference model for that agent, or a default preference model. The available information on the resulting products is communicated to the agent (e.g., author, title, year, topics, abstract, location, and reference).

Once an agent interest is known to the mediating agent, it is reactive with respect to any information providing agent that announces a product that fits the agent's scope, and has a sufficiently high predicted rating. In such a case the information on this product is communicated to this agent (i.e., to all relevant agents).

Pro-active behaviour occurs when the mediating agent has as a characteristic that it is pro-active with respect to certain agents. A pro-active mediating agent, from time to time, takes the initiative to ask provider agents for information on products which match some of its subscribed request profiles. It may focus on an agent's scopes of interest and actively select information providing agents and ask them whether they have products that fit in one of these scopes.

The behaviour of the mediating agent may depend on other characteristics of the mediating agent as well. In the above example, the knowledge used within own process control was kept rather simple. It is not difficult to extend this knowledge in such a way that more complex forms of pro-active social behaviour are initiated and controlled. For example, it is also possible that the mediating agent pro-actively determines an expected scope of interest of an agent and proposes products that fit this expected scope of interest.

6 Preference Modeling

In this section, we survey the field of user preference *modeling* and discuss some existing approaches and related working systems. Basically, the preference model of a user can be used to determine how interesting is an item to that user. The preference model of a user can thus be used to select and prioritise items that may be interesting to that user. For example, a user may like French or German cars and prefer to have a German car above a French car. The structure and properties of preference models depend on the application area in which they are used. For example, in multi-attribute decision systems (see [2],[21],[29],[36]) the user preference (utility) for an item is determined in terms of values of various attributes of the item and the preferences of the user towards those attributes (i.e., the importance of those attributes). In other application areas such as recommendation systems, the preference model may be defined either in terms of statistical correlation between users and their rated items or in terms of a set of attribute values that describe the items.

In general, the preferences of a user towards a set of items can be defined in terms of information concerning either the content of the items (content information) or the use of the items by a society of users (collaborative or social information). Roughly speaking, in the content-based approach a user is thought to like an item if the item is similar to other items that are liked by the user while in the collaborative-based approach a user is thought to like an item if the user is similar to other users who like the item. In the following, we use the term content-based preference model to indicate user preference models that are defined in terms of the content of items, and the term collaborative-based preference model to refer to user preference models that are defined in terms of collaborative information. In this paper, we assume that both the content information as well as the collaborative information can be used to construct user preference models for various kinds of applications, included automated negotiation in multi-agent systems where a model of user preferences is indispensable.

The construction of a preference model is usually a time consuming and cumbersome job. In applications such as information retrieval, information filtering, or automated integrative negotiation, the user has to express her preferences towards various (combinations of) attributes and attribute values. In other applications such as recommendation systems, a user may be asked to rate several, sometimes hundreds, of items before an item can be recommended. There are various methods to acquire information concerning user preferences. For example, in some systems a user may be asked to fill-out a form consisting of questions (usually a large number of questions) about her preferences every time she uses the system. Instead of forms, systems may also ask a user to answer consecutive multiple-choice questions in an interview-like interaction. Yet, other systems (see [14]) derive the preferences of a user by suggesting an item to the user and ask her to correct this suggestion. The user corrects system's suggestion by indicating why the suggested item does not match her needs. Based on these corrections, preference models of users are constructed or updated. Finally, some systems employ methods to induce the preferences of a user by observing the behaviour of that user over time (see [17],[23],[26],[30]). These methods are usually not intended to fully model user preferences, but to model the more frequent and predictable user preferences. It should be noted that applications that require huge efforts from their users risk to become ineffective and useless (see [24],[25]). Therefore, to model user preferences in an application a balance is to be found between the amount of interaction with the user and the necessary effectiveness of the constructed user profile.

Modeling user preferences on the basis of content or collaborative information can be considered as a learning problem where the aim is to learn the so-called preference function for a certain user. The preference function for a user maps items from a certain domain to some values that express the importance of those items for that user. In this way, the structure of the chosen range is imposed on domain items. It is important to note that various types of preference functions may exist. The type of a preference function characterises the structure of preference model (see [21],[36]). For example, the range of one preference function may be the set of real numbers where the order of real numbers reflects the degree of user interest. The range of another preference function may be the set consisting of two elements: LIKE and DISLIKE. In the first case, a partial order structure is imposed on the items and in the second case a nominal structure is imposed on the items, i.e. the preference function is a classification function.

6.1 Collaborative-Based Preference Modeling

In the collaborative approach the preference model of a user is constructed on the basis of the items that are previously used and rated by that user and the preferences of other users represented as sets of rated items. Intuitively, in the collaborative approach an item is thought to be interesting for a user if other users who have similar taste are interested in that item too. The taste similarity of users is determined by a statistical correlation between users and their rated items. In this way, a group of users that rate items similarly are considered as having similar taste or interest. This approach to user preference *modeling* is often called "word of mouth" propagation. For example, consider the following data table representing the rating (a number between 1 and 10) that four users $U_1,..., U_4$ have assigned to three papers $P_1,..., P_3$. An empty cell in the table indicates that the rating of a person for an item is unknown.

	U_1	U_2	U_3	U_4
P_1	4	-	5	9
P_2	1	9	-	8
P_3	8	1	7	2

It should be clear that persons U_1 and U_3 have similar rating and therefore can be considered as having similar taste. Likewise, U_2 and U_4 show similar taste. These similarities can be used to predict the interest of users towards papers for which the rating is unknown. For example, the taste similarity between U_1 and U_3 suggests that the interest of U_3 towards the second paper is low, while the taste similarity between U_2 and U_4 may suggest that the interest of U_2 towards the first paper is high.

Collaborative-based preference models have been used in retrieval and filtering systems to, respectively, retrieve and filter available items for certain users. In fact, the purpose of these systems is to assist a user by selecting, prioritising, and delivering available items according to the preferences of that user. In this way, the selected items are presented to a user in the order of their relevance for that user. These retrieval and filtering systems are often used as recommendation systems where users are informed about items that may be interesting to them. There have been several collaborative-based recommendation systems introduced in which the preferences of users are modelled automatically. Examples of online recommendation systems that employ collaborative approach are MovieFinder [46] and FireFly [43]. The preferences of a user are modelled automatically by observing the behaviour of that user and applying different statistical methods to the observed behaviour (see [3],[17],[18],[34]).

In collaborative-based recommendation systems, an item can be recommended to a user if the user has already rated a subset of items and thereby has expressed some of her preferences. For this reason, these recommendation systems construct an initial preference model for a new user by asking the user to rate a pre-selected set of items. However, a serious disadvantage of these systems is that new items cannot be recommended to anyone since items are recommended to users only when they are rated by some users. Note also that the quality of recommendations by systems that are based on collaborative approach increases as the number of users and the number of rated items increase.

6.2 Content-Based Preference Modeling

The content-based approach provides the preference model of a user on the basis of properties and attribute values of the items. Using content-based approach, an item is thought to be interesting for a user if that item has properties or attribute values as predicted by the preference model. It is important to note that, in contrast to the collaborative approach, the content-based approach can be applied only when items can be described in terms of properties and attribute values. Like collaborative-based preference models, the content-based preference models have been used in online recommendation systems such as BargainFinder [41] and Jango [44]. However, unlike collaborative-based preference models, the content-based preference models are also used in applications such as integrative negotiation where the utility function is defined in terms of user preferences towards various attribute values (see [2],[16],[21],[26],[36]).

In general, content-based preference models are constituted by a set of attributes. For example, the set M = {Topic, Author, Year} of paper attributes may constitute the preference model of users for scientific papers. Given a set of attributes constituting the user preference model, the preferences of a user are often modelled by providing some values and rates for each attribute. First, for each attribute a rate may be given to indicate how important is an attribute. Then, for each attribute a set of possible attribute values should be given. Moreover, a rate should be assigned to each possible attribute value to indicate how preferred is that value. The assignment of rates to attribute values depends on the type of attribute values (e.g. nominal, ordinal, interval, and ratio). In fact, for nominal and ordinal attribute values a rate is assigned to each attribute value while for interval and ratio attribute values the inherent order of those values can be used to assign a rate to only a subset of those attribute values. The rate for other attribute values can then be derived by means of the inherent order of attribute values and the assigned rates to the subset of attribute values. For example, given the above set M of paper attributes, the preferences of a user may be modelled by the following set:

    {Topic:9 = <Agent:9 , Negotiation:6 , AI:4>,
    Author:7 = <Jennings:8 , Zlotkin:8 , Maes:6>,
    Year:4   = <1999:9 , 1984:4>   }

The numbers attached to attribute names and attribute values indicate user's rates for those attributes names and attribute values, respectively. In this example, the values of the first two attributes (i.e. Topic and Author) have nominal type whereas the values of the third attribute (i.e. Year) have an interval type. Therefore, based on the rate of the two year values (i.e. 1999:9 and 1984:4) and given the internal interval order of year values the rate of other year values can be derived (e.g. 1987:5, 1990:6, 1993:7, etc.).

As the values of attributes may not always be known to a user, the user may also be asked to represent compensation values for the unknown attribute values, i.e. the loss of an attribute value is compensated by gain in the value of another attribute. The following table is an example of compensation values between paper attributes.

	Topic	Author	Year
Topic	-	0.9	0.3
Author	0.8	-	0.4
Year	0.5	0.5	-

Basically, this table shows how the loss of an attribute value should be gained in terms of other attribute. In this way, the compensation values can be considered as representing user preferences towards interdependencies between various attributes and can be used to determine the user preference towards an item for which some attribute values are missing. Note that these scenarios are quite usual in automated integrative negotiation system (see [2]).

Although content-based preference models play an essential role in both recommendation systems as well as automated negotiation and decision theory, there is little attention in these studies for *modeling*, especially automated *modeling*, of content-based user preferences. An obvious and non-automatic way to model user preferences is the so-called "deep interview" approach. In this approach, the user is asked to answer consecutive multiple-choice questions by means of which item attributes and their values are rated.

A more interesting and semi-automatic way to model user preferences is the so-called "suggestion-correction" approach. This approach assumes a partial preference model of user which may be a default model in the worse case, i.e. when user is new to the system such that nothing is known about user except some default knowledge. For example, in applications such as computer selling systems or a travel agency systems some default knowledge about user such as "need-a-computer" or "want-to-go-to-holiday" can be assumed. Based on partial user preference model the system may suggest an item to that user and, if needed, the user corrects this suggestion by indicating why the suggested item does not satisfy her needs. In the case that the suggested item satisfies the needs of user the system stops. Otherwise, based on user's correction response the system updates the preference model and suggests a new item, etc. This approach is employed in Eugene et. al. (see [14]) where user's correction responses are considered as constraints. The constraints are then linked together to form a network of constraints. The resulting network of constraints represents the preference model of user. Consequently, an item is thought to be interesting for a user when it satisfies the network of constraints that represents the preference model of that user.

Finally, a fully automatic content-based approach to model user preferences is by discovering regularities among properties and attribute values of the used and rated items. Neural networks, genetic algorithms, principle component analysis, and all kinds of inductive learning methods are alternative techniques in automatic content-based preference *modeling*. Although the systems that employ automatic methods usually expect little effort from users, a new user is expected to make some effort and provide feedback to the system in order to ensure reasonable performance from the start. This is also true for the systems that are based on collaborative-based user preference models. It should also be noted that automatic methods to model user preferences is not only interesting for minimising the effort of users, but it may also be interesting for discovering the preferences of other involved participants. This is especially important for intelligent mediating agents that have to discover the preference models of other involved agents automatically (see Sections 3,4, and 5). Also, in cooperative multi-agent negotiation processes where an agent, who does not have a direct access to the preferences of her negotiating agent, likes to propose a bid that may be interesting to the negotiating agent as well.

In the content-based approach preferences can be modelled independent of preference models of other involved participants. In fact, the preference model of a user can be constructed on the basis of the descriptions of the items for which the user preference are known. Moreover, the quality of the content-based preference models that are provided by automated methods depends on the number of items for which the user preferences are known. This quality is, however, independent of the number of other users or their preferences, as it is the case in collaborative approach. Another characteristic of the content-based approach, in contrast to the collaborative approach, is that a new item can immediately be decided to be interesting for a user without the need of being rated by other users.

6.3 An Integrated Approach

The collaborative-based and content-based approaches do not exclude each other and in fact they can be combined into an integrated approach to model user preferences (see [1]). Such a user preference model will be called integrated user preference model. An integrated user preference model is thus defined in terms of both collaborative as well as content information. In particular, an integrated user preference model is constructed in terms of a predefined set of attributes, as it is the case with the content-based user preference models. However, unlike the content-based preference models, there are two attributes in the integrated approach which are defined in terms of collaborative information. These attributes are called collaborative attributes. One collaborative attribute characterises a user and the second collaborative attribute characterises an item.

In order to construct automatically the integrated preference model of a user, an inductive learning method is applied to a set of data entries (see [1]). Each data entry is an n-tuple of attribute values and represents the information about one user and one item that is liked by that user. Note that one may also consider the set of data entries in which an entry represents the information about one user and one item that is disliked by that user. The value of the collaborative attribute that characterises a user is a set of items that is liked/disliked by that user and the value of the collaborative attribute that characterises an item is a set of users that like/dislike that item. Note that the values of the collaborative attributes are set values: their values are sets instead of individuals. In contrast to the collaborative attribute values, the values of other (non-collaborative) attributes are individual values. Given n users U_1 ,..., U_n and m

scientific papers P_1 ,..., P_m , the following is an example of a set of paper entries on which an inductive method can be applied.

{ < Agent , Jennings , 1997 , $\{P_2, P_4, P_9\}$, $\{U_1, U_7\}$ > ,
   < Negotiation , Zlotkin , 1994 , $\{ P_1, P_9, P_3, P_5\}$, $\{U_4, U_2\}$ > ,
   < AI , Maes , 1995 , $\{P_2\}$, $\{U_7, U_4, U_1\}$ > }

The sets containing scientific papers are values of the collaborative attribute that characterises a user and the sets containing users are values of the collaborative attribute that characterises a paper. In this way, collaborative information, which is translated into attribute values, together with content-based information, which is also represented as attribute values, constitute the data to which an inductive learning method is applied to extract user preferences. It is important to note that the values of collaborative attributes can be very large sets when the numbers of users and items get large. This is a serious disadvantage of this integrated method.

6.4 Effectiveness of Preference Models

The effectivity of collaborative-based and content-based preference models depends on the applications they are used in. For example, collaborative-based preference models are effective for applications where either it is unrealistic to collect a large amount of information about the preferences of an individual user, or the number of users is too large. Using collaborative-based preference models is also effective for applications where the content of the items neither is available nor can be analysed automatically by a machine (e.g. items like a picture, video, sound, etc.). However, the collaborative-based preference models are less effective for applications like integrative negotiation (see [2],[15],[29]) in retail Electronic Commerce where negotiation is considered to be a decision making process over items that are described as multiple interdependent attributes. As explained, collaborative-based preference models are not defined in terms of attribute values and therefore they are less effective for applications like integrative negotiation.

On the other hand, content-based preference models are effective in applications where data are represented in terms of attribute values such that no more information than available is required. Also, content-based preference models provide sound results even in situations where there is only one single user. When a content-based preference model is constructed automatically, it will provide sound results if it is constructed on the basis of a set of rated items that is large enough. Note that collaborative-based preference models will fail to provide sound results in such a case. Content-based preference models are thus appropriate for applications like integrative negotiation since they are in terms of various attribute values. Moreover, since the preference model of a certain user is in terms of attribute values, a new items which is not rated by any other users can be decided to be interesting for that particular user. As we mentioned above, providing a preference model by a user in terms of various item's attributes is a time consuming activity. Therefore, we believe that in these applications user preferences should be modelled automatically. In order to achieve this goal in a multi-agent setting, we employ inductive logic programming which enables an agent to induce the preferences of a user in terms of item's attributes during its interactions with the user.

7 Automatic Preference Modeling with Inductive Logic Programming

Inductive logic programming (see [28]) lies at the intersection of machine learning and computational logic, as used in logic programming. It combines inductive machine learning with the representations of computational logic. Computational logic (a subset of first order logic) is a more powerful representation language than the classical attribute-value representation typically used in machine learning. This representational power is useful in the context of learning user preference models, because in this way more complex types of user preferences can be detected and described. Another advantage of inductive logic programming is that it enables the use of background knowledge (in the form of Prolog programs) in the induction process. Given the fact that DESIRE uses first order logic as knowledge representation formalism, this allows for an easy integration of both systems.

An ILP system takes as input examples and background knowledge and produces hypotheses as output. There are two common used ILP settings which differ in the representation of these data: learning from entailment ([11] compares different settings) and learning from interpretation (see [12]). We will use the second setting because of the time efficiency of this setting. In learning from interpretations, an example or observation of actions performed by the user — in this application requesting and rating a paper — can be viewed as a small relational database, consisting of a number of facts (such as 'author(Smith)' or 'interest(high)') that describe the specific properties of the example. An example may contain multiple facts about multiple relations. This contrasts with the attribute value representations where an example always corresponds to a single tuple for a single relation. We will show later that the extra flexibility gained with the learning from interpretations setting is very useful in user preference *modeling* (see Section 6).

The background knowledge takes the form of a Prolog program. Using this Prolog program, it is possible to derive additional properties from the examples. Let us illustrate this by showing how we can introduce a taxonomy using background knowledge:

```
topic(T)      papertopic(T).
topic(T)      isa(It,T), topic(It).
isa(agentsemantics,agent).
isa(agentarchitecture,agent).
isa(agent,artificial_intelligence).
```

This Prolog program recursively defines the topic-relation: a paper has topic T if either T is the topic directly related to the paper (through the papertopic-relation) or T is above It (defined with the isa/2 relation), an other topic related to the paper, in the taxonomy-lattice. By introducing the above background information the system adds to each example automatically all topic information: if we observe the user rating a paper with as topic agentarchitecture, the learning system adds that agentarchitecture, agent and artificial_intelligence are topics for this paper and will use this information when learning hypotheses.

There are two forms of induction: predictive and descriptive induction. Predictive induction starts from a set of classified examples and a background theory, and the aim is to induce a theory that will classify all the examples in the appropriate class. On the other hand, descriptive induction starts from a set of unclassified examples, and aims at finding a set of regularities that hold for the examples. In the situation of a paper mediating agent, predictive induction could be used to predict the interest of a user in a paper. Descriptive induction on the other hand would try to find all regularities that hold in the set of examples, and would find rules such as:

If the author is Jennings and the user is interested, then the co-author is Wooldridge

Notice that these types of rules — although maybe revealing interesting and unknown knowledge — are not useful for predicting the user's interest. Since our aim is to predict the user's preference for unseen objects, we focus on predictive induction in the learning from interpretations setting, because in this system the focus is on finding rules useful for classification. This task can more formally be expressed as follows:

Given:

a set of classes C,
a set of classified examples E,
a background theory B
Find a hypothesis H such that:
for all e   E, H   e   B   = c, and H   e   B   c'
where c is the class of the example e and c'   C - {c}.

To make the discussion more concrete we focus on one ILP system: Tilde (see [4],[5]). This system performs predictive induction in the learning from interpretation setting by inducing logical decision trees from classified examples and background theory. Consider for example the background knowledge that is mentioned above. Suppose also a set of observations describing papers and the interest of a user in those papers. In this application we let the user rate his interest in a paper on a score from 1 to 10, where higher numbers indicate a higher interest. We build user models for each user individually, so we collect all observations from a certain user in one file. As a result there is no need to add information about which user made these observations to the data that will be given to the learning system. The following is an example of one such observation. Notice that attributes (such as author) can have multiple values.

```
    papertopic(agentarchitecture).
author('Jennings').
author('Mamdani').
aff('Jennings','Queen Mary & Westfield College').
aff('Mamdani','Imperial College').
interest(6).
```

We included the affiliation of the authors in the example. One could argue that such information can be stored in background knowledge. However the fact that an author can belong to different affiliations at the same time makes this a property which can't be computed from the other information in the example and hence can't be stored in background information.

Starting from the background knowledge and a set of observations Tilde can build hypotheses (represented as first-order logic decision trees) which predict the user's interest in a paper. The following is an example of such a hypothesis:

```
    topic(agents) ?
+---yes: author(A), A = 'Jennings' ?
|    +---yes: author(B), aff(A,C), aff(B,D), C * D ?
|    |     +---yes: interest(6)
```

```
|    |      +--no: interest(4)
|    +--no: interest(3)
+--no: interest(1)
```

Tilde uses the standard induction tree algorithm for building this trees: look for a test which best separates the examples in sets belonging to the same class and repeat this procedure in each leaf of this tree until a stopping criteria is reached. Notice that this is a greedy approach: selecting the best splitting test at each level of the tree doesn't necessary result in the best global tree. Using look ahead, Tilde can make conjunctions of tests and use these as single tests, as clearly illustrated in the third line of the above tree.

The above hypothesis states that the user has interest 1 in papers that are not about agents. If it's a paper on agents written by Jennings the predicted interest value is 4 unless there is a co-author from a different affiliation, then the interest prediction is 6. Agent papers not written by Jennings have a predicted interest-value of 3. As this example shows, hypotheses can contain constants as well as variables.

Notice that this very simple example shows the power of inductive reasoning. From a set of specific facts, a general theory containing variables is induced. It is not the case that the induced theory deductively follows from the given examples. The Tilde system has the benefits (like most ILP systems) of being able to build complex hypotheses (using first order logic) and using background knowledge in finding these hypotheses. Moreover experiments have shown that the Tilde system scales nicely on large datasets (see [5]). More details of the Tilde system can be found in [4] and [5].

7.1 User Preference **Modeling** with Tilde

Following Section 6, we may define a user preferences model for a certain user u as a function $_u$ mapping an observation o from the set of possible observations O onto a preference indicator value p from the set of possible preference indicator values P, a finite structured domain. Since Tilde can induce general hypotheses from specific observations and background knowledge, it can be used to induce $_u$ automatically. This can be done by building a set of examples E, each example consisting of an observation o and $_u(o) = p$, the preference user u has for observation o. As the set of classes C we use the set of possible preference indicator values p from P. In this way we transform the construction of $_u$ into a learning task. We can also add background knowledge B with information the system can use in constructing $_u$.

We illustrate this by an example. Consider again the task of building a preference model for a user who is looking for interesting scientific papers as discussed in Section 2. In this context each observation consists of information about a paper: title, author, year of publication, type of publication (journal, conference proceeding, workshop proceeding) and the topic. Attributes author and topic can be multi-valued. Other possible useful attributes are the affiliation of the author(s), the publishing company and the length of the article (number of words or pages). In background knowledge we put the general information that could help Tilde in constructing $_u$. As background knowledge we use an extension of the taxonomy on topics as introduced earlier in this section. However all other relevant information (e.g. background information on authors, publishers and affiliations) could be included as well. Finally one has to create a language bias, specifying which concepts Tilde is allowed to use in constructing $_u$.

We conducted three types of experiments to answer three questions we had in mind: can the system detect complex rules, can the system detect rules if there is noise in the examples and can we construct user preference models from a small number of observations. For the first two experiments a set of 375 observations was used. All these experiments were performed on machine generated data. We produced 375 examples of paper descriptions and let the computer label them according to criteria we defined. These examples (but not the criteria used to label them) were then given to Tilde to learn user profiles. The reason for this type of experiments is to determine whether the agent would be able to find user patterns under the assumption that these exist. The question whether useful user patterns do exist is not answered by these experiments because it is application and user dependent.

For the first experiment we labelled all our examples using increasingly more complex rules:

1. If published before 1992 then interesting else not interesting.
2. If published before 1992 or if it is a journal paper then interesting else not.
3. If published before 1992 or if it is not a journal paper then interesting else not
4. If published before 1992 or if it is a journal paper or it is a paper by Jennings then interesting else not.
5. If published before 1992 or if it is a journal paper written in 1998 then interesting else not.

No background knowledge was used in these experiments. Each time we labelled all 375 examples according to one of the above rules and let the system learn on all these examples. We then inspect the user preference model produced to see if they match the rule used to label the examples. When using rule 1 no problems are encountered. Rule 2 adds a disjunction, but this easy for the system to learn because it's just an adding another branch. Rule 3 complicates rule 2 by using a negation of one of the tests. But this as well is easy for the system to learn because negating a test is the same as switching both branches at the node that corresponds with this test. Rule 4 extends rule 2 by adding another disjunction. In the example set there were only three examples of non-journal papers by Jennings published after 1991 but even then Tilde was able to find the correct user preference model. The fifth rule could be learned by Tilde, but only when look ahead (testing conjunctions of tests in stead of single tests) is enabled. Look ahead however increases the time to build the decision tree so when we test Tilde on this data set without look ahead it finds an user preference model which nearly matches the correct hypothesis: it has one test more, and misclassifies 1 out of the 375 examples.

Most of the time, a user doesn't behave completely according to rules. For instance, a user may be interested in Jennings' papers, but some of these papers he will rate as non interesting for different reasons. For a user preference *modeling* system to be useful, it should be able to cope with such 'noise' in the observations. We tested this by introducing noise in the experiment mentioned above. We labelled examples according to rule 1 and added 5%, 10% and 15% of noise (this means that such a portion of the examples were random labelled[1]). To test the preference models we

---

[1] interest is indicated by an integer between 1 and 10, were we used 1 for uninteresting and 10 for interesting. With random, we don't mean random either 1 or 10 but a random integer between 1 and 10

performed a cross validation: the dataset is divided in equal sets, all but one set is used to learn a preference model, which is then tested on the remaining set. This procedure is repeated with another set as testset until every set has once been used as testset. We performed this experiment first with rule 1. The system found user preference models that were as accurate as possible: respectively 95%, 90% and 85% accuracy. The system had learned in each case the correct preference model (and so would have a predictive accuracy of 100% if there is no noise in the testset). If we repeat this experiment with rule 3 the accuracies are comparable. The time to induce these user preference functions doesn't increase when the percentage of noise increases. However, if we perform this experiment with a rule that has a disjunction only supported by few observations (as in the author is Jennings branch of rule 4) we see that the accuracy on the testset remain the same but the system doesn't find a correct preference model. This occurs when there are more observations supporting random patterns created by the noise than the regular patterns. However, if the noise level is so high, can we consider this part of the user's preference?

In a final experiment we try Tilde to learn from few examples. Simple   functions can be learned from as few as ten examples. When learning rule 4 in the first experiment we also noticed that, although only 3 out of the 375 examples supported this disjunction, the system was able to detect this and include it in the preference model. Tilde can be used to model the user preferences based on few examples and will build a simple model. When more observations become available that don't agree with the initial simple hypothesis, Tilde will construct a more complex hypothesis. From these experiments we can see that the Tilde system is able to learn simple user preference functions from few examples. Preference functions can be learned even when the observations are noisy. From previous experiments [32] we can conclude that in an attribute-value setting Tilde performs comparable with classic machine learning systems. In the next section we will elaborate more on the advantages and disadvantages of the ILP-approach compared with more classical machine learning algorithms in learning preference functions

7.2 Advantages and Disadvantages of ILP in User Preference Modeling

In the previous section we briefly illustrated the Tilde algorithm on a simple dataset. We will now introduce the specific ILP-features and illustrate how these are useful in user preference *modeling* by applying them to the above example.

Because in ILP examples are represented as a set of facts, it is easy to represent examples where attributes have multiple values. This is common in many electronic commerce applications: books can have multiple authors, songs can have multiple songwriters and performers, ..., movies have multiple actors,... . If you want to represent such information in an attribute-value setting, you have to introduce multiple attributes of the same type (e.g. author1, author2, ...). This however results in two problems: the number of these attributes has to be fixed in advance (e.g. maximum 5 authors) and attribute-value learners will take the order of the attributes into account (e.g. if author3 = Jennings then interesting) while in many applications this will be irrelevant. ILP systems can represent multi-valued attributes without these disadvantages: facts can occur more than once and are unordered. We illustrated this already in the paper example.

One can also easily extend the learning task just by extending the examples. Let's illustrate this. The user preference model learned in previous examples was solely based on features of the paper itself, there was no use of the collaborative *modeling* approach as discussed in Section 6.2. However, extending the learning task to incorporate this collaborative *modeling* is very easy: each example still consists of the paper observations o (authors, title, type, ...), but instead of one indication of the preference of one user, the example also contains the preference of all users who read this paper. An example could then look like this:

papertopic(agentarchitecture).
author('Jennings').
author('Mamdani').
aff('Jennings','Queen Mary & Westfield College').
aff('Mamdani','Imperial College').
interest(user12,6).
interest(user23,4).
interest(user76,4).

A possible resulting tree for user 23 could then be like this:
```
author('Jennings') ?
+--yes: interest(user12,A), A<5 ?
|     +--yes: interest(user23,8)
|     +--no:  interest(user23,4)
+--no:  interest(user23,1)
```
If it is a Jennings paper and user 12 has read it and had low interest in it, then the interest of user 23 will be 8, if user 12 had not read it or had an high interest in it, user 23 has an interest of 4. If it is no Jennings paper the interest of user 23 is 1. So the $_u$ function is based on a mixture of properties of the paper and the interests of other users.

First notice that this collaborative *modeling* approach is more flexible than other collaborative approaches in which for user u users u' are identified such that $_u$ (o) = $_{u'}$ (o) for many observations o, while in this approach we identify for user u users u' such that $_u$ (o) = $f_{u'}($ $_{u'}$ (o)) for observations o that obey to certain conditions (namely the tests higher up the decision tree), and $f_{u'}$ a function mapping the preferences of user u' onto the preferences of user u. Also notice that the above approach nicely merges the two approaches (collaborative and content based) into one integrated approach in a natural and easy way, due to the flexibility of inductive logic programming. Of course, in stead of information about specific users, information about clusters of users can be calculated using background knowledge (see next paragraph) and used (e.g. 'if the interest of the students in this paper is low then ...').

It is very common in ILP to extend the dataset by introducing background knowledge, formulated in the form of static facts (e.g. situated_in('Imperial College','London').) or in the form of rules (e.g. situated_in(A,C)   situated_in(A,B), situated_in(B,C)) which allow to infer new facts from the knowledge already available in the background knowledge and the example. We illustrated the use of background knowledge by introducing a taxonomy, but since Prolog is Turing complete, any computable information can be added to the example. This allows for easy integration of ILP systems with other systems. For instance, in the above example we could use a clustering algorithm to find descriptions for clusters of users. This information could be added to the background knowledge of Tilde so the system could use the result of the clustering algorithm. Another example of the flexibility is the fact that integrating Tilde with DESIRE was very easy: background knowledge translated information in DESIRE representation into the representation in which the learning task was expressed.

ILP is based on logic programming, a declarative programming formalism. Due to its declarative nature, input as well as output of ILP systems are readable (for humans as well as for computers), in contrast to sub-symbolic systems like neural networks. This is a very important feature in the context of agents for electronic commerce because ILP user models can easily be translated to English sentences. In this way the user can check and understand his preference model the agent has built. Users will probably be more likely to delegate tasks to agents they can understand and check than to 'black box' agents.

As illustrated above, ILP has some advantages compared with other concept learning methods. Due to the use of background knowledge and the use of first order logic as representation language, ILP is especially suited in knowledge intensive learning tasks where the data is mainly symbolic. If there is only few or no background knowledge used and the observations can easily be expressed in an attribute-value representation, traditional concept learning algorithms such as C4.5 [31] will result in a comparable user model while these systems require less computing power. Although the ILP method can handle numeric attributes, it's mainly focussed on symbolic datasets. If the observations of the user are expressed as numbers (for example sensor readings (blood pressure, brain activity, ...)) and the user preference model is a mathematical function of these readings, better techniques (such as neural networks) exist. Finally, because ILP systems search a larger space of possible solutions than other techniques, ILP systems require more computing power than most other techniques. Although ILP systems can handle large datasets [5], to our knowledge there doesn't exist a fast incremental ILP algorithm useful in time-critical applications.

So ILP systems have their limitations. But a broad range of electronic commerce applications deals with mainly symbolic data in an environment where useful background knowledge is common. ILP can not only build user preference models in such a setting, but is also able to provide this model in a representation that can easily be mapped on natural language, and in this way help the user understand and trust the system. Since electronic commerce applications are fairly new phenomena, these applications tend to change over time. ILP is a very flexible learning method which makes it easy to adapt the learning system to new situations. All these features makes ILP well suited to learn user preference models in electronic commerce applications.

8 Discussion

In this section, some of the recently developed and operational models of virtual market places and Web commerce based applications are briefly mentioned.

1.   Kasbah

Kasbah (cf. [9], [10]) is a web-based multi-agent system using agents interacting with each other within the virtual market domain. The agents act on behalf of their users [9]. Price Negotiation is one of the interesting features applied within Kasbah [10].

2.   Market Space

Market Space is an open agent-based market infrastructure. It is based on a decentralized infrastructure model in which both the humans and the machines can read information about the products and services, and everyone is able to announce interests to one another [13]. The aim in designing Market Space is to design a market place where searching, negotiation and deal settlement, e.g. interaction with users is done using agents. The AMP (Agent Marketplace Project) is a collaboration project between Uppsala University and Swedish telecom, Telia. Market Space has been developed mainly in Prolog. For the communication with the Web, the standard protocol (HTTP) has been used.

A difference with our approach is that these approaches have been implemented without using a principled design method, and do not use components as building blocks that are (formally) specified at a conceptual level. This is also a difference with the work described in [35]. The mediating agent architecture introduced here was designed and implemented in a principled manner, using the compositional development method for multi-agent systems DESIRE [6]. Due to its compositional structure it supports reuse; a flexible, easily adaptable architecture results.

Required properties or functionalities of agents can be formalised, and the relation between required properties and underlying assumptions can be established in a formal manner. An example of a result of such a formal analysis is the relation between basic functionalities (required properties) and available knowledge (assumptions) discussed in Section 5 (see *Figure* 2). In this paper the result of formal analysis was used in the agent model; the formal analysis itself was done by us as designers. To support this, a compositional verification method for multi-agent systems has been developed and successfully applied to verify the behaviour of a multi-agent system for one-to-many negotiation (see [7]), and to give a formal analysis of pro-activeness and reactiveness (see [20]). One of the more ambitious aims of our future research is to explore possibilities to include these formal analyses themselves in an agent model, and not only the results obtained by them.

On the basis of the above discussion of techniques to construct preference *modeling*, the following claims can be made. A proper approach for preference *modeling* in a multi-agent setting should:

1.   Allow agents to induce preferences of the involved participants automatically by observing their behaviour.

2.   Be capable of handling the changes in the interests of participants that take place over the time by adjusting their preference models accordingly.

3.   Be robust with respect to the partiality of information about preferences.
4.   Allow for re-use of a preference model in different domains and for different purposes.

Note that none of the approaches mentioned in Section 6 can handle the second aspect real time, i.e., without computing the whole preference model over again. Likewise, the ILP method introduced in Section 7 cannot handle this problem real time. The design in this study is such that the mediating agent applies the ILP method when enough new observations have been made. Furthermore, the approaches that are mentioned in Section 6 neither support the fourth facility. This facility may be realised by defining compositional preference models, i.e., various primitive preference models that can be composed to each other to form the preference model of a user. Each primitive preference model can then be reused in various configurations and thus for different applications. We will address this in more details in future studies.

Acknowledgements

Mehrzad Kharami and Pascal van Eck supported experiments with some early instantiations of the mediating agent model. This work was partially supported by the NWO project "Automatic and Dynamic Configuration of a Multi-agent system for Electronic Commerce, 612-060-004". Nico Jacobs is financed by a specialisation grant of the Flemish Institute for the promotion of scientific and technological research in the industry (IWT).

References

BASU, C. , HIRSH, H. , COHEN, W. Recommendation as Classification: Using Social and Content-Based Information in Recommendation. Proceedings of the fifteenth National Conference on Artificial Intelligence (pp. 714-720), 1998.

BENN, W. , GÖRLITZ, O , NEUBERT, R. Enabling Integrative Negotiations by Adaptive Software Agents. In Klusch, O. Shehory, and G. Weiss (eds.), Cooperative Information Agents III, Proceedings of the Third International Workshop on Cooperative Information Agents, CIA'99. Lecture Notes in Artificial Intelligence, vol. 1652. Springer Verlag. 1999.

BILLSUS, D. , PAZZANI, M. Learning Collaborative Information Filters. Proceedings of the Fifteenth International Conference on Machine Learning (pp. 46-54). Madison, WI: Morgan Kaufmann, 1998.

BLOCKEEL, H. , De RAEDT, L. Lookahead and discretization in ILP. In Proceedings of the 7th International Workshop on Inductive Logic Programming, volume 1297 of Lecture Notes in Artificial Intelligence, pages 77-85. Springer-Verlag, 1997.

BLOCKEEL, H. , De RAEDT, L. , JACOBS, N. , DEMOEN, B. Scaling up inductive logic programming by learning from interpretations. Data Mining and Knowledge Discovery, 3(1):59-93, 1999.

BRAZIER, F.M.T., DUNIN-KEPLICZ, B., JENNINGS, N.R., TREUR, J., Formal specification of Multi-Agent Systems: a real-world case. In: V. Lesser (ed.), Proceedings of the First International Conference on Multi-Agent Systems, ICMAS'95, MIT Press, Cambridge, MA, 1995, pp. 25-32. Extended version in: International Journal of Cooperative Information Systems, M. Huhns, M. Singh, (eds.), special issue on Formal Methods in Cooperative Information Systems: Multi-Agent Systems, vol. 6, 1997, pp. 67-94.

BRAZIER, F.M.T., CORNELISSEN, F. GUSTAVSSON, R., JONKER, C.M., LINDEBERG, O., POLAK, B., TREUR, J., Compositional Design and Verification of a Multi-Agent System for One-to-Many Negotiation. In: Proceedings of the Third International Conference on Multi-Agent Systems, ICMAS'98, IEEE Computer Society Press, 1998.

BRAZIER, F.M.T., JONKER, C.M., TREUR, J., Formalisation of a cooperation model based on joint intentions. In: J.P. Müller, M.J. Wooldridge, N.R. Jennings (eds.), Intelligent Agents III (Proc. of the Third International Workshop on Agent Theories, Architectures and Languages, ATAL'96), Lecture Notes in AI, volume 1193, Springer Verlag, 1997, pp. 141-155.

CHAVEZ, A., MAES, P., Kasbah: An Agent Marketplace for Buying and Selling goods. In: Proceedings of the First International Conference on the Practical Application of Intelligent Agents and Multi-Agent Technology, PAAM'96, The Practical Application Company Ltd, Blackpool, 1996, pp. 75-90.

CHAVEZ, A., DREILINGER, D., GUTMAN, R., MAES, P., A Real-Life Experiment in Creating an Agent Market Place. In: Proceedings of the Second International Conference on the Practical Application of Intelligent Agents and Multi-Agent Technology, PAAM'97, The Practical Application Company Ltd, Blackpool, 1997, pp. 159-178.

De RAEDT, L. Logical settings for concept learning. Artificial Intelligence, 95:187-201, 1997.

De RAEDT, L. , DZEROSKI, S. First order jk-clausal theories are PAC-learnable. Artificial Intelligence, 70:375-392, 1994.

Erikson, J. Finn, N., Market Space: an open agent-based market infrastructure. Master's Thesis, Computer Science Department, Uppsala University, Sweden, 1997.

Eugene, C. , Freuder and Richard J. Wallace. Suggestion Strategies for Constraint-Based Matchmaker Agents. In Principles and Practice of Constraint Programming - CP'98. Pisa, October, 1998. http://www.cs.unh.edu/ccc/papers1998.shtml.

GUTTMAN, R.H. , MAES, P. Agent-mediated Integrative Negotiation for Retail Electronic Commerce. Proceedings of the Workshop on Agent Mediated Electronic Trading (AMET'98), Minneapolis, Minneasota, April 9, 1998.

GUTTMAN, R.H. , MOUKAS, A.G. , MAES, P. Agent-mediated Electronic Commerce: A Survey. Knowledge Engineering Review, June 1998.

HILL, W. , STEAD, L. ROSENSTEIN, M. FURNAS, G. Recommending and Evaluating Choices in a Virtual Community of Use. Proceedings of the Conference on Human Factors in Computing Systems (CHI95), pp 194-201, Denver, CO, ACM Press, 1995.

HOFMANN, T. , PUZICHA, J. Latent Class Models for Collaborative Filtering. Proceedings of the Sixteenth International Joint Conference on Artificial Intelligence, Stockholm, Sweden, July 31- August 6, 1999.

JONKER, C.M., TREUR, J., Compositional Design and Maintenance of Broker Agents. Technical Report, Vrije Universiteit Amsterdam, Department of Mathematics and Computer Science, 1998.

JONKER, C.M., TREUR, J., Compositional verification of multi-agent systems: a formal analysis of pro-activeness and reactiveness. In: W.P. de Roever, H. Langmaack, A. Pnueli (eds.), Proceedings of the International Workshop on Compositionality, COMPOS'97, Springer Verlag, 1998.

KEENEY, R. , RAIFFA, H. Decisions with Multiple Objectives: Preferences and Value Trade-offs. Jhon Wiley and Sons, 1976.

KUOKKA, D., HARADA, L., On Using KQML for Matchmaking. In: V. Lesser (ed.), Proceedings of the First International Conference on Multi-Agent Systems, ICMAS'95, MIT Press, Cambridge, MA, 1995, pp. 239-245.

LANG, K. Learning to filter news. Proceedings of the twelfth International Conference on Machine Learning, Lake Tahoe, CA, 1995, (pp 331-339).

LANGLEY, P. Machine Learning for Adaptive User Interfaces. Proceedings of the 21st German Annual Conference on Artificial Intelligence (pp. 53-62). Freiburg, Germany: Springer, 1997.

LANGLEY, P. User Modeling in adaptive interfaces. Proceedings of the seventh International Conference on User Modeling, 1999.

LIEBERMAN, H. Letizia: An Agent that Assists Web Browsing. Proceedings of the 14th International Joint Conference on Artificial Intelligence (IJCAI'95). Montreal, Canada, 1995.

MARTIN, D., MORAN, D., OOHAMA, H., CHEYER, A., Information Brokering in an Agent Architecture. In: Proceedings of the Second International Conference on the Practical Application of Intelligent Agents and Multi-Agent Technology, PAAM'97, The Practical Application Company Ltd, Blackpool, 1997, pp. 467-486.

MUGGLETON, S. , PAGE, C.D. A learnability model for universal representations. In S. Wrobel, editor, Proceedings of the 4th International Workshop on Inductive Logic Programming, pages 139-160, Sankt Augustin, Germany, 1994. GMD.

OLIVEIRA, E. , FONSECA, J.M. , STEIGER-GARÇÃO, A. Multi-criteria negotiation on Multi-Agent Systems. The First International Workshop of Central and Eastern Europe on Multi-agent Systems (CEEMAS'99) International Conference , St. Petersburgh, June 1999.

PAZZANI, M. , BILLSUS, D. Learning and Revising User Profiles: The identification of interesting web sites. Machine Learning 27, pp 313-331, (1997).

Quinlan, J. R. , Programs for Machine Learning. Morgan Kaufmann, 1992.

Roberts, S. and Jacobs, N. and Van Laer, W. and Muggleton, S. and Broughton, J. A Comparision of ILP and Propositional Systems on Propositional Traffic Data. In: Proceedings of the 8th International Conference on Inductive Logic Programming, lecture notes on AI nr 1446, Springer verlag, 1998.

SANDHOLM, T., LESSER, V., Issues in Automated Negotiation and Electronic Commerce: Extending the Contract Network. In: V. Lesser (ed.), Proceedings of the First International Conference on Multi-Agent Systems, ICMAS'95, MIT Press, Cambridge, MA, 1995, pp. 328-335.

SHARADANAND, U. , MAES, P. Social Information Filtering: Algorithms for Automating "Word of Mouth". Proceedings of the CHI-95 conference, 1995.

TSVETOVATYY, M., GINI, M., Toward a Virtual Marketplace: Architectures and Strategies. In: Proceedings of the First International Conference on the Practical Application of Intelligent Agents and Multi-Agent Technology, PAAM'96, The Practical Application Company Ltd, Blackpool, 1996, pp. 597-613.

VINCKE, P. Multicriteria Decision-aid. John Wiley and Sons, 1992.

WOOLDRIDGE, M., JENNINGS, N.R., Agent theories, architectures, and languages: a survey. In: [38], pp. 1-39.
WOOLDRIDGE, M., JENNINGS, N.R. (eds.), Intelligent Agents, Proc. of the First International Workshop on Agent Theories, Architectures and Languages, ATAL'94, Lecture Notes in AI, vol. 890, Springer Verlag, 1995.

Amazon URL: http://www.amazon.com
AuctionBot URL:<http://auction.eecs.umich.edu>
BargainFinder URL:<http://bf.cstar.ac.com>
eBay URL:<http://www.ebay.com>
FireFly URL:<http://www.firefly.com>
Jango URL:<http://www.jango.com>
MarketMaker URL:<http://maker.media.mit.edu>
MovieFinder URL:<http://www.moviefinder.com>

Agent Technologies for the Development of Adaptive Web Stores

Liliana Ardissono, Anna Goy, Giovanna Petrone, Marino Segnan,
Luca Console, Leonardo Lesmo, Carla Simone, and Pietro Torasso

Dipartimento di Informatica, Università di Torino
Cso Svizzera 185; 10149 Torino; Italy
{liliana, goy, giovanna, marino, lconsole, lesmo, simone,
torasso}@di.unito.it

Abstract. With the increasing popularity of Web shopping, the personalization of the front-end of on-line stores has become a critical issue: these systems are accessed by customers with different backgrounds, expertise and preferences; therefore, their usability can only be improved by personalizing their interfaces to the needs of each specific user.
In this paper, we describe the architecture of SETA, a prototype toolkit for the creation of adaptive Web stores, where user modeling and flexible hypermedia techniques are exploited to personalize the interaction with the user, dynamically generating the catalog pages on the basis of the user's features. The SETA architecture is composed by different specialized agents, which cooperate to the management of the interaction with the user; we will discuss how the application of agent-based techniques has been essential to the design and development of this system.

1 Introduction

The research on electronic commerce has opened several scenarios where agent-based technologies can be exploited in the design of open systems having auction, negotiation and brokering capabilities. For instance, in the business-to-business area there is a lot of on-going work on the development of complex architectures for enabling an automatic management of the supply chain [16,33,37,45]. Moreover, in the business-to-customer area, agent-based technologies are exploited in the development of complex systems where agents search for products and services on behalf of a user, compare the solutions offered by different providers, and so forth [19,22].

In addition to the above issues, agent-based technologies can be successfully applied to the enhancement of other features of electronic commerce systems, among which the adaptability of the interfaces to the users' needs: the popularity of Web shopping is increasing and very different types of customers purchase goods by accessing on-line catalogs on their own, without relying on intermediaries. Noticeably, this trend does not only concern traditional domains like air-flight booking, or the market of movies and music, but also other domains, like the electronic power trade: in these domains, the user needs information

F. Dignum and C. Sierra (Eds.): Agent Mediated Elec. Commerce, LNAI 1991, pp. 194–213, 2001.
© Springer-Verlag Berlin Heidelberg 2001

about the alternative services offered by the providers, the advantages and disadvantages of the various options, their cost, in order to compare them and identify those satisfying her needs and constraints at best [44]. To comply with these requirements, several commercial tools for the creation of on-line stores, like Microsoft Merchant, IBM's Net Commerce and ATG's Dynamo, have been extended to offer more or less sophisticated personalization functionalities for tailoring the suggestion and the presentation of goods to the specific user. One major goal of these systems is to improve the interaction with the customer, in order to establish a long-term relationship with her, in contrast to the typical one-shot type of interaction supported by the first electronic commerce systems.

The customization of on-line stores is a complex activity and requires very different types of expertise, such as knowledge about users and products, and techniques to personalize the layout and content of the catalog pages; therefore, complex software architectures are needed. The exploitation of agent-based technologies can help to manage this complexity in an effective way. In particular, multiagent systems can be designed, where several agents offer specialized services, interacting with each other to produce the overall, complex service to the user (e.g., see [3,39]). In principle, the agents devoted to specific services can exploit very different technologies, so that heterogeneous multiagent architectures are designed.

The work described in the present paper concerns the development of adaptive Web stores, capable to assist the customer during the selection of goods, varying the interaction style and the suggestions of the system on the basis of the user's preferences and needs. In the last three years, we have developed a prototype toolkit for the creation of Web stores supporting personalized interactions with users [8]. We have focused on the design and development of the front-end of a Web store, concentrating on the management of a flexible interface, and we have pursued two main goals:

1. The definition of the requirements of an adaptive Web store, concerning the interaction with the customer and the management of the system's resources, and the design of a system architecture meeting such requirements. To this extent, we have designed the system architecture by identifying a set of main roles to be filled and by associating a specialized agent to each role. The first testbed of the architecture is a prototype system presenting telecommunication products [7].
2. The design of a toolkit for the development of new adaptive Web stores. In order to reach this goal, we have revised the system architecture and developed a second prototype, where knowledge representation techniques and agent-based technologies are exploited to improve the configurability of the system and its scalability [5,8].

Our current system, SETA, includes a customizable store shell and some configuration tools needed to help the store designer to set up a new Web store [5, 6,8]. An on-line demo of a Web store created using SETA is available at the following URL: http://www.di.unito.it/~ seta. This store presents telecommunication products, like phones, switchboards, and so forth, and will be used in the rest of the paper as a concrete example to describe the functionalities of SETA.

The paper is organized as follows: section 2 discusses the issue of personalizing interactions in Web stores. Section 3 introduces the main ideas on which our approach is based, while section 4 describes the SETA architecture, outlining the main roles identified in our Web store architecture and the agents filling them. Section 5 discusses the way how agent-based technologies have been useful in the design and development of SETA and section 6 provides some technical details about the system. At last, section 7 concludes the paper.

2   Personalization Issues

With the expansion of the Internet, not only business users, but also a huge number of home users are browsing the Web and accessing on-line stores. As discussed in [12], users differ with respect to many characteristics, such as their status, expertise, preferences and the reason for connecting to the Web store, which should be taken into account to enhance the usability of systems. Therefore, while the initial research on electronic sales mainly focused on back-end activities like the provision of efficient order processing and secure payment transactions, other aspects, concerning the personalization of the interaction with the customer, are now becoming important. For instance:

- Since an on-line store is accessed by heterogeneous users, it should satisfy different needs and preferences in the selection of goods; this ability requires filtering capabilities, to identify the items most suited to the specific customer (e.g., see [35]).
- The advertisements included in the catalog pages should be targeted to the customer base and, in particular, selected on the basis of the interests and life style of the specific user accessing the system (e.g., see [2]).
- Furthermore, since Web stores are hypermedia systems, they should meet the users' needs in what concerns the interaction style [28].
- Finally, in addition to the customers' interactional needs, also their technological constraints should be taken into account to facilitate their access to the stores. For instance, they should be allowed to select alternative media for the delivery of the information about goods, depending on the efficiency of their connections to the Web (e.g., see [21,25]).

The customization of a Web store involves many tasks: on the one hand, a detailed description of product features is essential to support a flexible selection of items suiting the customers' needs; on the other, the features characterizing the customers to which the store products are directed have to be identified, and an effective personalization can be reached if the peculiarities of the customer accessing the store are learned by observing her behavior.

By personalizing the interaction with the customer we mean that the relevant products should be selected for presentation and their description should be tailored to the user's expertise and interests, so that she can evaluate items more accurately than just looking at a raw product catalog. This aspect influences the selection of the information to be presented and its linguistic (or pictorial) form [14]; for instance, descriptions might use more or less technical terms and include images to improve their comprehension; the product descriptions should be focused on the features relevant to the users. Customers could even be helped by virtual sales assistants, who guide them in their browsing and product selection activity (e.g., see [24,32]).

In some works, very general techniques, like those exploited in the information filtering research (e.g., collaborative filtering, or TF/IDF - term frequency/inverted document frequency) have been used to select interesting items in environments where heterogeneous information sources are exploited, or little information is available about the user's needs; for instance, see [9,13,35].

While those techniques are suited to deal with large-scale applications, such as information retrieval on the Web, other works show that more specific techniques can be applied to personalize the interaction with the user in applications where the domain-specific information is at least partially structured. For example, [34] exploit the typical structure of movie databases in a VOD recommender system to analyze the user's selections and evaluations of the items. They use the collected information to learn which product attributes affect the user's choices, so that user modeling techniques [27] can be applied to customize the suggestion of other items. However, the lack of knowledge about the meaning of the attributes and the relations among them does not support the adoption of effective strategies for tailoring the description of products to the individual user, taking into account aspects such as her interests and domain expertise.

Other researchers have adopted sophisticated approaches based on the application of natural language generation techniques for the dynamic production of personalized descriptions in the catalog pages. For instance, [17] exploit the structure of the records describing the items of a museum to analyze their content and dynamically generate summaries of the descriptions; the summaries may focus on different concepts, depending on the user's interests. Although these approaches support highly personalized interactions, they are not easily applicable in system shells, which have to be instantiated on different domains: in fact, these approaches require the definition of very detailed domain ontologies, which impose a strong overhead at configuration time.

3 Our Approach

The description of the related work in the previous section supports the idea that a deep representation of the knowledge about products and customers is the basis for effectively personalizing the interaction with the customer. However, to face the trade-off between offering highly adaptive systems and constraining the effort in setting up these stores on the various sales domains, we have defined a relatively compact representation of the domain-specific knowledge, concerning users and products: this representation supports the exploitation of powerful

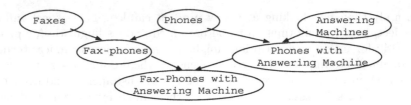

Fig. 1. Portion of the Product Taxonomy.

personalization strategies, without requiring that the store designer characterizes the semantics of each domain concept in too much detail.

3.1 Representation of the Knowledge about Products

As far as product classes are concerned, we superimpose on the products database (which stores the information about the individual items available in the store) a conceptual representation of the domain: the Product Taxonomy contains the definition of all the products of the Web store and of their relations. In this representation, the relations among products are explicitly declared: for instance, similar products are grouped together; moreover, several basic products can be related to the products which offer the same functionalities in a single, integrated solution. This representation supports the generation of a rational sequence of catalog pages, making the navigation of the catalog easier; in particular, the taxonomy graph represents the structure underlying the hypertext forming the Web catalog. Figure 1 shows a portion of the product taxonomy of our prototype.

The Product Taxonomy specifies the features characterizing the items of each product class. The product features are represented in a declarative way, as structured entities with the following attributes:

- *Type*: the features concern different aspects of the product description. Since a detailed specification of the semantics of each feature would require an extremely detailed definition of the domain knowledge, we have characterized features in an abstract way, by defining the following feature types:
  - *Functionalities* are basic facilities representing the purposes for which a product has been designed; e.g., phones support vocal communication, while faxes are designed to transmit documents.
  - *Technical features* concern technical details (e.g., the resolution of a fax).
  - *Functional features* include minor facilities offered by the product (e.g., the agendas offered by phones).
  - *Aesthetic features* concern aesthetic aspects, such as color and size.
  - *Generic features* include information not belonging to the previous types, such as the price.
- *Importance*: this slot specifies to which degree the feature represents a mandatory piece of information in the description of a product.
- *Domain*: this slot represents the range of values that a feature can take.

```
Record 1:
  Name: Facile;
  Code: I00025;
  Type: phones;
 Features:
  Price: LIT. 108000;
  Color: grey, black;
  Agenda: 20;
  ...
 Properties:
  Quality: high;
  Ease of use: high;
  Cheapness: medium;
  Design: high;
  ...
```

Fig. 2. Representation of an item.

3.2   Representation of Items

The Products DB stores the description of all the items available in the store. Each item is described by means of a record with attributes specifying the features and properties of the item: the features correspond to the set of features associated in the Product Taxnonmy to the product class to which the item belongs. Consider, for instance, the record of the "Facile" phone item, shown in Figure 2: the description includes the internal code and the external name of the item, and the product class of the item ("Type" field); moreover, it includes information about the features of the item (e.g., its price, color, etc.); finally, for each product property (e.g., quality, etc.), the record includes a value representing a qualitative evaluation of the item with respect the property.[1]

3.3   Representation of the Knowledge about Users

The knowledge about users is represented in a declarative way, by specifying the user features to be modeled and their possible values. A user model contains:

- Descriptive information about the user, concerning personal data, like the user's age, education level and job, provided by the user by filling a registration form.
- Predictive information, concerning the user's preferences for the properties of goods, like quality and ease of use, and user features such as her receptivity, domain expertise, and so forth. These data are represented by means of parameters characterized by an *Importance* slot and a list of <*Linguistic Value, Likelihood*> pairs [40]: the importance slot specifies how relevant is the property to the user and takes values in the range [0..1], where "0"

---

[1] While the description of the features is standard for a product database, the specification of the properties represents supplementary information that has to be embedded into the database by the store designer, after an evaluation of the product.

Identification:
    First Name: George;
    Family Name: Smith;
Personal data:
    Age: 55-64;
    Job: employee;
    Education Level: high_school;
    ...
User features:
    Receptivity:
        Values: low: 0.5; medium: 0.25; high: 0.25;
    Domain Expertise:
        Values: low: 0.5; medium: 0.3; high: 0.2;
    Technical Interest:
        Values: low: 0.1; medium: 0.5; high: 0.3;
    Aesthetic Interest:
        Values: low: 0.3; medium: 0.3; high: 0.4;
    ...
Preferences:
    Quality:
        Importance: 0.8;
        Values: low: 0; medium: 0.4; high: 0.6;
    Ease of Use:
        Importance: 1;
        Values: low: 0; medium: 0.25; high: 0.75;
    ...
User classification:
    life style:
        Values: yuppie: 0.2; average: 0.6; modest: 0.2;
    domain expertise:
        Values: ...

Fig. 3. An example user model.

denotes an irrelevant preference, while "1" denotes a maximally important one. Each <*Linguistic Value, Likelihood*> pair contains a linguistic value that the parameter can assume and the likelihood that the user prefers that value for the related product property. For instance, in Figure 3, George's preference towards the products quality is rather important (0.8) and he prefers high-quality products (<low, 0>, <medium, 0.4>, <high, 0.6>).

The data specified in the user models are domain-dependent and have to be defined for each Web store instance; however, the same data could be exploited in several Web stores, if the systems are instantiated on similar sales domains.

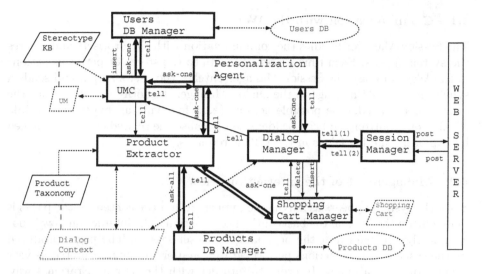

Fig. 4. The Web store architecture: rectangles denote agents; solid parallelograms denote knowledge bases; dashed parallelograms represent the session-dependent contextual information handled by the agents. Bold (thin) arrows represent synchronous (asynchronous) messages between agents.

4   The SETA Architecture

In the design of the architecture of our system, we identified a number of functionalities that an adaptive Web store should offer while interacting with a user; then, we isolated the activities necessary to obtain the desired system behavior. The result of this analysis is the identification of a set of basic roles: for instance, the maintenance of the user models containing the customers' preferences and needs, the application of personalization strategies to tailor the generation of the hypertextual pages and the personalization of the suggestion of items. The identified roles are necessary to offer a personalized navigation of a Web catalog, but are not exhaustive: depending on the requested system functionalities, the architecture might need to be further extended; for instance, we did not include the management of orders and payment transactions in the set of basic roles we have developed.

We designed a multiagent architecture where each agent fills a role [43], offering the other agents the services associated to the role. Our multiagent architecture is shown in Figure 4, where the boxes denote agents; the parallelograms represent the knowledge bases used by such agents to retrieve the domain-dependent knowledge (e.g., the description of user and product features); the databases are represented as dashed ovals. Each agent has its own context, denoted by a dashed rectangle, that keeps the session-dependent data: every agent maintains a single context for each active user session. The arrows among agents represent the types of messages they can exchange. In the following, we will describe the main roles and their associated agents.

4.1 Communication with the Web

The Session Manager handles the communication with the browsers and creates the system agents. Each time a user connects to the store (or performs actions in the Web catalog), the Session Manager catches the user's action and sends a synchronous "tell" message to the Dialog Manager, to notify the agent that the event has occurred. The possible actions (e.g., following an hypertextual link, clicking on a button, etc.) can be identified because the related events are tagged by exploiting hidden labels in the HTTP requests.

4.2 Management of the Interaction Flow

Since the system appears as a dynamic hypertext and the content of the pages is planned "on the fly", on the basis of the user's actions, the interaction flow is not completely determined at the beginning of a user session. The pages produced by the system and the actions performed by the user can be interpreted as very generic turns of a dialog. In order to interact with the user in a rational way, it is important to maintain the (logical) interaction context and decide how the dialog should continue, given its status and the user's previous actions.

In our architecture, this task is performed by the Dialog Manager, that handles the interactions and maintains the contextual information. The Dialog Manager monitors the user's actions, by interpreting the generic events caught by the Session Manager. These events are used to decide how to continue the dialog and to collect data about the user's interests.

From the system's viewpoint, each page represents a dialog turn. Thus, the admissible sequences of turn types can be represented by means of a finite-state automaton which specifies, for each page type, which user actions can be performed (such actions are available via buttons and hypertextual links in the displayed page) and which page type must follow each action type. For instance, from a page describing an item of a product class, the user may follow a "more information" link, in which case, the same type of page has to be displayed next.[2] However, she can also inspect the technical details, create a comparison table, and so forth; in these cases, a parallel page, showing the requested information, is handled by the system.

4.3 Management of the User Models

A basic role in an adaptive system is the management of the user models: the characteristics of the specific user have to be identified to apply the appropriate personalization rules and adapt the interaction as a consequence. In SETA, various types of user models can be used: e.g., static user models, instantiated on the basis of the user's features, or dynamic user models, continuously updated on the basis of the user's behavior [26,41].

---

[2] If the "more information" link is followed on a page, the page is redisplayed by the system, showing the whole list of features characterizing the item, instead of showing only the most relevant ones.

In the SETA architecture, a User Modeling Component (UMC) creates and maintains the models of customers. When a user accesses the store, her model is initialized either by retrieving her record from the User's DB, or by exploiting stereotypical information about customers available in the Stereotype Knowledge Base (KB). This KB contains a hierarchical taxonomy of stereotypes which cluster typical properties of customer groups [36]. The stereotypes are characterized by a classification part and a predictive part. The classification part concerns socio-demographic characteristics, corresponding to the personal data asked to the user when she first accesses the Web store. The predictive part concerns user features and preferences towards product properties. The user is classified by matching her personal data with the classification part of the stereotypes. Then, her features and preferences are initialized by merging the predictions of the best matching stereotypes [6].

In addition to the stereotypical information, dynamic user modeling techniques have been recently introduced in the system to update the user models on the basis of the users' behavior during the interaction. The UMC maintains in its working memory the history of all the relevant events delivered by the Dialog Manager. The events may regard clicks to hypertextual links and clicks on buttons to perform specific tasks (e.g., putting an item into the shopping cart). The UMC periodically analyzes the event history to refine the user model, so that it represents a description of the user consistent with her recent behavior.

In other approaches, such as [18,25,31], the user models are instantiated and updated on the sole basis of an unobtrusive observation of the customer's behavior. While we recognize that the minimization of questions is essential to improve the acceptability of the system, we believe that the exploitation of both implicit and explicit information is crucial to handle precise user models, which can hardly be obtained on the sole basis of the observation of the user's behavior. In particular, in our system the exploitation of the stereotypical information about customers is essential to initialize the user models and start a personalized interaction immediately after a customer accesses the store. Then, while she browses the catalog, dynamic user modeling techniques are exploited to revise her model on the basis of her individual behavior.

4.4   Generation of the Catalog Pages

Once the next interaction step is decided, the appropriate hypertextual page has to be dynamically generated. On the basis of the purpose of the system, the content displayed in the pages may strictly depend on the dialog context, or it may also vary on the basis of the user's interests; for instance, specific product features can be highlighted, or presented in a more or less technical way.

In our architecture, the Dialog Manager invokes the Personalization Agent, specifying the type of page to be produced and the product to be described. The Personalization Agent applies a set of customization rules and dynamically generates the HTML code for the hypertextual pages.

All the decisions about the layout and the content of a page are made on the basis of the user model, at the granularity level of the single product fea-

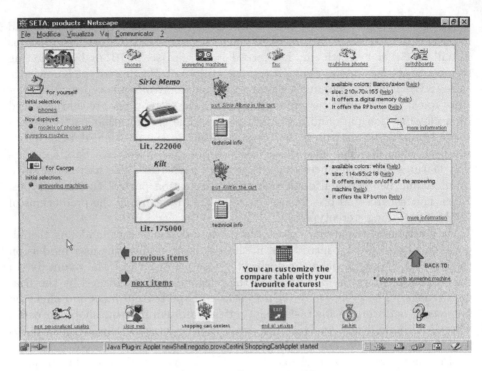

Fig. 5. A page dynamically generated by our system.

ture; moreover, the data to be included in the presentations are selected from the Products DB, which contains the whole information about the items. Thus, significantly different descriptions may be produced when presenting the same product to different users; furthermore, no additional (and redundant) information is needed to generate the product descriptions.

Figure 5 shows a page produced by the Personalization Agent of our prototype instantiated on the telecommunication domain. The page describes two phones with answering machine and contains both navigation buttons and presentation areas. More specifically:

- The upper bar in the page allows the user to inspect the main product classes described in the catalog: the bar can be used to select further products to be examined.
- The lefthand side area is a synthetic description of the interaction context: the products initially selected by the user for inspection are listed ("Initial selection"), specifying the intended beneficiary ("for yourself", "for George") and use (home vs. business, represented by means of icons). Moreover, for each selection, the last product displayed by the system is reported ("last visited", not shown in the figure), so that she can remember which hypertextual node she visited most recently in that context. Finally, the active context, associated to the product displayed in the main area of the page,

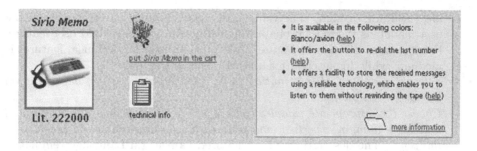

Fig. 6. A page dynamically generated by our system.

is highlighted ("Now displayed"). In this example, the user is looking for a phone with answering machine for her office (business use); she is also looking for a simple answering machine for her friend George (home use).

- The central area of the page describes the available models. For each of them, the area contains the name, a picture, the price, a button to put the item into the shopping cart, another one to get the technical details, and a description of the main features of the item itself: the system may display a subset of the features describing the item, to focus on those most interesting to the user.
- The rest of the page contains links and buttons available to perform actions like browsing the catalog, creating a personalized comparison table, inspecting the content of the shopping cart, and so forth.

The page shown in Figure 5 is tailored to an expert user, supposed to understand technical terms (like "digital memory", "RP button") and to be able to absorb relatively large amounts of information: for example, the system shows two items in a single page, instead of one. The description of item "Sirio Memo" in this page may be compared with that of Figure 6, representing the area describing the same item, extracted from a page generated for a non-expert user. As it can be noticed, the language used in Figure 6 is much simpler, the complex concepts are explained (e.g., consider "digital memory" vs. "It offer a facility to store the received messages..."), and fewer features are described to let the user focus on the most important ones.

The Personalization Agent plans the content and layout of a page by exploiting a set of personalization rules [6], used to:

- *Rate the relevance of the information items on the basis of the user's interests and of the intrinsic importance of the features to the presentation of the item.* There is a direct correspondence among the user's interests and the types of features defined in the Product Taxonomy. The features of an item are ranked by combining their importance with the user's interest in an additive formula: $score_F = w_1 * Imp_F + w_2 * Interest_T$
  where Imp_F is the importance of F and (given the category T of features to which F belongs) $Interest_T = 1(2, $ or $3)$ if the user's interest in T is

low (medium, or high). The value of the user's interest is retrieved from the user model, as the most probable linguistic value of the related user feature. For instance, referring to Figure 3, George's interest for technical features is medium, while his interest for aesthetic features is high.

- *Select the amount of information to be included in the page, depending on the user's receptivity.*
- *Choose the appropriate complexity level for the descriptions, on the basis of the user's domain expertise, and produce the descriptions to be included in the page.* The descriptions are structured as Natural Language templates, characterized by a difficulty level which basically depends on their technicality. For each feature to be described, the system extracts from the Products DB the values of the feature offered by the item and then it generates the complete linguistic description by filling in the place-holders of the template with the linguistic expressions of such values. For instance, the description of the "color" feature is generated by exploiting its template ("It is available in the following colors: #0") and replacing the place-holder ("#0") with the linguistic description of the colors offered by the item (e.g., "white").
- *Refine the layout of the features, choosing special sizes and styles (e.g., the boldface), depending on their ratings.*

4.5   Suggestion of Items

An important role in the architecture is the retrieval of the items to be suggested on the basis of the user's preferences. In our system, the Product Extractor assists the user's selection of items, interacting with the Products DB Manager to retrieve the internal description of the items which might be suggested. In order to let the user inspect all the items available for a product class, the system does not filter out any item: thus, the suggestion consists of sorting the items, so that the most promising ones are shown to the user before the others.

The Product Extractor ranks the items by evaluating how close their properties match the beneficiary's preferences [6]. An individual item is ranked by evaluating its properties one by one and combining the results of such evaluation into an overall score, used to place the item in the sorted suggestion list. The general requirement is that an item should be preferred if it matches all the preferences important to the user; in contrast, the item could mismatch irrelevant user preferences. The individual score of a property A is a number in $[0..1]$, where "0" denotes the fact that the item mismatches the related user preference, while "1" denotes a full match. This second value can occur in two main cases: either the preference is important to the user and the item matches it perfectly, or the preference is totally irrelevant and thus it should not be considered in the evaluation process. For each item property (A), we compute the individual score by applying a formula which combines the importance of the related user preference (Imp_A) with the likelihood associated in the user model to the linguistic value of A fitting the item (p_{a_i}):

$$sc_A = Imp_A * p_{a_i} + (1 - Imp_A).$$

Basically, we want that an irrelevant property receive scores near to "1", independent of how close it reflects the user's preferences: in this way, the influence of the property on the matching degree decreases proportionally to the importance of the user preference. In contrast, a score near to "1" should be given to a very influent property only when the likelihood that the user prefers products with that property value is very high.

The individual scores of the properties are then combined in a fuzzy AND: given two properties A and B, and their individual scores, sc_A and sc_B, the overall score for the item is calculated as follows:

$$SCORE(sc_A, sc_B) = sc_A * sc_B / (sc_A + sc_B - sc_A * sc_B).$$

This formula produces matching degrees in $[0,1]$: if at least one of the individual scores is null, the overall score is null (in fact, the related property is totally incompatible with the user's preferences); in contrast, an item perfectly matching the user's preferences has an overall score equal to "1".

4.6   Management of the Databases

A Web store architecture needs to store into a database the data about the specific items available in the store, as well as the information about its customers; the last information concerns the customer's previous connections to the store, purchases, preferences, and so forth. The data about customers enhance the system's capability to personalize the interactions, because they enable it to load precise user models at the beginning of the interaction.

In our architecture, we have designed two database managers (Products and Users DB Manager) that handle the Products and Users databases respectively. The Products database contains the information about the goods sold in the store (price, technical features, etc.), while the Users database contains the records of the customers who have accessed the store, including the goods that they purchased in previous visits.

4.7   Management of the Customer's Selections

A Shopping Cart Manager keeps track of the items selected by the user during an interaction: at any time, items can be put into the cart, or removed, and the cart always displays its content and the total amount of money to pay.

5   Comments

In addition to the roles described in the previous section, the architecture of a Web store should include other essential roles, such as the management of the orders and payment transactions, stocks, and so forth. We have omitted the roles concerning the management of the supply chain, and we have just sketched the one regarding the purchasing activity (see the Shopping Cart Manager). However, the design of the architecture as a multi-agent system supports the extension of this architecture to include such back-end activities as well.

Indeed, the exploitation of agent-based technologies has been very useful for the design of our architecture, as well as for the implementation of our Web store shell, for the following reasons:

- Components filling very different roles have to be coordinated within a single architecture and this fact may create serious organizational problems: these components may use heterogeneous knowledge sources and technologies; still, they have to cooperate with one another to offer the overall service to the user. For instance, the Session Manager handles the multi-user access to the store. This component operates in a strict event-driven way and works on low-level data which represent the events occurring in the active user sessions. On the other hand, other components carry on inferential processes; these components work on complex data structures and perform high-level reasoning tasks by applying different approaches, like for example the exploitation of production rules.
- Some of the roles fit well in a traditional Object-Oriented programming paradigm; however, others require that the components filling them are proactive and may initiate tasks although their methods are not explicitly invoked [30]. For example, the shopping cart might be monitored to check whether the customer's selections are consistent (for example, items such as a computer and a printer, which have to work together, must be compatible): in case of inconsistencies, the controller should autonomously trigger a dialog to warn the user about the problem. Although not all the components have to be represented as agents [42], the overall system architecture needs to exploit the technologies developed in the design of multiagent architectures.
- For efficiency purposes, the activity of the agents has to be performed in parallel whenever possible. Therefore, a sequential interaction model has difficulties in scaling up. On the other hand, agent-based technologies offer different types of communication, including synchronous and asynchronous messages, that enhance the parallelism in the execution of tasks.
- Although we have developed the architecture of a single marketplace, an interesting extension is the possibility provide broker agents with information about the items available in the Web store. This scenario raises interoperability issues, that can be faced thanks to the exploitation of agent communication languages and, at a lower level, of the facilities to interact in heterogeneous communication platforms (CORBA, RMI), offered by several tools to build multiagent systems.
- Although the integration of a new component into a complex system requires a careful design of its interaction with the rest of the system, the exploitation of agent-based technologies facilitates the task, by supporting the communication among the components in a seamless way.
- Other technical reasons have influenced our design decisions. For instance, the seamless distribution facilities offered by many agent-based technologies: in fact, given a complex system, the distribution of its components on several computers may be desirable and our experience showed that the exploitation of agent-based communication techniques and specific tools to build multiagent systems allows the developer to distribute agents easily and efficiently.

6   Technical Details

The system architecture, described in detail in [5], is a parallel architecture where synchronous, asynchronous and multicast messages can be exchanged and handled by the agents. The asynchronous messages are exploited to enhance the efficiency of the system: we selected the activities that could be carried on in parallel and we identified a number of messages that can be handled asynchronously by the agents. We described the messages as performatives in a speech-act based agent communication language. Figure 4 shows the types of messages exchanged by the agents during a working session: the thin arrows denote asynchronous messages, while the thick ones denote synchronous messages. Each arrow has associated the message type sent by the agent; we have labeled the message types with names derived from the KQML performatives [20].

We have implemented this architecture by exploiting Objectspace Voyager [29], a tool for developing multiagent systems which provides system components with basic agent capabilities, such as distribution and communication protocols. The agents of our system are Java objects which offer all the services necessary to carry on the personalized interactions with customers; moreover, we have exploited Voyager's facilities to allow the agents' distribution over different computers and their communication. While synchronous messages are handled by the main thread of an agent, the multithread environment supported by Voyager enables the agents to spawn in order to handle the asynchronous messages; in this way, they can also manage the active user contexts in parallel. In this way, we can handle in a homogeneous way an almost complete parallelization of the activity of the various agents within a user session, as well as different sessions.

The only exception is the Session Manager, which is implemented as a Servlet. Servlets are used to enhance the functionalities of Web-based systems, by extending Web server capabilities. In particular, we have exploited them to handle the communication with the browsers (catching users' actions and sending to the users' browsers the Web pages of the store) and to conveniently manage concurrent user sessions (by exploiting session tracking) in our Session Manager.

We have considered several tools for building multiagent systems in a Java-based environment: all these tools offer communication and distribution facilities, and introduce an abstraction level with respect to the communication protocol, which might be RMI, DCOM, CORBA, or other. We have selected Objectspace Voyager [29], which best suited the needs of our architecture, allowing a convenient object distribution: objects created by the Voyager compiler can be remotely executed. Moreover, Voyager supports an almost seamless transformation of a Java object, which can only exchange synchronous messages, into an agent able to send and receive various types of messages (noticeably, although different message synchronization types are supported, the Java method declaration does not change). Voyager offers synchronous, oneWay, oneWayMulticast and "future" messages ("future" messages correspond to asynchronous messages, which do not involve the sender and the receiver in a rendez-vous). Messages are exchanged among agents by method invocation; however, the object invoking a method has to specify in which way it wants to synchronize with the receiver. While synchronous communication corresponds to traditional Java method invocation, the other types of messages can be delivered by objects by invoking specific Voyager methods.

Other systems, like JAFMAS [15] and JATLite [1], would allow our agents to be distributed on a network and communicate in a standard agent communication language based on Speech Acts [38,20,30]. However, following KQML, they impose that the contents of the speech acts are represented, in an appropriate content language, as strings. Therefore, they make the exchange of messages containing structured information a complex task.[3] On the other hand, in the development of our system, we have experienced that a huge portion of the information which the agents need to send to each other is embedded into complex objects and a conversion of such data into very general String patterns would reduce the efficiency in agent communication.

Since we need flexibility in agent communication, we excluded other well known agent building tools, specifically focused on the management of agent mobility, which handle agent communication at a rather low level: e.g., MOLE [11], and IBM Aglets [23]. At the same time, other tools for building open multiagent systems, which also provided negotiation and coordination primitives to enable an active cooperation between the agents, proved to exceed our needs: for instance, the Agent Building Shell [10]. In fact, in our system, the agents offer fixed services, and there is no need to dynamically distribute tasks among them.

It should be noticed that the SETA architecture represents a quite well-established architecture for complex Web-based systems. In particular, the most recent research has triggered the development of other frameworks for the creation of these types of systems. For instance, the Jackal tool for the development of multiagent systems [4] supports a rich, KQML-based communication among agents; moreover, the Java 2 Enterprise Edition by Sun Microsystems provides the developer of a distributed, Web-based system with all the facilities for the management of parallel user sessions and also supports a transactional access to databases. Such frameworks were not available when we developed SETA; however, our approach is compatible with the one adopted by these tools; thus, the SETA system could be updated to exploit such environments, if needed.

7   Conclusions

In this paper, we have discussed the importance of the personalization of the interaction with customers in electronic commerce, specifically referring to the case of adaptivity in Web stores. In particular, we claim that these stores need to be adaptive and to tailor the description of the catalogs to the needs and capabilities of the specific customer. In fact, customers are heterogeneous and have different demands, ranging from the amount of information that they want

---

[3] Object serialization could be used to transmit messages containing object parameters, but a sensible effort is required to decode and parse the content of messages on the receiver's side.

to receive, to the content of the descriptions, that may be more or less compact, technical, or may focus on different product features, depending on the customer's interests.

In the paper, we have also discussed the importance of the exploitation of agent-based technologies in the design of adaptive Web stores: these stores requires the design of complex architectures, where differentiated roles can be identified. Agent-based technologies are very important to manage this complexity: in fact, they support the development of heterogeneous, possibly distributed systems; moreover, they offer powerful communication languages, that can be exploited to deliver different types of messages, such as synchronous and asynchronous messages. Finally, they support the interoperability with respect to the communication platform, therefore making the development of open systems an easier task.

Acknowledgments. This work has been developed in the project "Servizi Telematici Adattativi" (http://www.di.unito.it/~ seta), carried on at the Dipartimento di Informatica of the University of Torino within the national initiative "Cantieri Multimediali", sponsored by Telecom Italia.
Many thanks to R. Meo, C. Barbero and all the students who have contributed to the development of the SETA system.

References

1. JATLite. http://java.stanford.edu/java_agent/html.
2. AIMedia. @media, communicating on interactive media. http://www.aimedia.org, 1999.
3. M. Albers, C.M. Jonker, M. Karami, and J. Treur. An electronic market place: generic agent models, ontologies and knowledge. In *Proc. of the Agents'99 Workshop: "Agent-based decision-support for managing the Interned-enabled supply-chain"*, pages 71–80, Seattle, WA, 1999.
4. IBM alphaWorks. Jackal. http://jackal.cs.umbc.edu/, 1999.
5. L. Ardissono, C. Barbero, A. Goy, and G. Petrone. An agent architecture for personalized web stores. In *Proc. 3rd Int. Conf. on Autonomous Agents (Agents '99)*, pages 182–189, Seattle, WA, 1999.
6. L. Ardissono and A. Goy. Tailoring the interaction with users in electronic shops. In *Proc. 7th Int. Conf. on User Modeling*, pages 35–44, Banff, Canada, 1999.
7. L. Ardissono, A. Goy, R. Meo, and G. Petrone. An agent architecture for personalized interaction with customers in virtual stores. In *Proc. Int. IFIP/GI Working Conf. on Trends in Distributed Systems for Electronic Commerce (TrEC'98)*, pages 137–148. Dpunkt Verlag, Heidelberg, Germany, 1998.
8. L. Ardissono, A. Goy, R. Meo, G. Petrone, L. Console, L. Lesmo, C. Simone, and P. Torasso. A configurable system for the construction of adaptive virtual stores. *World Wide Web*, 2(3):143–159, 1999.
9. M. Balabanovič. Exploring versus exploiting when learning user models for text recommendation. *User Modeling and User-Adapted Interaction*, 8:71–102, 1998.
10. M. Barbuceanu and R. Teigen. Higher level integration by multi-agent architectures. In P. Bernus, editor, *Handbook of Information System Architectures*. Springer Verlag.

11. J. Baumann, F. Hohl, N. Radouniklis, K. Rothermel, and M. Straβer. Communication concepts for mobile agent systems. In *Proc. 1st Int. Work. on Mobile Agents (MA'97)*, 1997.

12. D. Benyon. Adaptive systems: a solution to usability problems. *User Modeling and User-Adapted Interaction*, 3:65–87, 1993.

13. D. Billsus and M. Pazzani. A personal news agent that talks, learns and explains. In *Proc. 3rd Int. Conf. on Autonomous Agents (Agents '99)*, pages 268–275, Seattle, WA, 1999.

14. P. Brusilovsky. Methods and techniques of adaptive hypermedia. *User Modeling and User-Adapted Interaction*, 6(2-3):87–129, 1996.

15. D. Chauhan. *JAFMAS: A Java-based Agent Framework for Multiagent Systems Development and Implementation.* PhD thesis, University of Cincinnati, Stanford, CA, 1997.

16. Y. Chen, Y. Peng, T. Finin, Y. Labrou, S. Cost, B. Chu, J. Yao', R. Sun, and B. Wilhelm. A negotiation-based multi-agent system for supply chain management. In *Proc. of the Agents'99 Workshop "Agent-Based Decision-Support for Managing the Internet-Enabled Supply-Chain")*, pages 15–20, Seattle, WA, 1999.

17. R. Dale, S.J. Green, M. Milosavljevic, and C. Paris. Dynamic document delivery: Generating natural language texts on demand. In *Proc. 9th Int. Conf. and Workshop on Database and Expert Systems Applications (DEXA'98)*, Vienna, 1998.

18. M. Dastani, N. Jacobs, C.M. Jonker, and J. Treur. Modelling user preferences and mediating agents in electronic commerce. In *Proc. of the Agent-Mediated Electronic Commerce (AMEC) SIG-Meeting of AGENTLINK*, Barcelona, 1999.

19. O. Etzioni. Moving up the information food chain: deploying doftbots on the World Wide Web. In *Proc. 14th Conf. AAAI*, pages 1322–1326, Portland, 1996.

20. T.W. Finin, Y. Labrou, and J. Mayfield. KQML as an agent communication language. In J. Bradshaw, editor, *Software Agents*. MIT Press, Cambridge, 1995.

21. J. Fink, A. Kobsa, and A. Nill. Adaptable and adaptive information for all users, including disabled and elderly people. *New review of Hypermedia and Multimedia*, 4:163–188, 1998.

22. A.R. Greenwald, , and J.O. Kephart. Shopbots and pricebots. In *Proc. 16th IJCAI*, pages 506–511, Stockholm, 1999.

23. IBM. Aglets. http://www.trl.ibm.co.jp/aglets/whitepaper.htm.

24. A. Jameson, R. Shäfer, J. Simons, and T. Weis. Adaptive provision of evaluation-oriented information: tasks and techniques. In *Proc. 14th IJCAI*, pages 1886–1893, Montreal, 1995.

25. T. Joerding. Intelligent multimedia presentations in the web: Fun without annoyance. In *Proc. of the 7th World Wide Web Conference (WWW7)*, Brisbane, Australia, 1998.

26. R. Kass and T. Finin. Modeling the user in natural language systems. *Computational Linguistics*, 14(3):5–22, 1988.

27. M.F. McTear. User modelling for adaptive computer systems: a survey of recent developments. *Artificial Intelligence Review*, 7:157–184, 1993.

28. M. Milosavljevic and J. Oberlander. Dynamic hypertext catalogues: Helping users to help themselves. In *Proc. the 9th ACM Conference on Hypertext and Hypermedia (HT'98)*, Pittsburgh, PA, 1998.

29. ObjectSpace. Voyager. http://www.objectspace.com/index.asp, 2000.

30. C.J. Petrie. Agent-based engineering, the web, and intelligence. *IEEE Expert*, December:24–29, 1996.

31. W. Pohl and A. Nick. Machine learning and knowledge representation in the LabouUr approach to user modeling. In *Proc. 7th Int. Conf. on User Modeling*, pages 179–188, Banff, Canada, 1999.

32. H. Popp and D. Lödel. Fuzzy techniques and user modeling in sales assistants. *User Modeling and User-Adapted Interaction*, 6:349–370, 1996.

33. A. Preece, K. Hui, and P. Grey. KRAFT: supporting virtual organizations through knowledge fusion. In *Proc. of the Agent-Mediated Electronic Commerce (AMEC) SIG-Meeting of AGENTLINK*, Barcelona, 1999.

34. B. Raskutti, A. Beitz, and B. Ward. A feature-based approach to recommending selections based on past preferences. *User Modeling and User-Adapted Interaction*, 7:179–218, 1997.

35. P. Resnick and H.R. Varian, editors. *Special Issue on Recommender Systems*, volume 40. Communications of the ACM, 1997.

36. E. Rich. Stereotypes and user modeling. In A. Kobsa and W. Wahlster, editors, *User Models in Dialog Systems*, pages 35–51. Springer Verlag, Berlin, 1989.

37. N.M. Sadeh, D.W. Hildum, D. Kienstad, and A. Tseng. MASCOT: an agent-based architecture for coordinated mixed-initiative supply chain planning and scheduling. In *Proc. of the Agents'99 Workshop: "Agent-based decision-support for managing the Interned-enabled supply-chain"*, pages 133–138, Seattle, WA, 1999.

38. D. Steiner. An overview of FIPA 97. http://drogo.cselt.stet.it/fipa/#Papers, 1997.

39. K.P. Sycara, A. Pannu, M. Williamson, and D. Zeng. Distributed intelligent agents. *IEEE Expert*, December:36–45, 1996.

40. P. Torasso and L. Console. *Diagnostic Problem Solving*. North Oxford Academic, 1989.

41. W. Wahlster and A. Kobsa. *User Models in Dialog Systems*. Springer Verlag, Berlin, 1989.

42. M.J. Wooldridge and N.R. Jennings. Pitfalls of agent-oriented development. In M. Wooldridge and N.R. Jennings, editors, *Proc 2nd Int. Conf. on Autonomous Agents (Agents98)*, pages 385–391. ACM Press, Minneapolis, 1998.

43. M.J. Wooldridge, N.R. Jennings, and D. Kinny. A methodology for Agent-Oriented analysis and design. In *Proc. 3rd Int. Conf. on Autonomous Agents (Agents '99)*, pages 69–76. Seattle, WA, 1999.

44. F. Ygge. Software agent for electronic power trade. In *Proc. of the Agent-Mediated Electronic Commerce (AMEC) SIG-Meeting of AGENTLINK*, Barcelona, 1999.

45. D.D. Zeng and K.P. Sycara. Agent-facilitated real-time flexible supply chain structuring. In *Proc. of the Agents'99 Workshop "Agent-Based Decision-Support for Managing the Internet-Enabled Supply-Chain")*, pages 21–28, Seattle, WA, 1999.

Constraint Satisfaction for Modelling Scalable Electronic Catalogs

Marc Torrens and Boi Faltings

Artificial Intelligence Laboratory (LIA)
Swiss Federal Institute of Technology (EPFL)
IN-Ecublens, CH-1015, Lausanne
Switzerland
torrens@lia.di.epfl.ch, faltings@lia.di.epfl.ch

Abstract. Many information systems are used in a problem solving context. Examples are travel planning systems, catalogs in electronic commerce, or agenda planning systems. They can be made more useful by integrating problem-solving capabilities into the information systems. This poses the challenge of *scalability*: when hundreds of users access a server at the same time, it is important to avoid excessive computational load.

We present the concept of *smart clients*: lightweight problem-solving agents based on constraint satisfaction which can carry out the computation- and communication-intensive tasks on the user's computer. We present an example of an air travel planning system based on this technology.

1 Intelligent Information Systems

The world today is full of information systems which make huge quantities of information available. A good example is the travel domain, where information systems accessible through the Internet provide information about schedules, fares and availability of almost any means of transport throughout the world.

The first generation of information systems provided simple database access facilities such as SQL which allow a user to access specific information. The current generation provides some intelligence for locating the right information, for example by searching for flights at a certain fare or with certain schedule constraints.

However, all information systems are ultimately used not to just provide information, but to *solve problems*. Thus, we believe that the next generation of intelligent information systems should provide explicit support for the problem-solving activities that a user carries out with them. For example, a travel information system should help the user plan an entire trip according to constraints and preferences, and not just give information about certain airline schedules.

One dimension of this new generation will be the integration of various information systems into a uniform framework using agents. Such integration is

F. Dignum and C. Sierra (Eds.): Agent Mediated Elec. Commerce, LNAI 1991, pp. 214–228, 2001.
© Springer-Verlag Berlin Heidelberg 2001

apparent for example in shopping robots such as Jango [Jan98], or in the integrated travel information system designed by Siemens as a demonstration within the FIPA [FIP98] consortium.

Another dimension will be to provide explicit problem-solving capabilities: help with configuring a complete solution, possibly consisting of many parts. For example, a travel planning system would *configure* an entire trip with matching outgoing and return flights, ground connections, etc. An insurance planner could configure a suitable insurance package from offers of different companies with different parameters. Such problem solvers will be essential to help people deal with the complexity of the information provided by the servers. The following section describes Constraint Satisfaction technology which is the key issue of our approach.

2   Java Constraint Library (JCL)

We implemented the Java Constraint Library (JCL), which allows us to package constraint satisfaction problems and their solvers in compact autonomous agents suitable for transmission on the Internet. We will first give a brief introduction to constraint satisfaction techniques and then describe JCL.

2.1   Constraint Satisfaction Problems

Constraint Satisfaction Problems (CSPs) are ubiquitous in applications like configuration [SM89,SF96], planning [Ste81], resource allocation [Cho94,SF89], scheduling [Fox87] and many others. A CSP is specified by a set of variables and constraints among them. A solution to a CSP is a set of value assignments to all variables such that all constraints are satisfied. There can be either many, 1 or no solutions to a given problem. The main advantages of constraint based programming are the following:

- It offers a general framework for stating many real world problems can be stated in a succinct and elegant way.
- A constraint based representation can be used to synthesize solutions of the problem as well as for verification purposes (i.e. showing that a solution satisfies all constraints).
- The nature of the representation allows a formal description of the problems as well as a declarative description of search heuristics.

A finite, discrete Constraint Satisfaction Problem (CSP) is defined by a tuple $P = (X, D, C)$ where $X = \{X_1, \ldots, X_n\}$ is a finite set of variables, each associated with a domain of discrete values $D = \{D_1, \ldots, D_n\}$, and a set of constraints $C = \{C_1, \ldots, C_l\}$. Each constraint C_i is expressed by a relation R_i on some subset of variables. This subset of variables is called the *connection* of the constraint and denoted by $con(C_i)$. The relation R_i over the connection of a constraint C_i is defined by $R_i \subseteq D_{i1} \times \ldots \times D_{ik}$ and denotes the tuples that satisfy C_i. The *arity* of a constraint C is the size of its connection.

A large body of techniques exists for efficiently solving CSPs. For more details see [Tsa93].

2.2 The Java Constraint Library (JCL)

We have implemented a library of common constraint satisfaction techniques in
the Java Constraint Library (JCL). It provides services for:

- creating and managing discrete CSPs
- applying preprocessing and search algorithms to CSPs

JCL can be used either in an applet[1] or in a stand-alone Java application. The
purpose of JCL is to provide a framework for easily building agents that solve
CSPs on the Web. JCL is divided into two parts: A basic constraint library
available on the Web and a constraint shell built on the top of this library,
allowing CSPs to be edited and solved. JCL allows the development of portable
applications and applets using the constraint mechanisms. It can be downloaded
from `http://liawww.epfl.ch/~torrens`.

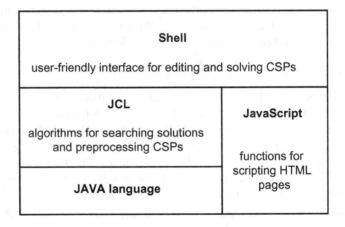

Fig. 1. The components of the JCL environment.

The library contains search and preprocessing algorithms. The search algorithms allow us to find the solutions of a CSP, while the preprocessing algorithms are used to simplify a CSP by eliminating values and compound labels
that do not affect its solutions. Several search algorithms are implemented in
JCL. There are three main algorithms derived from *Chronological Backtracking*
(BT) that are: *Backmarking* (BM), *Backjumping* (BJ) and *Forward Checking*
(FC) [KvB97]. Some combinations of them are implemented in CSPLib [vB95]
and adapted in JCL. Figure 2 shows a hierarchy of the algorithms in JCL.

The following two preprocessing algorithms are implemented in JCL: *Arc-
consistency* (AC) and *Path-consistency* (PC) [Mac77].

---

[1] An *applet* is an application designed to be transmitted over the Internet and executed
by a Java-compatible Web browser.

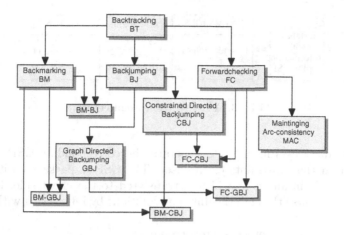

Fig. 2. A hierarchy of the search algorithms implemented in JCL.

3   Smart Clients

Another issue which has to be faced in information systems is *scalability*: the ability to support large numbers of simultaneous users. Client-server computing allows such scalability by distributing the computational load to the client computers. The concept of *thin clients* has extended client-server computing to much larger systems, in particular the Internet.

Traditional wisdom would say that in order to make a client intelligent, it will have to include a lot of complex code and data, i.e. be a very fat client. The point of this paper is to show that constraint satisfaction allows us to have smart (intelligent) clients that are also smart (thin), by marrying two characteristics:

- constraint satisfaction provides search algorithms which are both very simple and compact to implement, and at the same time very efficient.
- constraints allow representing complex information in a compact form.

As a result, smart clients are efficient autonomous problem-solvers which at the same time are small enough to be sent through a network in a short time.

Such problem-solvers are particularly useful for catalog-type systems, where user has to select from a range of possibilities: this set can be represented as a CSP (Constraint Satisfaction Problem) and solved by incremental constraint posting.

However one can imagine similar smart clients for designing and planning applications.

4   Architecture

The architecture supporting smart-agent methodology is shown in Fig. 3. The client sends a request containing the user constraints to the server. The server

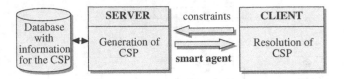

Fig. 3. A smart-agent architecture.

will access databases in order to generate the corresponding CSP taking into consideration the constraints of the user. The CSP is packaged with a search algorithm to form an agent which is transfered to the client side. In this way the user can browse through the different solutions by interacting with the agent locally.

We decompose the process into two parts:

– the information server compiles all relevant information from the database and the user constraints (query) into the corresponding CSP. The CSP is a compact representation of all solutions that the problem can have given the initial restrictions of the user.
– the server sends a smart agent consisting of the CSP and search algorithms to the client. This allows the user to browse through all the possible solutions. Since the agent executes on the client, response time can be very fast and the user can compare different alternatives without placing unnecessary load on the server.

Building the CSP requires only a small fraction of time compared to solving the CSP, so having the agent executed on the client significantly reduces server overload. After having generated the CSP there is no longer need of accessing the server, so the agent sent by the server is completely autonomous.

Note that this architecture is protected by a pending patent.

5   Representing Solution Spaces

Combinatorial problems can have an enormous number of solutions, arising through the combinations of variable values. For a problem with n variables of uniform domain size d, there can be up to d^n different solutions. A complete list would require nd^n units of storage.

If variables are completely independent, the space can be represented as a cross product of all their values. This would require only $n \cdot d$ units of storage.

However, in most cases the admissible combinations are restricted by constraints. In the worst case, a constraint can be stored as a list of all the admissible tuples. In such a case, a k-ary constraint can require up to d^k units of storage. In a network with n variables, there can be at most $n \cdot (n-1) \cdot (n-k+1) \le n^k$ such constraints, so in the worst case we require at most

$$(n \cdot d)^k$$

units of memory to store a network of degree k. If k is relatively small with respect to n, this is *exponentially better* than storing all admissible combinations. The price to pay, of course, is that solutions can only be accessed by solving the NP-complete problem of constraint satisfaction. We call a space of solutions described in this way a constraint space.

6   Example: Air Travel Planning

We are all faced with the problem of arranging trips. Typically, we have to meet with a set of people in different cities. Each of the people has certain days on which they are available for a meeting. Transportation schedules impose additional constraints.

In the current state of affairs, schedule information can only be obtained by queries to travel agents or Web servers for particular routes, dates and times. Thus finding the optimal plan would require separate queries for every part of every alternative itinerary. Since each query implies response times on the order of 1 minute, this makes travel planning very tedious. The prototypical business Air Travel Planning (ATP) system is a kind of personal assistant designed to facilitate arranging these kinds of trips using the concept of smart agents.

Consider the following example of a travel planning problem:

I live in Bern, Switzerland, and would like to visit colleagues in Princeton, New Jersey, and London. I would like to spend at least two days in each place, and will need to travel in the first two weeks of February.

Of course, I also have some preferences about airlines, departure times, transfer airports and so on, but these are too complicated to state in a first query.

Since I live in Bern, I can leave from any of three Swiss airports (Zurich, Basel, Geneva, abbreviated as ZRH, BSL, GVA). Also, for Princeton I can fly to two New York airports (JFK, EWR) or to Philadelphia (PHL), and there are three airports in London to consider (LGW, LHR, LCY). Finding the best plan for my trip involves checking all combinations of flights between these airports. Considering only direct flights (except flights from London to Philadelphia, where we consider one-stop flights because there are no direct flights), there are in fact more than 4 million solutions for this problem. An intelligent tool would be of great help to manipulate this large set.

There are two important questions about efficiency in this kind of information systems:

1. How many server accesses are required ?
2. How much information has to be sent from the server to the client ?

Let us analize these two questions in the traditional flight information systems and in our smart-agent based system. In table 1 we show the approximated answers to the example describe above.

Table 1. Conventional systems vs. Smart Agents

	Conventional	Smart agents
Server access	447039.6	1
Size of 1 transfer	$\approx 60\,Kb$	$\approx 180\,Kb$
Size of total transfers	$\approx 26.82\,Gb$	$\approx 180\,Kb$

Conventional approach. Let us consider planning such a trip using the systems currently available on the WWW. One type of system, most commonly offered by airlines themselves, allows simply to inspect flights or connections for one particular leg at a time. On a multi-leg trip such as this one, this would require the customer to carefully note down all solutions for the different legs and finally put together a solution by hand - not a very satisfactory way of planning such a trip.

Fortunately, tools such as Travelocity [Tra98] allow us to configure multi-leg trips. Complete itineraries are constructed on the server and returned to the customer for selection. In an example such as the one given above, we could in principle browse through all the 4 million possible solutions, evaluating each manually as to whether it satisfies our constraints. Considering that solutions are displayed in web pages with about 10 solutions at a time, this would involve an enormous number of transfers. Each web page sent back has about 60 Kbytes, so in total we need to transfer (and look at) about 24 Gbytes ($4 * 10^6/10 * 60$ Kbytes) of information to see the complete solution space.

However, a smart user can save some time by exploiting regularities of the domain, such as the fact that most flights operate daily and usually have space available. But this means precisely that the tool is not very intelligent: it still requires the customer to do most of the work.

Smart clients. Smart clients offer the possibility to support the customer's decision-making process with an intelligent scratchpad. In contract to conventional tools, it can keep track of all options and choices and avoid having to reload information which had already been requested earlier.

In this example, the smart client collects information about *all* flights which could be part of a solution in one single server access. Since the information is encoded as a CSP, it only needs to record the *sum* of the information for each possible flight, not all their combinations. In this example, there are 795 possible flights, each of which is encoded in a text line containing no more than 80 bytes. Thus, the entire CSP takes up no more than 63 Kbytes ($795 * 80 bytes$). Added to this the size of the JCL (100 Kbytes) and the graphical interface (20 Kbytes), the complete smart client is no longer than 183 Kbytes. Considering that the size of an average response page from a conventional server such as Travelocity is already 60 Kbytes, this is not a particularly large agent. It can be transmitted through the internet in less than 1 minute.

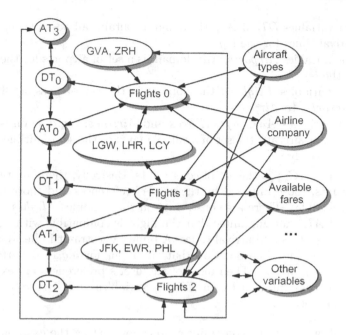

Fig. 4. The constraint graph representing all the possible solutions for the given example. Nodes represent variables and the edges are the constraints. The constraints guarantee that the user's preferences are taken into consideration and the flight schedules are satisfied.

Let us formalise the problem of arranging travel plans using a constraint-based formalism. We define an itinerary as a sequence of legs or segments between different destinations: $itinerary = \{leg_0, leg_1, \ldots, leg_n\}$. Then, the CSP encoding the travel planning problem with n legs is defined by a tuple $P = (X, D, C)$ where:

- $X = \{DT_0, \ldots, DT_n, AT_0, \ldots, AT_n, Airports_0, \ldots,$
  $Airports_n, Flights_0, \ldots, Flights_n, AirCrafts,$
  $Fares, Airlines, \ldots\}$ is a set of variables. There are several kind of variables:
  - DT_i and AT_i represent the dates and times where the traveller could depart and arrive respectively.
  - $Airports_i$ represents the possible airports near the destination of leg_i of the itinerary.
  - $Flights_i$ stands for the possible flights in between the destinations of leg_i and leg_{i+1}.
  - The problem can have more variables for encoding the user's preferences. For example, variable $AirCrafts$ is used for encoding the type of aircraft, variable $Fares$ for encoding the different types of fares, $Airlines$ for the different airline companies, etc...
- $D = \{D_1, \ldots, D_n\}$ is the set of domains. There are several kind of domains depending on the type of the associated variable:

- For variables DT_i or AT_i: the domain contains all possible departure and arrival times for the leg_i.
- For variables $Airports_i$: the domain is a set of airports for the departure of the leg_i.
- For variables $Flights_i$: the domain is the set of possible flights from $Airports_i$ to $Airports_{i+1}$.
- For variables $AirCrafts$, $Fares$ and $Airlines$: the domain is the set of different aircraft, the set of available fares or the set of airline companies respectively.

- $C = \{C_1, \ldots, C_k\}$ is the set of constraints. Basically, there are two kinds of constraints: those imposed by the user's preferences and those imposed by flight schedules. There are constraints on the variables $Flights_i$, $Airports_i$, DT_i and AT_i that guarantee that the flight is compatible with the airports, departures times and arrival times. A binary constraint in between AT_i and DT_{i+1} takes into consideration that the flight for leg_{i+1} departs after the flight for leg_i arrives. Then most of the user's preferences are expressed by means of constraints between $Flight_i$ variables and $Aircrafts$, $Airlines$, $Fares$ and others.

In Fig. 4, we show the constraint graph representing the example described above.

The CSP in the smart client implicitly contains all 4470396 possible solutions. Because it runs locally on the customer's computer, these combinations can be searched using advanced techniques without overloading the server even if there are hundreds of users using the system.

Once the customer has decided on a particular solution, the smart client generates a new request to the server, which can then initiate a booking process.

7   Browsing Solution Spaces

Very often, the initial constraints given by the customer define a very large space of possible solutions. For example, even if I want to travel on a particular day, there is often a bewildering number of possible flights and combinations of them that I could take. While it is possible to optimize for a single criterion, such as price or travel time, this might cause the user to miss solutions which would have been preferred: a small increase in price might be acceptable in return for an advantage in another criterion. Interactive *browsing* is necessary to find the right solutions in such a multi-criteria problem.

Formulating solution spaces using the CSP formalism offers interesting possibilities for this browsing process. In particular, users can narrow down their choices by *posting* additional constraints on the solutions they see. These constraints could be formulated on any attribute or combination of attributes of the solutions. For example, in an airline travel problem, it would be possible to formulate constraints such as "minimum layover time has to be 90 minutes" and filter flight combinations in this way. Since the constraint satisfaction algorithms are completely uniform, such additional constraints can be incorporated at any moment before searching again new solutions.

The smart client can thus implement approaches similar to that in [LHL97], where sample solutions are proposed to the customer and stimulate formulation of additional constraints to rule out undesirable features. However, with smart clients this mechanism can be much more efficient and faster, since it is not limited by the need to communicate with the central server.

When posted constraints become contradictory, techniques such as partial constraint satisfaction ([FW92]) can be used to help the user decide which constraints can be dropped to make the problem consistent again. In fact, within the constraint satisfaction framework there are numerous techniques for multi-criteria tradeoff which can be applied in this context. In our model, we associate a penalty to each tuple of the constraints according to the user's preferences. Then, it is possible to combine constraint satisfaction techniques and branch and bound algorithms to find out optimal solutions.

Figure 5 shows how the user inputs his initial constraints for the prototype we have developed for planning air travels on the web. Figure 6 shows how the user can post constraints on any attribute of the solutions in order to find the best solution according to his/her preferences. After solving the problem considering the new posted constraints, the user can see more solutions, post new constraints and solve the problem again. This process is repeated until a good enough solution is found. Figure 7 shows solutions that take into account earlier posted constraints (Fig. 6).

8   Future Work
Networked Information Systems

Often, problem solving requires information from many different servers. For example, in travel planning I do not only have to consider the air travel, but also:

- schedules of ground transportation to and from airports,
- the availability of people that I want to meet, and
- my own availability.

Travel planning requires finding a combination of meeting time, ground and air transportation that meets the constraints of the participants as well as the transportation means.

One can figure out that information about schedules and agendas is available through different agents accessible through a network. The planning problem could then be solved in the following steps:

- gather information about schedules and availability from each of the servers,
- construct the combined problem, and
- solve this combined problem in a single process.

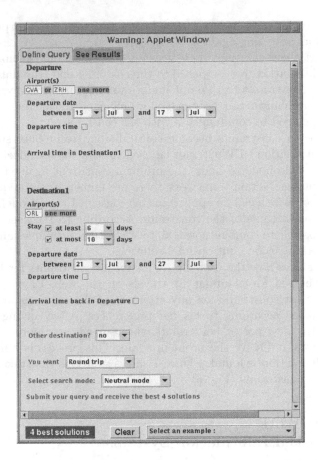

Fig. 5. In the Air Travel Planning prototype the user gives an initial specification according to his needs. In the example, the user wants to go from GVA or ZRH to Orlando. He wants to leave from 15th July to 17th July. He would like to stay in Orlando at least 6 days and at most 10 days.

Here again, the formulation of solutions spaces as CSP can be of great help. The planning agent can combine the CSPs obtained from different servers into a single CSP which represents the entire problem.

Consider the following example: Bill, living in Bern, Switzerland, has to arrange a 3-hour business meeting with John, who is located in Princeton, USA. Both have agenda agents which can be queried for time intervals when they are free, and the airline provides its schedules on a server. Bill can then leave the job of planning the entire trip to his agent. Figure 8 shows the CSP that this planning agent would have to construct and solve. Any solution to this CSP will be a consistent combination of times and flights.

To construct this complete CSP, the planning agent will have to obtain parts of its from different servers: Bill's agenda, the airline, and John's agenda. If

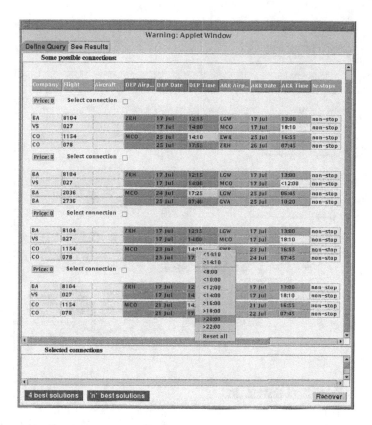

Fig. 6. Yellow cells indicate that there is a constraint in this attribute -in the example the user wants to arrive to Orlando (MCO) before 12:00. Pink cells indicate that the user is posting a constraint in the attribute -in the example, the user wants to leave from Orlando after 20:00.

each of them can provide its information as a CSP, it becomes easy for the planning agent to compose them into a single problem. It would also be possible to integrate other CSPs representing for example, ground transportation, hotels, etc. The solutions to the combined problem can then be generated and browsed using a smart client just as in the case of a single server. It would be extremely difficult and inefficient to provide such a service without the CSP formalism.

9   Conclusions

The modern world overwhelms people with massive information overload. We believe that Artificial Intelligence techniques have an important role to play in dealing with it. Up to now, much work has concentrated on techniques for retrieving or filtering information as such. We believe that the next step is to actively support the user in the problem-solving process. Only in this way can

Warning: Applet Window

Define Query | See Results

Some possible connections:

Company	Flight	Aircraft	DEP Airp...	DEP Date	DEP Time	ARR Airp...	ARR Date	ARR Time	Nr stops
Price: 0	Select connection								
AF	1543		GVA	17 Jul	09:00	CDG	17 Jul	10:05	non-stop
AF	002			17 Jul	11:00	JFK	17 Jul	08:45	non-stop
DL	1601		LGA	17 Jul	10:25	MCO	17 Jul	13:00	non-stop
VS	28		MCO	23 Jul	20:40	LGW	24 Jul	09:45	non-stop
BA	728		LHR	24 Jul	12:45	GVA	24 Jul	15:15	non-stop
Price: 0	Select connection								
BA	723		GVA	17 Jul	08:45	LHR	17 Jul	09:30	non-stop
BA	001			17 Jul	10:30	JFK	17 Jul	09:20	non-stop
US	259		LGA	17 Jul	11:00	MCO	17 Jul	13:39	non-stop
VS	28		MCO	23 Jul	20:40	LGW	24 Jul	09:45	non-stop
BA	728		LHR	24 Jul	12:45	GVA	24 Jul	15:15	non-stop
Price: 0	Select connection								
BA	709		ZRH	17 Jul	08:05	LHR	17 Jul	09:00	non-stop
BA	001			17 Jul	10:30	JFK	17 Jul	09:20	non-stop
US	259		LGA	17 Jul	11:00	MCO	17 Jul	13:39	non-stop
VS	28		MCO	23 Jul	20:40	LGW	24 Jul	09:45	non-stop
BA	728		LHR	24 Jul	12:45	GVA	24 Jul	15:15	non-stop
Price: 0	Select connection								
AF	1543		GVA	17 Jul	09:00	CDG	17 Jul	10:05	non-stop
AF	002			17 Jul	11:00	JFK	17 Jul	08:45	non-stop
US	259		LGA	17 Jul	11:00	MCO	17 Jul	13:39	non-stop
VS	28		MCO	23 Jul	20:40	LGW	24 Jul	09:45	non-stop
BA	728		LHR	24 Jul	12:45	GVA	24 Jul	15:15	non-stop

Selected connections

4 best solutions | 'n' best solutions | Recover

Fig. 7. Red cells indicate that a constraint in this attribute is unsatisfiable. Yellow cells indicate that there was a constraint posted in this attribute which is satisfied.

we achieve further substantial reductions in the complexity a user has to deal with.

Since most problem-solving is either compute- or knowledge-intensive, providing such functionality poses severe scalability problems. In an information system that has to serve thousands of users with small response times, the time that can be allotted to each individual user is very small. Smart clients offer a way out of this scalability problem by making available the computation capacity of each user, thus linearly scaling the available capacity with the total load. The work we presented shows that contrary to what one might assume, this paradigm is very manageable for real applications. We hope to encourage others to investigate such an architecture for other problems as well.

Another important aspect of our work is the use of the constraint satisfaction paradigm. It allows us to represent complex problems and their solution algorithms in a very compact way. While constraint satisfaction is extreme in its compactness and simplicity, declarative techniques used in AI are in general more compact than traditional software. In networked environments where size

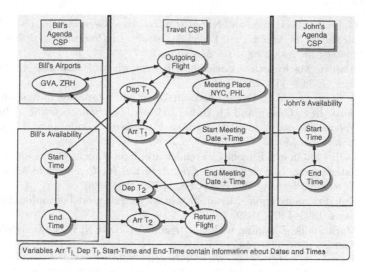

Fig. 8. A CSP for a complete travel planner combining information from several servers. Ovals are variables, the arcs are constraints. Note that Bill is living in Bern (Switzerland), so he can leave from both Geneva or Zürich airports. On the other side, Bill can arrive at New York or Philadelphia because both are equally convenient for reaching Princeton. The Travel CSP uses same formulation of the problem such as the one described in Fig. 4.

of applications becomes important, this is another interesting feature which can be exploited in many other applications.

Smart clients are a new way of applying constraint satisfaction techniques. Rather than focusing on efficient solvers, we exploit the possibilities of representing spaces of solutions as constraint satisfaction problems. This possibility is important for information systems, where problem solving is based on comparing or synthesizing large numbers of solutions from a set given by an information system server.

References

[Cho94] Berthe Y. Choueiry. *Abstraction Methods for Resource Allocation.* PhD thesis, Swiss Federal Institute of Technology in Lausanne, 1994.

[FIP98] FIPA. *Foundation of Intelligent Physical Agents. http://www.fipa.org,* 1998.

[Fox87] Mark Fox. *Constraint-Directed Search: A Case Study of Job-Shop Scheduling.* Morgan Kaufmann Publishers, Inc., Pitman, London, 1987.

[FW92] Eugene C. Freuder and Richard J. Wallace. Partial Constraint Satisfaction. *Artificial Intelligence,* 58(1):21–70, 1992.

[Jan98] Jango. *Excite Product Finder. http://www.jango.com,* 1998.

[KvB97] Grzegorz Kondrak and Peter van Beek. A Theoretical Evaluation of Selected Backtracking Algorithms. *Artificial Intelligence,* 89:365–387, 1997.

[LHL97]   G. Linden, S. Hanks, and N. Lesh. Interactive Assessment of User Preference Models: The Automated Travel Assistant. In *Proceedings of Sixth International Conference on User Modeling*, 1997.

[Mac77]   Alan K. Mackworth. Consistency in Networks of Relations. *Artificial Intelligence*, 8:99–118, 1977.

[SF89]   A. Sathi and M. S. Fox. Constraint-Directed Negotiation of Resource Allocations. In L. Gasser and M. Huhns, editors, *Distributed Artificial Intelligence Volume II*, pages 163–194. Pitman Publishing: London and Morgan Kaufmann: San Mateo, CA, 1989.

[SF96]   Daniel Sabin and Eugene C. Freuder. Configuration as Composite Constraint Satisfaction. In *Proceedings of the Artificial Intelligence and Manufacturing Research Planning Workshop*, pages 153–161, 1996.

[SM89]   Felix Freyman Sanjay Mittal. Towards a generic model of configuration tasks. pages 1395–1401, 1989.

[Ste81]   Mark Stefik. Planning with constraints (MOLGEN: Part 1). *Artificial Intelligence*, 16(2):111–140, 1981.

[Tra98]   Travelocity. *http://www.travelocity.com*, 1998.

[Tsa93]   Edward Tsang. *Foundations of Constraint Satisfaction*. Academic Press, London, UK, 1993.

[vB95]   Peter van Beek. *CSPLib : a CSP library written in C language.* ftp://ftp.cs.ualberta.ca/pub/vanbeek/software, 1995.

Encrypting Java Archives and Its Application to Mobile Agent Security

Volker Roth[1] and Vania Conan[2]

[1] Fraunhofer Institut für Graphische Datenverarbeitung
Rundeturmstraße 6, 64283 Darmstadt, Germany
vroth@igd.fhg.de
[2] Thomson-CSF Communications
66, Rue du Fossé Blanc
BP82, 92231 Gennevilliers Cedex, France
Vania.Conan@tcc.thomson-csf.com

Abstract. In this article we describe an extension of Java Archives that allows to keep data encrypted for multiple recipients. Encrypted data is accessible only by selected access groups. Java archives may be used as containers of mobile agents, which allows agents to keep confidential data unaccessible while residing on untrusted hosts. However, additional protective measures are required in order to prevent Cut & Paste attacks on mobile agents by malicious hosts. One such mechanism is described. The usefulness of the concepts is illustrated by an example application for user profile management in an electronic commerce setting.

Keywords: mobile agent security, Java Archives, encryption, malicious hosts

1 Motivation

Mobile agents [22] push the flexibility of distributed systems to their limits since not only computations are distributed dynamically, the code that performs them is also distributed. A number of mobile agent systems are in existence at present; basic information on about 60 such systems was collected[1] in the run-up to the ASA/MA'99 Conference that took place at the beginning of October in Palm Springs, FL, USA.

Adequate security has been identified numerous times by different researches as a top criterion for the acceptance of mobile agent technology. Despite advances in conceptual mobile agent security issues [20,21], few agent systems actually seem to offer security mechanisms beyond transport layer security. In mobile agent systems,

1. agents must be protected against malicious hosts,
2. hosts must be protected against malicious agents,

---

[1] See URL <http://www.informatik.uni-stuttgart.de/ ipvr/ vs/ projekte/ mole/ mal/ mal.html >

F. Dignum and C. Sierra (Eds.): Agent Mediated Elec. Commerce, LNAI 1991, pp. 229–239, 2001.
© Springer-Verlag Berlin Heidelberg 2001

3. agents must be protected against other agents,
4. both agents and hosts must be protected against the rest of the world.

The problem of malicious hosts is generally agreed to be the most challenging one of those noted above. A number of protection schemes have been devised to protect certain aspects of mobile agents against malicious hosts, yet most of them are very restricted or fail to be applicable in a general setting. In this article we describe another mechanism falling into the category "restricted but applicable".

Our philosophy is that good servers should help good agents to protect themselves against bad servers. In particular, mobile agent servers should offer some transparent security services to agents. This also has the advantage that bad servers can not make agents "forget" to take care of their security on their subsequent hops.

Once a mobile agent leaves the trusted haven of its owner's computer and hops off to another host, it is more or less on its own (unless it co-operates with other agents in protecting mutual security objectives [13]) and at the mercy of its hosting server. Even though an agent may compute certain functions in privacy while being on an untrusted host [17], the general rule holds: If data needs to be confidential then it must be encrypted and the encryption key must be unavailable even to the agent itself. Decryption, and hence disclosure of the encryption key, may be delayed until the very last moment [11] but ultimately the host may learn it when the data is being used.

However, if data of an agent need only be accessed on particular hosts then it may be encrypted in such a way that it is unavailable to other hosts when the agent passes by them. Contemporary agent systems occasionally advertise encryption of agents as a security feature but in general this means encryption of agents that are in transit between host systems (for instance using SSL). While this is the state-of-the-art protection mechanism against network-based eavesdroppers this does not prevent individual hosts from spying on agents at all. We are aware of only one mobile agent system which supports partial encryption of agent data for particular recipient servers. This agent system is called *Ajanta* [8,9].

Ajanta provides a number of mechanisms which are comparable to the ones we describe in this article. Agents can have a *read-only* state which is protected by means of digital signatures. A *targeted state* is used to reveal parts of the agent's state to selected recipients. However, Ajanta appears to be vulnerable to *cut & paste* attacks on the targeted state. This type of attack is described in Section 3.

In this article, we describe an addition to the Java Archive (JAR) Format that supports transparent selective encryption of archive contents for multiple recipients (Section 2). In Section 3, we describe the use of such JARs as containers for mobile agents (initial work on this subject is described in [14]), and show how *cut & paste attacks* on encrypted contents can be prevented.

2   Java Archive Extensions

The Java Archive (JAR) Format [18] devised by Sun Microsystems builds on the popular ZIP archive format. It supports multiple signatures and multiple signers on subsets of a JAR's contents. Multiple signatures are computed and verified efficiently through a two-stage process that avoids re-hashing of JAR contents for each signature. JARs are frequently used to distribute Java class packages, Applets and Java Beans. The original JAR Format devised by Sun does not provide mechanisms for encrypting parts of the archive; only digital signatures are covered. In this section we describe an extension to the Java Archive Structure that allows to keep partial archive data encrypted for multiple recipients.

The extension consists of an additional meta–folder with the name *SEAL-INF*. This folder stores the additional files required for:

- meta-information for the management of encryption and decryption (one file with the name *INSTALL.MF*).
- encrypted archives, identified by the extension *EAR*.
- data structures containing the encrypted data encrypted keys, identified by the extension *P7*.

The encryption mechanism used for encrypting EARs is a hybrid one. An encryption key is chosen randomly for a suitable symmetric bulk encryption cipher such as DE-Sede/CBC/PKCS5Padding [5,6,16]. This key is used to encrypt the compressed plain text. For each recipient, this *bulk encryption key* (BEK) is encrypted in the recipient's public key using an asymmetric cipher such as RSA [12]. This process is also called *sealing*, hence the name SEAL-INF for the meta-information folder. The sealing information and EARs are not located in the META-INF folder such that this information may itself be signed through the ordinary signing process defined in the JAR format. This is crucial for the application of Java Archives as containers of mobile agents as described in Section 3.

We chose PKCS#7 [15] as the standard for representing the encrypted BEK and recipient information. This blends well with the Java Archive Format, which mandates the use of PKCS#7 for DSA and MD5/RSA signatures. In choosing PKCS#7, we implicitly adopted X.509 [7] as the certificate format, which is the de-facto standard for the representation of certificates in the World Wide Web.

On creating a JAR, the user defines *access groups*, and assigns a name to each group. Each access group G with name $name_G$ consists of a set of valid recipients $r_1, \ldots, r_n$ and a randomly generated symmetric BEK k_G. Recipients are represented by their valid public key certificates. For each access group G, a PKCS#7 *EnvelopedData* structure is created, wrapped into a PKCS#7 *ContentInfo*, and stored in folder **SEAL-INF** under the name $name_G$.**P7**. This file contains a *RecipientInfo* for each intended recipient, holding k_G encrypted in the recipient's public key.

The user then may assign folders in the JAR to access groups. Each folder may be assigned to at most one such group. For each folder V that is assigned to an access group

G, a corresponding entry is stored in the INSTALL.MF file, which is stored in the SEAL-INF folder of the JAR. This file is similar to MANIFEST.MF files in that it contains sections of name/value pairs formatted like header fields in RFC822 [4] messages. Each section is separated from its successor by an empty line. Each section contains the entries described below, quotation marks denote literal strings:

Name	Value
"Name"	V
"EAR"	$name_V$
"Group"	$name_G$

The unique EAR name $name_V$ is generated by the sealing software. The encryption process takes each folder V that is assigned to an access group G, compresses its contents recursively into a ZIP archive, and encrypts it with k_G. The resulting file is stored in the SEAL-INF folder under the name $name_V$.EAR. The plain text folder V is then deleted.

The decryption process first tries to recover as many bulk encryption keys as possible by verifying the RecipientInfos in the P7 files against the public key certificates corresponding to the available private decryption keys. Each RecipientInfo contains the unique issuer name and serial number of the certificate [7] that was used to create that entry. This establishes the groups to which the processing entity belongs. For each folder that is assigned to such groups, the corresponding EAR is decrypted with the recovered BEK, and its contents are decompressed to folder V.

3   Encrypted JARs and Mobile Agents

A number of agent systems represent agents simply as a stream of serialised objects that encapsulate virtually all the information in the agent, including any data the agent may have collected on previous hops. Classes are either downloaded on demand or the serialised stream is annotated with the byte code. Often, RMI is used as means of transporting the agent from one hop to the next. While this bears advantages such as simplicity and elegance, it puts strains on security mechanisms. Since data and object state is cluttered throughout the serialised stream and many alternative orderings exist for a serialised object graph, it is hard to apply e.g. digital signatures to portions of an agent's data transparently for an agent.

Moreover, it is complicated to infer any information from the agent's representation before the agent is actually deserialised. This is unfortunate because during deserialisation the agent's classes are installed and the agent may seize control over the deserialisation thread by implementing the readObject and writeObject methods described in the documentation of class *ObjectInputStream*.

On the other hand, the JAR Format already offers well-defined processes for the signing and signature verification of archive contents. An agent's JAR may be loaded in its entirety and verified and/or processed in a number of ways transparent to the agent even

Table 1. The extended structure of a JAR used as a container for mobile agents

META-INF/ MANIFEST.MF
alias.SF
alias.(DSA|RSA|PGP)
SEAL-INF/ INSTALL.MF
name$_V$.EAR
name$_G$.P7
static/ agent.properties
mutable/ instance.ser
classes

before the agent is run. The basic layout that we use for such JARs is shown in Table 1. Once an agent is admitted to the system, its JAR is decompressed and installed in a file system folder that is reserved for that particular agent. The location of this folder is passed to the mobile agent. The Agent is granted access to this folder and can use it as storage space for data that it acquires. We encourage agent programmers to use this feature because this reduces the amount of data that is occupied by agents in the memory of the server's VM. Moreover, it is persistent storage that is not lost in case of a server crash. On migration, the agent's folder is compressed into a JAR again.

However, the mechanisms described in Section 2 do not yet suffice to assure the protection of the encrypted data. Malicious hosts and other attackers that get a copy of the agent JAR may launch a *cut & paste attack*. The following example illustrates the attack:

1. Alice prepares a search agent. The agent collects stock quotes from Bob's server and the server of Mallet, but Alice does not want Mallet to know which quotes her agent collected from Bob. So she creates an access group G with Bob as its sole recipient and assigns the folder **secret** to this group. The agent is programmed to store the quotes in that folder if it is at Bob's server.
2. Alice sends her agent to Bob. Bob decrypts and installs the folder **secret** because he is a legal recipient. The agent collects the stock quotes and sets its next hop to the server of Mallet. Bob re-encrypts the folder and sends the agent to Mallet.
3. Mallet copies the INSTALL.MF, $name_G$.P7 and $name_V$.EAR files from the agent to an agent of its own and sends it to Bob.
4. Bob decrypts and installs the folder **secret** in Mallet's agent because he is a valid recipient. The agent then copies the plain text data to another folder and sets its next hop to Mallet. Bob re-encrypts folder **secret** and sends the agent back to Mallet.
5. Mallet reads the plain text returned by his agent.

The attack is successful because the encrypted archives are not linked to the agent instance and Alice. Signing the encrypted archive is of no help since the signature may simply be stripped away by Mallet. One way to forge such a link is to request a non-interactive proof of knowledge of k_G from the entity that claims to be the rightful owner of the agent. In addition to this, the agent must have a unique static kernel that can be signed by its owner as proof of ownership and authorisation. The information in the kernel must be sufficient in order to assure that the agent can be bootstrapped securely, e. g. by starting only a class that the agent's owner trusts to keep confidential information in the appropriate folders. Below, we describe an approach to create a safe link.

Let $cert_A$ be the certificate of the signing key of Alice. Let MAC be a suitable *Message Authentication Code* (see [10], Section 9.5). Alice adds one additional section with the reserved name "GROUPS" to the INSTALL.MF file of the agent. For each defined access group G_i she puts an entry into this section as shown below; quotation marks denote literal strings:

Name	Value
"Name"	"GROUPS"
$name_{G_1}$	$MAC(k_{G_1}, cert_A)$
$name_{G_2}$	$MAC(k_{G_2}, cert_A)$
$\ldots$	

Alice signs the static parts of her agent including the agent properties, the file IN-STALL.MF, and the agent's classes with her secret signing key. The properties contain the agent's unique name, the name of its main class, and any other properties Alice wants to define in a way that cannot be tampered with without breaking the signature and hence Alice's assertion of ownership of her agent. Bob verifies the validity of access groups in Alice's agent as described in Algorithm 1.

Algorithm 1 The algorithm for verifying access group validity.

1: { Let $cert_B$ be the certificate of Bob's decryption key. }
2: { Let $cert_A$ be the certificate of Alice's signing key. }
3: **for all** $name_G$ **do**
4:     Bob loads the EnvelopedData structure SEAL-INF/$name_G$.P7;
5:     **if** it contains a RecipientInfo matching $cert_B$ **then**
6:         Bob recovers k_G with the private key corresponding to $cert_B$;
7:         Bob computes $MAC(k_G, cert_A)$;
8:         Bob compares the result with the value of attribute $name_G$ in section GROUPS;
9:         **if** both are equal **then**
10:             accept G;
11:         **else**
12:             reject G;
13:         **end if**
14:     **end if**
15: **end for**

Subsequent to this test, Bob iterates through the sections in file INSTALL.MF; for each folder V that is assigned to an accepted access group G Bob decrypts the appropriate $name_V$.EAR and installs it in folder V of the agent.

4   Security

The technical security of the encrypted data in the agent is based on the security of the weakest link in the chain of cryptographic primitives consisting of a symmetric cipher, the signature scheme, the weakest asymmetric encryption used within a RecipientInfo, and the MAC algorithm.

The MAC is crucial for the prevention of cut & paste attacks. In order to launch a successful attack, Mallet has the following choices. He may:

- Convince Bob that he produced the EAR by forging a MAC with his own certificate as the input and without knowing k_G (otherwise Mallet may simply decrypt the cipher text).
- Impersonate Alice, which requires forging Alice's signature on the kernel of an agent of his own.
- Modify the state of Alice's agent such that it leaks the plain text data. Copying the P7 and EAR files to a different agent of Alice won't work because the INSTALL.MF file is covered by Alice's signature.

Even if Mallet convinces a certificate authority Bob trusts to issue a certificate with Alice's identity and Mallet's public key, this will be detected by Bob, because the MAC is computed by Alice on her original certificate, which includes her public key and which is used to verify her signature on her agent's kernel.

Mallet cannot substitute a class of his own as the principal agent class because the class and its name is covered by Alice's signature. However, he may modify the serialised instances of Alice's agent such that a Trojan horse class is called by it, which leaks the plain text data. Therefore, it is of utmost importance that access to the agent's folder is granted only to classes that are authorised by Alice, using the Java 2 AccessController mechanisms and the digests stored in the Manifest file of the JAR.

5   Transparent Implementation

We integrated a reference implementation of the mechanisms described in Sections 2 and 3 into our experimental mobile agent server SeMoA. Transport of agents in SeMoA is handled by two principal services: the so-called *ingate* and *outgate*. Both make use of other services that may be registered in the server dynamically and at boot time. Services are grouped according to functionality and level of confidentiality on a number of configurable *service levels*. On such level is the *transport level* on which services are registered that have to do with transporting agents. A second level is the *security level* on which services are registered that provide security services. The ingate and outgate scan the security level for particular classes of services implementing *filters* for incoming and outgoing agents. They arrange such filters in a pipeline that must be passed by each agent before it is admitted to the server and before it is sent to its next hop. This is illustrated in Figure 1.

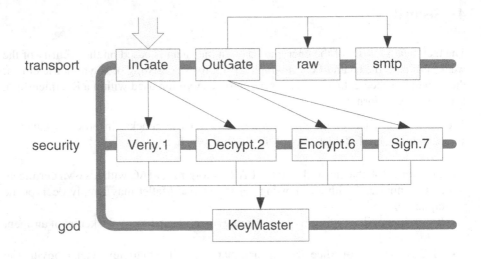

Fig. 1. An excerpt of the service levels in the experimental SeMoA server.

We implemented four security filters, two for incoming agents and two for outgoing agents:

Verify filter: This filter expects and verifies two signatures per agent. The first signature covers the static part of the agent, the signer is assumed to be its owner. The second signature covers the entire agent, the signer is assumed to be the last sender of the agent. The valid certificate chain of the signer's certificate must end in a trusted CA certificate.

Decrypt filter: This filter implements the decryption mechanisms described in Sections 2 and 3, including the verification of the access groups as set forth in Algorithm 1.

Encrypt filter: This filter re-encrypts the agent's contents according to the scheme described in Sections 2 and 3, and deletes the plain text folders.

Sign filter: This filter binds the new execution state of the agent to its kernel by signing the complete agent with the server's secret signing key.

Each server has two key pairs, one for signing and another one for encryption and decryption. The agent passes the incoming filter pipeline before it is started. On execution of the agent, the accessible data is already installed in the agent's folder. Apart from setting up the access groups and assigning the appropriate folders, the agent creator is not bothered with the encryption and decryption anymore. This is handled transparently by the server on behalf of the agent.

6   Application Example: Profile Protection

Privacy protection is an important feature for agent applications [3]. Mobile agents which carry personal information are able to carry out personalised tasks on their owner's behalf. The richer the profile information, the more personalised the agent's response. Securing the profile data is thus a means to insure privacy protection.

Privacy protection is guaranteed in the European Union by national laws, and national data protection organisations. All national regulations implement the same European privacy protection principles, as expressed in EU directive 95/46 [1], which is a legally binding document since October 1998. The directive proposes a formal framework for privacy protection, which is not available for instance in the USA. The directive considers personal data as information on which the data subject has a number of rights such as right of access to the data, opt out opportunity and protection on international data flow. A detailed list is given in the directive.

For instance if a netizen (the data subject) provides his name and address (personal data) to the web site of a software vendor (the data controller), he automatically reserves said rights on this data, and the data controller implicitly agrees to adhere to these rights. In addition, the data controller has a number of obligations. Only legitimate data may be collected and the collected data must be adequate to the purpose for which it is collected.

Apart from legal issues involved in processing personal data, technical means must be provided to facilitate the management and control of such data in particular for the data subject. The W3C put forward a proposal named *Platform for Privacy Preferences* [2] (P3P) that aims at providing a protocol for reaching agreements between a Web user and a Web site on the exchange and use of personal data. P3P is reaching its final state in early 2000. Prototypes of P3P compliant servers and client applications are available, and are now ready for a widespread dissemination of the standard.

P3P consists of a negotiation and data exchange phase. The protocol is designed for a client server system. At first sight, mobile agents may not profit from a standard such as P3P since negotiating personal information while being disconnected from a trusted computing base is extremely risky in the face of a potentially malicious host.

However mobile agents can benefit from the on-line P3P negotiation phase. The agreement reached by the two parties, the data subject (netizen) and the data controller (retailer), is valid on a number of profile elements over a given period of time. An agreement id is stored on the netizen's side with the corresponding time stamp. Agreements with regular retailers may last up to six months or one year. Mobile agents can then carry the relevant agreement id and the corresponding profile elements using selective encryption as presented above. Only the authorised retailers will thus be allowed access to the information.

We are implementing this scheme for personalised product brokering mobile agents. Upon visiting the retailer's sites, answers to mobile agents are personalised, taking into account both the specific request and profile information.

7   Conclusions

In this article, we presented an extension of the JAR format that allows to encrypt contents in a JAR for multiple recipients, and its application to mobile agents. Using extended JARs as containers for mobile agents requires additional security precautions in order to detect and prevent cut & paste attacks on the encrypted contents. We presented an approach to solving this problem. In conjunction with the signing scheme we devised, we are now able to support a number of access rights to portions of an agent. Folders in the agent's structure may have one of the following access rights:

Read–only: This data can be read on each host but cannot be modified without breaking the agent's verifiable integrity.

Read/write committed: This data can be read and modified on each host but hosts have to commit to the new state. The changes can be (in principle) be checked and linked to that host on the agent's next hop.

Group read: This data can be read only on a predetermined set of authorised hosts. Modification of the data breaks the agent's verifiable integrity.

Group read/write: This data can be read and modified only on a predetermined set of authorised hosts.

Groups may be defined flexibly. The selective encryption scheme that we presented is highly useful to protect data a mobile agent gathers. Hosts not belonging to the access group of a given folder cannot eavesdrop on data in such folders. We realised a reference implementation of the encryption, decryption, signing, and verification steps including cut & paste detection and prevention; these operations are transparent for mobile agents. Hence, agents can remain completely unaware of the security operations performed on them as these operations are part of the agent server's security services.

For illustration, we described an application scenario that makes use of the selective encryption scheme for protecting personal information within mobile agents such that this information is made available only to the intended recipients.

References

1. Directive 95/46/EC of the European Parliament and of the Council of 24 october 1995 on the protection of individuals with regard to the processing of personal data and on the free movement of such data. published in OJEC, November 1995.
2. Platform for Privacy Preferences (P3P) Specification. Available from URL <HTTP://www.w3.org/ TR/ 1999/ WD-P3P-19990826/>, August 1999.
3. CONAN, V., FOSS, M., LENDA, P., LOUVEAUX, S., AND SALAYN, A. Legal issues for personalised agent mediated electronic commerce: The aimedia case study. In *Agent Mediated Electronic Commerce*, C. Sierra, Ed. Springer Verlag, Berlin, 2000. Issued for review, book is to appear.
4. CROCKER, D. RFC 822: Standard for the format of ARPA Internet text messages, Aug. 1982. See also STD0011. Obsoletes RFC0733. Updated by RFC1123, RFC1138, RFC1148, RFC1327, RFC2156. Status: STANDARD.

5. FIPS46. Data Encryption Standard. Federal Information Processing Standards Publication 46, U.S. Department of Commerce/National Bureau of Standards, National Technical Information Service, Springfield, Virginia, 1977. revised as FIPS 46-1:1988; FIPS 46-2:1993.

6. INTERNATIONAL ORGANIZATION FOR STANDARDIZATION. *Information Processing – Modes of Operation for an n–Bit Block Cipher Algorithm*. Geneva, Switzerland, 1991. ISO/IEC 10116.

7. INTERNATIONAL ORGANIZATION FOR STANDARDIZATION. *Information technology – Open Systems Interconnection – The Directory: Authentication Framework*. Geneva, Switzerland, nov 1993. ISO/IEC 9594-8, equivalent to ITU-T Rec. X.509, 1993.

8. KARNIK, N. M., AND TRIPATHI, A. R. Agent server architecture for the Ajanta mobile-agent system. In *Proceedings of the 1998 International Conference on Parallel and Distributed Processing Techniques and Applications (PDPTA '98)* (Las Vegas, July 1998).

9. KARNIK, N. M., AND TRIPATHI, A. R. Security in the Ajanta mobile agent system. Technical Report TR-5-99, University of Minnesota, Minneapolis, MN 55455, U. S. A., May 1999.

10. MENEZES, A. J., VAN OORSCHOT, P. C., AND VANSTONE, S. A. *Handbook of Applied Cryptography*. Discrete Mathematics and its Applications. CRC Press, New York, 1996. ISBN 0-8493-8523-7.

11. RIORDAN, J., AND SCHNEIER, B. Environmental key generation towards clueless agents. In Vigna [20], pp. 15–24.

12. RIVEST, R. L., SHAMIR, A., AND ADLEMAN, L. M. A method for obtaining digital signatures and publi–key cryptosystems. *Communications of the ACM 21* (1978), 120–126.

13. ROTH, V. Mutual protection of co-operating agents. In *Secure Internet Programming* [21].

14. ROTH,V., AND JALALI, M. Access control and key management for mobile agents. *Computers & Graphics, Special Issue on Data Security in Image Communication and Networks 22, 3* (1998).

15. RSA LABORATORIES. Cryptographic message syntax standard. Public Key–Cryptography Standards 7, RSA Laboratories, Redwood City, CA, USA, 1993. Available at URL: `ftp://ftp.rsa.com/pub/pkcs/`.

16. RSA LABORATORIES. Password–based encryption standard. Public Key–Cryptography Standards 5, RSA Laboratories, Redwood City, CA, USA, 1993. Available at URL: `ftp://ftp.rsa.com/pub/pkcs/`.

17. SANDER, T., AND TSCHUDIN, C. F. Protecting mobile agents against malicious hosts. In Vigna [20], pp. 44–60.

18. SUN MICROSYSTEMS, INC. *Java^{tm} Archive (JAR) Features*. in [19], relative URL: `file:/docs/guide/jar/index.html`.

19. SUN MICROSYSTEMS,INC. *JDK 1.2 Documentation*, 1998. Available at URL: http: //java.sun.com.

20. VIGNA, G., Ed. *Mobile Agents and Security*, vol. 1419 of *Lecture Notes in Computer Science*. Springer Verlag, Berlin Heidelberg, 1998.

21. VITEK, J., AND JENSEN, C. *Secure Internet Programming: Security Issues for Mobile and Distributed Objects*, vol. 1603 of *Lecture Notes in Computer Science*. Springer-Verlag Inc., New York, NY, USA, 1999.

22. WHITE, J. E. *Mobile Agents*. AAAI/MIT Press, 1997, ch. 18.

Author Index

Lecture Notes in Artificial Intelligence (LNAI)

Lecture Notes in Computer Science